JONI MITCHELL
both sides now

Edited by: Debbie Poyser
Design: David Houghton
Printed by: Staples of Rochester

Published by: Sanctuary Publishing Limited, The Colonnades, 82
Bishops Bridge Road, London W2 6BB.

ISBN: 1 86074 160 6

JONI MITCHELL
both sides now

by Brian Hinton

Acknowledgments

My thanks go to Penny and Michelle at Sanctuary Publishing Limited, to Debbie Poyser, and to the following for providing ideas, contacts and information: Julian Bell, Emma Bradford, David Caddy, Mark Cooper, Charles Everest, Henrietta Garnett, Neil Hammerton, Amanda Hemingway, David Harris, Jeff Lewis, Eileen McManus, Phil McMullin of the Ptolemaic Terrascope, Neil Philip, KV Skene, Martin Stone, Harry Verey, Geoff Wall, and the large number of magazines, interviews, and journalists, whose work has served as source material for this book, and whom I acknowledge in my bibliography.

Special thanks to Michelle Meaby and Ben Cunliffe.

For Jean and Amanda

Contents

Introduction:

Here Today And Gone Tomorrow

It's 1970, three years after the summer of love, and all that it had unleashed. Joni Mitchell has returned to her native Canada to play at the Mariposa Folk Festival. She stands backstage, shyly unsmiling, a mixture of apprehension and watchfulness, dressed simply in black, her long blonde hair loosely plaited.

Fellow Canadian Larry LeBlanc provides a verbal snapshot for *Rolling Stone*. "Joni sat watching, curiously and quiet, nodding hello now and then. With her chin resting on her crossed legs, she seemed just a little self-conscious but inwardly serene. So perfect, with high soft cheekbones, great bright blue eyes, bittersweet blonde hair dribbling past her shoulders. She has a tremendous vanilla grin which makes her almost magical."

Once barely known even among a small group of professional folk singers in the musical outpost of Toronto, Joni is now one of the most famous people in the world. She uses her wide range as a singer to give women a new voice – soaring, conversational, witty and yearning. As a songwriter, her pre-eminence is challenged only by Dylan and Leonard Cohen, though unlike either she can sing in tune, a nightingale compared to Dylan's prairie dog vocals or Cohen's froglike moans. Her bohemian lifestyle in upmarket Los Angeles is a matter of worldwide envy and speculation. She is already a millionairess from her songwriting alone, a hippie capitalist who owns two corporations which market her songs. Her clothes, the antiques and fabrics with which she furnishes her home in Laurel Canyon, her look of chic simplicity: all have become role models for a generation.

For all that, she seems here a lonely, unemphatic figure. At the

11

previous Mariposa Festival – in summer 1969 – she had sailed to Toronto's Centre Island on a small boat with Graham Nash. Onstage, she began to perform a new song she had written for him, 'Willie', but found herself unable to finish it. It was like an omen. Within a few months, the affair with Nash had ended, and she had decided to take a year off from music. "I needed new material. I need new things to say in order to perform, so there's something in it for me. You just can't sing the same songs."

Already half-written by the summer of 1970 is her most personal and emotionally tortured album, *Blue*, which strips her love life down to the bare bone. As a performer, she has semi-retired, taking a year's sabbatical to work out a new direction: "I was being isolated, starting to feel like a bird in a gilded cage. I wasn't getting a chance to meet people. A certain amount of success cuts you off in a lot of ways. I like to live, be on the streets, to be in a crowd and moving freely."

Behind her are years of scuffling for money on a dying folk circuit, kept going only by a burning self belief, taking control of her own career in a way that no woman in rock has before her. Already endured and lived through is a childhood up-ended by contracting polio, a brief and unsuccessful marriage, a daughter born out of wedlock and reluctantly given up for adoption. Her highly public love life – as chronicled in her own songs – has seen no relationship, however stellar, which endures. In front of her is a long and dark road. The frail, uncertain figure here is about to take her music into areas – both lyrically and through a strange blending of genres – where no-one else has ever dared to go. On a makeshift stage on the Isle of Wight, within weeks, in front of half a million people, she will confront nightmare, and the dark side of the sixties dream; she will indeed be driven to tears and – for a while – silence.

Joni will also painfully fight her way to some kind of self-definition – musically, emotionally, and in a return to her first love of painting. Conversely, she will also lose much of her audience, and appear as an ambigious, semi-fulfilled figure. The part she has played in allowing a whole generation to dream of a better life is now misrepresented, sidelined, and betrayed.

Joni Mitchell's life has been a strange journey. Because of her innate privacy, it is one previously told only in hints and whispers, although she herself has scattered clues, like Ariadne in the maze. It is my job in this book to begin re-assembling them.

Whatever else flickers across that watchful, beautiful face which so warily confronts *Rolling Stone* (as if predicting the campaign of insinuations and critical attack which that magazine was soon to launch at her), there is a strong sense of self-awareness. As the critic Robert Christgau shrewdly observed, "In a male performer, such intense self concern would be an egotistical cop-out: in a woman it is an act of defiance." Linda Rondstadt, a close friend and neighbour, described Joni as "the first woman to match a man on his own terms as songwriter, guitar player and incredibly magnetic human being." In this, she made the template for generations of singer-songwriters to come, influencing both her own age group, and younger musicians as otherwise diverse as Prince, Madonna, Seal, Suzanne Vega, and Annie Lennox. Her importance as a role model for women singers in particular has been profound, and never properly acknowledged, not least by feminist rock critics.

For all that, there is something haunted and other-wordly about Mitchell, perhaps because – like Neil Young, the musician closest to her, geographically, spiritually and in terms of sheer self-determination – she had an early tussle with polio, a living death. As Paul Gambaccini once noted, "If angels sang, they would probably have voices like Joni Mitchell," though immediately pointing out that her subject matter was hardly angelic! *Music World* once described her voice as "airbrushed gold leaf." It was a conscious abandonment of the 'high folky' sound of Joan Baez, or the fluty purity of Judy Collins, both early influences who Joni was to later eclipse. As Bob Sarlin once tellingly observed, "In abandoning folk classicism, Mitchell has achieved an immediate effect, her lyrics are much more accessible to the casual listener." The fact that Joni is known so readily by her Christian name to a generation of fans – as compared to Baez and Collins, or indeed Dylan – says it all.

She gave a particular voice to her own sex. With the exception of Carole King (herself given second billing in the Goffin-King writing partnership) it is difficult to think of a songwriter in rock before who so obviously wrote out of the female experience: Janis Joplin, for all her other breakings of the mould, largely relied on the songs of others. As Stephen Stills recognised, "Joni exorcises her demons by writing these

13

songs – and in so doing she grabs the essence of something very private and personal for women." This from the man who wrote 'Love the One You're With', and all kinds of other blustering macho bluff!

Mitchell herself saw her role not so much as a spokeswoman but as someone crafting great art, which endures. "My music is not designed to grab instantly – it's designed to wear a lifetime, to hold up like a fine cloth." For her, art ultimately supersedes life, and certainly the conventional path of settling down, of raising a family. She has often compared the process of making an album to giving birth, and in her rare interviews, returns time and time again to her determination to remain herself, to guard her secrecy. "Freedom is the luxury of being able to follow the path of the heart. I think that's the only way that you maintain the magic in your life, that you keep your child alive. Freedom is necessary for me to create, and if I don't create, I don't feel alive."

The clash of such freedom and the views of her fans was an accident waiting to happen. Their devotion to her was so great that they assumed ownership: "Joni Mitchell was their best friend, their more articulate mirror, their sin eater." Love so soon turns to jealousy, worship to sacrifice, and the response to Joni Mitchell's later work – including, perhaps, her masterpiece, *The Hissing of Summer Lawns*, was semi-hysterical, like that of wolves deprived of their meat. John Lennon provoked the same jealous devotion, and on that wooden cockpit on the Isle of Wight, Joni Mitchell came close to sharing his martyrdom.

With all that yet to come, Joni Mitchell stares out from the yellowing pages of *Rolling Stone*, daring past and future, the years of celebrity and the years of neglect, alike. Here is someone both hauntingly fragile and as tough as a backwoods pioneer. She will survive.

In one of those tiny ironies of history, at roughly the same time – June 1970 – a minstrel troupe of musicians, over 130 of them packed onto a train and drinking, drugging and fornicating as they go, is traversing the endless prairies of rural Canada. The Grateful Dead, Janis Joplin, New Riders of the Purple Sage, the Band, Delaney and Bonnie, Tom Rush, Buddy Guy, Ian and Sylvia, Mountain: a weird mixture of Californian head-cases and Canadian exiles, now largely resident in the millionaire valleys of Los Angeles. They soon drain the bar dry, and in a nowhere place called Saskatoon, hold a collection and spend four hundred dollars restocking with alcohol, including the largest bottle of Canadian Club whiskey that anyone had ever seen. As Joel Selvin was later to write in his definitive book on *The Summer of Love*, "The train ran from Toronto through some mighty remote outposts on its way to the final destination of Calgary. To these bejewelled hippies... Saskatoon was as exotic as Outer Mongolia."

Largely unknown to these revellers, it was in Saskatoon that the young Joni Mitchell grew up, survived death and learnt to embrace life, and stored deep in her memory the endless prairie, its weird patterns of light, its huge sky with clouds piled high like fairy palaces, wind howling across its wastes, ice crackling in the winter night. Here was the basis for a lifetime spent largely in exile, but recapturing in words, music and paint this primal world, half tamed by man, half untameable. Here is the first step in any attempt to find her.

chapter 1:

Urge For Going

J oni Mitchell was born Roberta Joan Anderson on November 7th, 1943 in Fort MacLeod, Alberta, Canada. She was part of an extraordinary generation: Leonard Cohen had first seen daylight in Montreal in 1934, novelist Margaret Atwood in 1939, while Neil Young was born in Toronto in 1945.

Speaking to Timothy White for *Billboard* magazine over fifty years later, in Bel Air, Los Angeles, Mitchell noted with an "uneasy chuckle" that she is "a Scorpio with Scorpio rising, which... gives you resilience to bounce back from dire adversity." That ominous astrological combination is shared with the poet John Milton – who could create within himself both heaven and hell – and Sigmund Freud, explorer of the dark continent of human desire. Its endless see-sawing between the sensual and the spiritual was seen by White as a template for her whole career, not least in her song 'Shadows and Light', with its eternal war between "blindness and sight."

Joni's first memory, at the age of 18 months, was of just this dichotomy, of light glimpsed through darkness. "Above my crib as a baby was a roll-up blind. This was a poor household, and they had those kind of blinds that came in beige and dark green. This one was dark green, and it was perforated and cracked in a lot of places from frequent rolling. I can remember lying in my crib, seeing the filtered little stream of light and the fluffs of dust floating in it." Few of us could remember our childhood so meticulously. Only a painter could recall the exact colour of the blind and only a poet remember with such pin-sharp precision quite why it was letting in the sun, and how. Mitchell recalls her family living at the time in a single room, shared with another couple, only divided from them by a sagging curtain. It was the end of the Second World War, and Joni's parents were sharing cramped Canadian airforce quarters above a drugstore on Main Street, Fort Alberta.

Joni, "a tall, clear-eyed girl of Scots and Irish ancestry," was the only child of William and Myrtle Anderson. Bill, an instructor with the Royal Canadian Air Force Academy, had met his young wife, Myrtle 'Mickey' Marguerite McKee while she was working in a bank in Regina, Saskatchewan. They quickly eloped to Medicine Hat, Alberta for a hasty wedding. Less than a year later, their daughter Roberta Joan was born. "They wanted a boy named Robert John," Joni wryly notes. Her later song, 'The Tea Leaf Prophecy', is a direct retelling of her own parents' courtship. Without the courtship, there would have been no song, and no Joni!

Talking to Timothy White, she filled in the story, which is so strange that it has to be true. It reads like a folk-tale: "My mother had been a country schoolteacher and she had come to the town of Regina to work in a bank. It was wartime and nearly all the men in the town had been shipped overseas. So there weren't many prospects for her, and she was a good-looking woman, thirty years old – which was old for that time. There was a fancy hotel in that town that served high tea, and you had to wear hats and gloves in those days to get in. One day she and her girlfriend went over there just for the dress up of it all. When they were finished, a gypsy came over and read her teacup and said "You will be married within the month, and you will have a child within the year, and you'll die a long and agonising death."

"My mother laughed in her face. She said 'This is ridiculous. Look at this town. There's no men left, just frail boys and babies.' Two weeks went by and a friend of a friend had a friend from out of town and they put my mother and father together on a blind date and it was instant chemistry. My father had two weeks leave. He said 'I know this is sudden, Myrtle' – her name was Myrtle McKee, in the song it's Molly – 'but would you marry me?'

"So they ran off to Moose Jaw, and got hitched. I was born within the year, and to this day she feels a little funny about the rest of the prophecy, considering the odds of the other parts coming true. She's seventy-six, and she's never been sick a day in her life. I mean she's a

18

real germ fighter because she's convinced it's a germ that's gonna knock her down. She does yoga, Tai Chi, cross country skiing, and doesn't even have a quaver in her voice yet.

"I say to her 'Don't worry about the gypsy, Mom. Two out of three ain't bad.' The gypsy got it wrong, it's me who's gonna die the long and agonising death, with my bad habits. But I had to ask her. 'What made you marry Dad? You were so picky.' And she said, 'Because he looked so cute in his uniform.' So that's in the song too."

Joni has elsewhere spoken about her parents with the kind of verbal precision she also invests in her songs. On her mother's side, the McKees were homesteaders in Creelman, Saskatchewan. "Before meeting my dad, my mother had been a Depression-era country school teacher – making her own books by hand, instructing all grades in one room. My family was accustomed to hardship. These were people reared in a complete pioneer setting, and nobody thought to complain."

Indeed, Joni's grandfather James McKee, an Irishman ploughman, was one of the first white settlers on the prairie, at the turn of the century. The new railroads were opening up access to these desert plains. "They were giving away sections of land for pennies, and all you had to do was build a house, so he built a twelve by fourteen foot place." Joni's own wanderlust has its ancestry, her ability to move to where her brand of work was available: the folk clubs of Toronto and New York, the valleys of Bel Air, the concert halls of the world. Pioneer days.

Again, like mother, like daughter. In Joni's description of Myrtle, one can see in embryo her own love of high romance, of the mystery of past things – "an old-fashioned woman, presser of flowers, scrapbook keeper" – of a love for the great outdoors. It is the daughter's gift to be able to put these things into words, and so preserve them. "My mother was a romantic – she encouraged me in old-fashioned things. I used to keep pressed flowers in a scrapbook. We Canadians are a bit more nosegay, more old-fashioned bouquet than Americans. We're poets because we're a reminiscent kind of people. My poetry is urbanised and Americanised, but my music is influenced by the prairies. When I was a kid, my mother used to take me out to the fields to teach me bird calls. There was a lot of space

19

behind individual sounds. People in the city are so accustomed to hearing a jumble of different sounds that when it comes to making music they fill it up with all kinds of different things."

Music takes many forms. Mitchell's father was the son of a violin maker who emigrated to Alberta from Norway at the end of the century, earning a living in the New World as a carpenter and cabinet maker. Bill himself played the trumpet in a marching band. From him, Joni must have taken her Scandinavian blonde looks, and much more besides. As she told Alan Jackson in 1985, "I had a good relationship with my father. He taught me a lot of things that, had he had a son, he would have taught a boy. How to make a bow and arrows, and so on. I enjoy men's company, and I grew up enjoying it. My best friendships, generally speaking, that I've made in my life were with men."

Joni remains close to her parents, and still pre-censors her interviews so as not to upset them. During a gypsy life, this kind of close family support system (particularly intense for an only child) has kept her grounded. The affection and respect with which she speaks of her forebears extends to her grandmothers, both of whom she knew, and who seem, as role models, to apply to two different strands of her own life. Both were "frustrated musicians in different ways." From her father's mother, Mrs Mitchell, one can guess why Joni herself was at first so wary of long-term relationships. "She came from Norway, and the story has it that the last time she cried in her life she was 14, and she was crying because she knew she would never have a piano. And she became a stoic. She had a miserable, nasty life. She had 11 kids and married a mean, poor drunk, but she never wept through all the hardship in all her adult life, that anyone knows of."

On her mother's side, James McKee had married Sadie Henderson, whose father was one of the canoe brigades inherited from Canada's original French colonists. The 'canots de maitre' helped build a nation, transporting goods and railway building materials up river. In those pioneer days, distance was measured by the time it took to smoke a pipe's worth of tobacco.

Joni herself has credited Sadie McKee with bequeathing her a love of music. Sadie was an oxen-ploughing pioneer. She also played the organ, wrote poetry, and owned a gramophone player on which she would crank out grand opera and symphonic works, echoing over the newly-dug prairies. A real spitfire, by all accounts, and the kind of trail-blazer so movingly and properly evoked by David Ackles – a great songwriter, too, in his own narrowly defined sphere of sadness and loss – on 'Montana Song'.

Joni remembers her well. Again, one senses her refusal to be trapped in the same way, learning lessons from the history of her own family: "My maternal grandmother, on the other hand, was a classical musician who came East when the prairies opened up by train. She was Scottish-French and a poet and musician, but she still kicked the kitchen door off its hinges out of her frustration at being trapped in the role of a housewife." The album *Clouds* is dedicated to Sadie. Indeed, Joni credits her grandmother's greatest inheritance as her own talents as a poet. She reckons to have "got the bard" from Sadie, "a fine musician who wrote poetry in a thick Scottish brogue like Robert Burns, about the lifestyles of the French and Indian traders: 'Oh the sighing o the pines/'tis a lowerin' winter's nicht'." (sic)

Joni Mitchell has the purest folk credentials. Sadie's great grandfather had once been employed by Sir Walter Scott, himself a noted collector – and rewriter – of Scottish ballads. He even "gave her ancestor a medal for ploughing the fastest furrows in the shortest time." Thus does the folk tradition continue.

Bloodlines are not a fashionable thing to currently discuss, but they leave their mark. I remember seeing the Sussex folk-singing family, the Coppers – as traditional and upright as oak – performing in folk clubs in the late sixties with their son in long hair and hippie threads (which immediately made me identify with their music, unaccompanied drones from a century-old songbook, as far from Jimi Hendrix as can be imagined). Currently, a whole generation of the children of folk singers of the sixties is making its own mark – Eliza Carthy, daughter of Martin, and Norma Waterson; Nick Harper, son of Roy; UB40 is led by two sons of Ian Campbell; Kirsty MacColl is the daughter of Ewan.

Joni Mitchell's musical ancestry is therefore not all that surprising, though certainly intriguing. Despite an initial reputation as a trainee Joan Baez, she learnt early to write and perform her own songs, and abandon the traditional material she at first had to depend on. She has never recorded traditional material on any of her albums: indeed, her only cover versions have been of jazz standards. Nevertheless, that

Scottish lilt and fatalism is embedded in her own songs and performances, as are her complex tunings, which make her songs difficult for others to imitate, but derive from the rich diet of folk, classical, rock and jazz musics on which she was raised. If this is robbery, it is of the most distinguished kind.

The Anderson family moved on from Fort MacCleod to airforce bases in Calgary and Maidstone, a two-church town with a population of 400. After demob, Bill Anderson opened a grocery store in North Battleford – here Joni started school, at the age of six – and later moved on to Saskatoon, a small town on the plains of Saskatchewan. It was in these prairie towns that Joni grew up, in a post-war world of drabness and poverty, but surrounded by love, a far more precious heritage.

Her artist's eye caught the textures of her childhood surroundings, rural outposts left behind as riches grew in distant, almost unimaginable cities, garnered by corporate wealth. Here are the roots of Mitchell's ambivalence towards city streets, shared in different ways by Gram Parsons – 'Sin City' – and Neil Young. One thinks also of Dylan, also raised in a denuded landscape (near the Canadian border), and who, in songs like 'North Country Blues', skewers a community economically raped and then abandoned. Joni, as ever, is more positive, noticing how people make the best of things, make their own art. "Fort MacCleod was coming out of the Great Depression and into the war, so every house was weathered-out and derelict looking, with no paint on it. There had been a drought too, so gardens were non-existent. Some of the people who had no money for paint would try to brighten things up by stuccoing their houses with chicken feed and broken brown, green and blue bottle glass."

In another interview, she reveals how she could make the best of such surroundings – making jewels from junk – and, in passing, how she walked unharmed through the natural perils of childhood. "From an early age I always liked to look at light through transparent colours, so when I was let out into the yard to play I would collect the glass that had fallen off onto the ground. Coming back into the house on more than one occasion with my cheeks bulging, my mother would say 'open up' and my mouth would be full of this broken coloured glass.

But I never cut myself."

For someone who prefaces the above quote with the sharp self-observation "I was born materialistic," magic was everyday. When still a little girl, "I tried for weeks to change candle wax into jewels after I saw an alchemist do it in the *Tales of Hoffmann*." One can only speculate how much that weird Powell/Pressburger movie haunted her imagination. A typically strange mixture of beauty and the macabre, it combines classical music, film, and magic into a dense soup, from which an imagination as fresh as the young Joni's could drink endlessly. She might have been growing up in a remote township, but through the cinema screen, the world was already hers.

Whatever the mental nourishments, physically it was a tough existence, one generation away from the first pioneers, and still geographically living out on the edge. Post-war rationing was still in place. As Joni recalled for *Q*, "It was a strange, surrealistic time. Stocks on the shelves were dwindling down to nothing. You were lucky to get soap, and when you did get it, you washed your dishes and your hair and your clothes with it, whether it was detergent or shampoo." It was also a time when children could still safely play and wander in the streets at night.

In retrospect, a time of innocence. Family photographs recently published in *Billboard* show Joni aged two-and-a-half years old, looking winsome in a woolly dress, but a few years on she stands on her front porch, a defiant tomboy dressed as a cowboy. (Here is the start of her occasional fetish for cross-dressing: after all, her family did at first expect a son!) Like all right-on people, Joni's instinctive support now would be for the original settlers: her friend-to-be Buffy Sainte-Marie was meanwhile growing up on a nearby Cree reservation.

From Fort MacLeod, the Andersons moved to Calgary. Here, they rented a room from a Mrs Crow, who sounds like something out of Dickens. She was, for all that, the first person to recognise the young genius, and prime her verbally. "She was a Cockney and realised you could programme me, like a mynah bird, full of stanzas of poetry. Which is interesting, because she probably prepared me for all of this. 'Barber, barber shave a pig, how many hairs to make a wig, four and twenty that's enough, give the barber a pinch of snuff.' God knows what else she made me say."

A rich compost, from which would flower new and more profound stanzas. The family first put down roots in North Battleford, where Anderson managed a store for a grocery chain, and his wife taught school. Fellow Canadian Larry LeBlanc captures best how this landscape buried itself deep within her: "The flat prairie of Saskatchewan, a have-not province plagued by droughts and wavering wheat prices, holds things that must be seen and touched. Crocuses spreading a mauve mist along railway ties before the last patch of snow was melted, wheat fields merging into a wave-surfaced golden ocean, and telephone wires strung like popcorn."

Any true poet carries Eden inside them, a perfect world before the fall learnt in childhood. Recent Nobel prize winner Seamus Heaney has spent a lifetime trying to recapture and understand such images, from rural Ulster. In Joni's sphere, both Leonard Cohen, and more notably, Neil Young have also captured this vast emptiness, an existential space where the lone individual can confront his or her destiny, a cinematic landscape charged with meaning. Joni told Mick Brown that "I spent a lot of my childhood just sitting in the bush all by myself, watching the light come through the leaves. I always was thrilled by colour and landscape." As LeBlanc notes, in winter plains, dwellers "might see the skyline mirages of grain elevators 20 miles away, since frigid morning temperatures in the far North can literally bend light rays over the curvature of the Earth."

In such a landscape, human contact could be fleeting and gain an importance never glimpsed at on (still lonelier) city streets. A recent song, 'Love Cries', with its refrain "when that train comes rumbling by," draws on a primal childhood memory. "The only recreation I had was waving from our living-room picture window in Maidstone to the steam locomotive that blew its whistle at the bend in the tracks as it entered town – but at least that gave me a curiosity about going places." This was the big event, to watch the only train of the day passing through. Of course, the regular service has now been abandoned, as part of the cost-cutting 1990s, when accountants rule everything, even record labels. Joni later updated the story: "Several years ago, my mom and dad met a conductor on that railroad. He said 'The only thing I remember about Maidstone was that there was a house with a big window where they left the Christmas tree lights up, and a little girl used to wave to me.' It was the same guy! So we had this ritual, he and I. It really makes you want to think that every prayer, every message we send, eventually gets answered."

The family moved on to Saskatoon, a small dry, proud town marooned in an ocean of wheat, deeper still into the prairie. Here, Joni attended high school. As a community, Saskatoon has been described as sober to the point of dullness. It was founded around the turn of the century by the Ontario Methodist Colonisation Society, as a teetotal zone far from corruption. No wonder Joni escaped as soon as possible! Meanwhile, she led the life of a conventional teenager – when that definition was just coming into focus. She won trophies for ten-pin bowling, singing in the church choir, and enjoyed swimming and dancing, as she does to this day. She showed an early talent for art, and would provide the decorations for school hops or amateur dramatics.

From an early age, Joni was inwardly preparing to move on, to use her talent to escape the educational programming implicit in becoming a local housewife and doer of good works. "I always had star eyes. I had one very creative friend and we used to put on circuses together, and he also played brilliant piano. I used to dance around the room, and say that I was going to be a great ballerina, and he was going to be a great composer, or he was going to be a great writer, and I was going to illustrate his books. My first experience with music was at this boy's house, because he played the piano and they had old instruments like auto-harps lying around. It was playing the piano that made me want to have one of my own to play with, but then as soon as I expressed interest (and my parents made me take lessons) that killed it completely."

Talking to Kristine McKenna for *NME*, she named this childhood friend. Frankie was a "piano prodigy who could play the church organ when he was seven years old. He and I were the only artists in what was basically a real jock community." At a school reunion, a classmate told her that she and Frankie were the only creative people in a town "where everyone threw balls and stones."

Tomboy Joni fitted into that as well. Her first idol was James Dean, that perfect image of teenage rebellion. For all her artiness, she was also adopted as a mascot by the tough guys on the streets. Nothing much has changed there, as anyone foolish enough to slight her has found from her Laurel Canyon neighbours. All in all, though, it was a fairly standard childhood. Joni puts it all concise and clear: "I was born in Fort MacLeod, Alberta, in the foothills of the Canadian Rockies – an area of extreme temperature and mirages. When I was two feet off the ground I collected broken glass and cats. When I was three feet off the ground, I made drawings of animals and forest fires. When I was four feet off the ground I discovered boys and bicycles. When I was five feet off the ground I began to dance to rock 'n' roll and sing the top ten and bawdy service songs around campfires."

The start, though she hardly knew it then, of a lifetime's creative agony. As she later told Sean O'Hagan, "My work reflects the migration of my life. I was brought up in a tiny hamlet, a place where teams of horses delivered the fresh water for the village. When I was ten, I moved to the town, but I still lived a life on the outskirts. I have a love of raw land that's stayed with me even in New York and LA. For a long time I found cities tragic. I was a girl from the prairies with a severe case of the bends."

This is not quite the whole picture: she also kept a certain distance. As Joni later told Kristine McKenna: "Every summer all the kids that threw balls and stones would hang out at the lakes, but my family would pile into the car and drive someplace like Minnesota." It would have been just too piquant for them to there run into the young Bob Dylan, two years her elder. She continues: "I had a lot of childhood illnesses, and we moved a lot. You can see in early pictures of me that I started out as an extroverted, hammy kid. But a number of moves, then polio, scarlet fever, chicken pox bordering on smallpox, nearly dying with measles – all of that isolated me a lot."

Joni's light has always been set off by equally strong shadows, and a particularly dark one fell across her life at this point. Polio was to mark her out as different, but it gave her, too, the time and space to delve into her own soul for the first time. It was also the culmination of a youthful career of ill-health. For Timothy White, in the most revealing interview of her career, Joni elaborated further: "I was a sickly child. At three, my appendix burst and they rushed me to the hospital. Then I had German measles and red measles, one of which nearly killed me. At eight, I had chickenpox and scarlet fever, plus the arbitrary tonsillitis.

We were living in small rented rooms and shacks with outdoor toilets, in tiny towns without running water that had names like Maidstone, leading a life almost like on the Russian tundra. Drinking water was delivered, and bathing water was captured off the eaves of the houses."

Joni contracted polio at the age of nine in the same 1952 epidemic which also struck Neil Young. Joni shows her extraordinary ability to recall exactly what she was wearing at her life's high and low points: "I vividly remember the day I got polio. I was nine years old and I dressed myself that morning in pegged grey slacks, a red and white gingham blouse with a sailor collar, and a blue sweater. I looked in the mirror, and I don't know what I saw – dark circles under my eyes or a slight swelling in my face – but I said to myself 'You look like a woman today'." It is almost as if a life-threatening illness is the price she must pay for reaching sexual maturity, make of that what you will.

"After I got outside, I was walking along with a school friend, and at the third block I sat down on this little lawn and said 'I must have rheumatism' because I'd seen my grandmother aching and having to be lifted out of the bathtub. I complained a little bit more, but still went and spent the day in school. Next day I woke and my mom said 'Get up, come!' I said 'I can't.' She didn't believe me and yanked me out of bed, and I collapsed. They rushed me to the St Paul's Hospital in Saskatoon. The infectious part of the disease lasts two weeks, and it twisted my spine severely forward in a curvature called lordosis, and then back to the right in a lateral curve called scoliosis, so that I was unable to stand. One leg was impaired, but the muscles didn't atrophy, so there was no withering, thank God. I was put in the children's ward, and with Christmas rolling up, it became apparent I wasn't going home. Someone sent me a colouring book with pictures of old-fashioned English carollers and the lyrics to all these Christmas carols."

It doesn't take her fellow Scorpio Freud to find here the seeds of Joni's later creativity, with words, with sounds, and with paint. The poet Fiona Sampson is currently pursuing front-line research on the healing powers of art. Recently, hospitals have been far more instrumental in covering their walls with new paintings, and populating their therapy rooms with poets and artists teaching their craft. It seems a given scientific fact that immersion in one's own suppressed creativity can help both body and mind recover, and make them as one.

27

For all that, Joni's recuperation was both slow and horrifying. "I had ulcers in my mouth that they'd come and swab [with] an antibacterial solution called gentian violet, and they'd leave the swabs behind, so I used the swabs to colour the carollers purple. And I sang those carols to keep my spirits up. My mother came with a little mask on and put a little Christmas tree in my room with some ornaments. The first night they allowed me to leave it lit an hour after lights-out. And I said to the little tree 'I am not a cripple' and I said a prayer, some kind of pact, a barter with God for my legs, my singing."

While Joni was dredging all this back up for Timothy White – whose tactic is not to interrupt this stream of primal therapy – he reports that she spoke "weakly, drained by the remembrance." Although not expected ever to walk again, Mitchell gamely withstood the excruciating treatments then current, almost as emotionally withering as the disease itself. Scalding flannel rags would be applied to her bare legs with insulated gloves and then stripped off with tongs, blistering the raw skin. Obviously, this had an effect on her, if one not expected by her doctors.

One day – like the hero of Dennis Potter's *The Singing Detective* – she suddenly announced that she was ready to walk, and the sceptical nuns wheeled her to a ramp with long railings. "If the disease spread to your lungs, you were doomed to pass the rest of your life reclining in an iron lung with your head sticking out. As I rose to make my walk, I could hear the iron lungs wheezing in the background." It was perhaps the most important moment of her whole life, and one to be faced alone. Miraculously – and I do not use that word lightly here – she summoned up every ounce of her strength, and gradually began to stagger, inch by painful inch, to the end of the ramp.

From there on in, everything was an improvement, and Mitchell was soon discharged home. There, she refused her corrective shoes, braces or wheelchair, putting herself through a self-imposed, year-long rehabilitation programme. As if in reaction, and in defiance of medical advice, Joni also became a secret cigarette smoker – that most incorrect of current political positions – hopelessly hooked on nicotine before the age of ten. The whole experience made the experience of adolescence indescribably poignant and joyful, like that of someone brought back (literally) from the dead. It's therefore no surprise that her early songs have a freshness and delight in the minutiae of existence – the breakfast of "milk and toast and honey and a bowl of oranges, too" in 'Chelsea Morning', a baptismal feast – and an innocence which can only arise from deep suffering, painfully overcome.

Her singing was at first, literally, a form of self-healing. As a nine-year old stranded in a polio ward over Christmas, she had certainly needed something: "So I started to sing Christmas carols, and I used to sing them real loud. When the nurse came into the room I would sing louder. The boy in the bed next to me used to complain. And I discovered I was a ham. That was the first time I started to sing for people." The boy in the next bed probably grew up to become a rock critic! Illness – and recuperation – also brought Joni far closer to her mother, the effect on whom of almost losing her only child can also barely be imagined.

Having stopped work, Mrs Anderson taught her daughter at home for a whole year, before she was well enough to return to school. As Joni told *Q*, "She had this blackboard, and when I didn't understand something, she would say 'For Pete's sake, Joan, do I have to draw you a diagram?' And that was exactly it. I needed pictorial references." This enforced time off gave young Joni the chance to indulge an already obvious creative talent. She painted and wrote poetry almost constantly, as if in relief. Regaining her strength, she plunged with almost demonic energy into her previous hobby of dancing, organising weekly Wednesday night get-togethers. Being able to walk again, she wanted to do nothing but dance.

Joni specialised in rock 'n' roll, jiving with the door handle to hit parade shows on the radio. As intensely competitive as she was to prove in other areas, she began to win local teen contests in Saskatoon, with her speciality, the Lindy Hop. It was also her first experience – literally – of going downtown. She would take the bus, dressed in smart frock and posh gloves, down to juke-box hideaways, public dances, to brothels, even: "If you've seen pictures of me when I was 25, you'll know I looked 12 then, so you can imagine what I looked like when I really was 12. Awfully wholesome to be in those places. The kids used to say to me 'you look too innocent. Smoke'."

A further part of the learning process was her work as a professional model, another self-imposed regime which aided her recovery. It partially explains her poise on stage, and her self-command. It also helped her bank balance, even if now it all seems a little undignified. "There were no fashion shows in the region, but I worked in dress shops in Saskatoon, and travelling salesmen came through town and hired 'wholesale models' locally, who were basically quick-change artists exhibiting clothes for retail buyers. You wore a black slip and changed behind a screen because you were a young woman working in a hotel room with a traveller, and you had to be a size eight. But the pay was pretty good, and that's how I got the money to go to art school." As she grew older, painting became more and more important, and – as later with music – she was always looking to extend herself, and learn new things. Even at high school, she studied abstract art and figurative realism on an extra-curricular basis. Her seventh grade teacher, Arthur Kratzman, complimented her on the drawings she was pinning up at a PTA gathering, adding prophetically that "if you can paint with a brush, you can paint with words."

Unfortunately, while attending Queen Elizabeth Public School, and then Nutana and Aden Bowan high schools, Joni showed scant interest in mainstream academic work. She was compelled to resit classes in senior maths, chemistry and physics on a part-time basis. Most important of all was her self-identity as an artist. The first step was some kind of personal trademark, and that too came from school art classes: "I changed the spelling of my name to Joni at 13, because I admired the way the last name of my art teacher, Henry Bonli, looked in his painting signatures." Can we imagine an alternative world with Joni Baez, or Judi Collins? Like Bob Dylan (born Robert Zimmerman), Joni knew instinctively how to fashion her own identity for popular consumption. It is interesting that close friends still tend to call her Joan. The surname was to come later...

When Joni bought her first record, at the age of nine in 1953, it was classical music as interpreted – and broadcast – through the movies, a Rachmaninoff theme used in the score of the Ethel Barrymore-James Mason movie *The Story of Three Loves*. Talking to Cameron Crowe, she could – and did – still hum the entire melody.

This was her first experience of music as an addiction. "Every time it used to come on the radio it would drive me crazy. It was a 78. I mean, I had 'Alice in Wonderland' and 'Tubby the Tuba', but the first one that I loved and had to buy? *The Story of Three Loves*." The music that really enthused her during adolescence, however, was amplified rock with a heavy backbeat, though one would not guess this from her early LPs, in which drums never intrude and an electric bass only appears in passing. At first, this kind of music was hard to track down. "You see, pop music was something else in that time. We're talking about the fifties now. When I was thirteen, The Hit Parade was one hour a day – four o'clock to five o'clock. On the weekends they'd do the Top Twenty. But the rest of the radio was Mantovani, country and western, a lot of radio journalism. Mostly country and western, which I wasn't crazy about. To me it was simplistic. Even as a child, I liked more complex melody. In my teens I loved to dance. That was my thing. I instigated a Wednesday night dance 'cause I could hardly make it to the weekends. For dancing, I loved Chuck Berry, Ray Charles' 'What I'd Say'. I liked Elvis Presley. I liked the Everly Brothers."

As we will see, the folk boom rendered rock music neanderthal and inane, "greasy kids' stuff" in Bob Dylan's sneered aside – this from a man who came across at the start of his career like a hillbilly acoustic folk bard, not someone once thrown off the stage at a school dance for playing electric guitar too loud. Dylan got his revenge on the 1966 world tour with the Hawks, playing a confrontational rock music – the folk messiah now a 'Judas' – for which Mitchell never felt the need.

Her own version of amplified rock was to be more subtle, jazz-flecked, using new technology to fit traditional forms. Both, though, were true children of the fifties, growing up in a world transformed by the animal rhythms of early rock 'n' roll artists like Elvis Presley. Interestingly, it is now black artists that Joni quotes mainly as early influences. For her, this was no passive love affair. Rock music was to get up and dance to, not a cheap substitute for poetry. "I guess I liked the hit parade in those days 'cause I was looking at it from the view 'Can you dance to it?' There wasn't much to the lyrics, although 'Get out in the kitchen and rattle those pots and pans', that's great music, great. I love 'Shake, Rattle and Roll', the Coasters, Chuck Berry. I've been with rock 'n' roll from the beginning."

In his history of the mighty Sun label, which rose over the mid-

31

fifties like an atom cloud, Colin Escott relates an extraordinary anecdote. Johnny Cash is now – rightly – an emperor of country music (to which he turned on a Bob Dylan shakily recovering from the excesses of 1966!), appearing on U2's *Zooropa* as a voice of authority and vengeance. Back in the late fifties, he was still a quiffed, greasy rocker, playing anywhere he could to turn an honest dollar. (No one, of course, thought that rock 'n' roll would last, nor turn out to be anything more important than, say, the hula hoop.) Cash even played the backwoods towns of Canada, during a fifteen-day tour which took him from Prince Edward Island to Vancouver. It was a real hick show, featuring Cash impersonating Elvis, performing calypsos, and engaging in comedy routines with his musicians. What happened next was far from comic – prophetic and spooky all at once. Over to you, Johnny: "We filled every hall, but more than that we sold over 100,000 singles. My last promo appearance was to draw a name out of a box at a large department store's record counter and name the Teenage Queen and the runner-up. One requirement to enter the contest was to prove the purchase of the record. I autographed hundreds and sometimes thousands of copies of that record in every city. During my concert that evening, I crowned the queen and announced the first runner-up. In the city of Saskatoon, the Teenage Queen died tragically, leaving the runner-up to be enthroned. That runner-up was already writing songs and singing. Her name was Joni Mitchell." 'Teenage Queen' entered the Billboard Hot 100 in February 1958, and peaked at number 16, also giving Cash his first number 1 country record, though he left Sun records soon after. Indeed, it seemed that such music had died and gone to heaven, with Elvis in the army, Chuck Berry in prison, and the likes of Eddie Cochran and Buddy Holly literally in another world. After the Lord Mayor's show came the horse manure, a seemingly endless parade of Bobby Vinton, Pat Boone, and Brian Hyland. In England, even *Childrens' Family Favourites* with Uncle Mac was more exciting. Loud boys with guitars were definitely out of bounds. As Joni later said, "Rock 'n' roll went through a really dumb, vanilla period. And during that period, folk came in to fill the hole."

The young Joni had to seek out other forms of excitement. "When I was 14, I remember sitting in the beauty parlour, having my hair set for the senior prom. I was reading a fan magazine about Sandra Dee and Bobby Darin, and I thought 'how awful to have your life in headlines'." How ironic. Mitchell has largely lived her life in headlines, and at times seems to resent the fact that she now rarely attracts such front-page attention. She has tried to guard her privacy, while still giving out so many clues in her songs to highly personal feelings and lovers that no listener thus drawn in – and who could fail to be? – is content to leave things at that. Equally ironic, for perhaps the most cerebral and intellectually precise rock star (admittedly a small field, led by the likes of Bowie and Sting) was her self-confessed failure at school.

"I was pretty much a good-time Charlie. I was a bad student. I failed twelfth grade. I did my book reports from classic comics. I was anti-intellectual to the max. Basically I liked to dance and paint and that was about it. As far as serious discussions went, I found them boring. I figured, all things considered, I'd rather be dancing." She updated the story for Cameron Crowe: "I went back later and picked up the subjects that I lost. I do have my high-school diploma – I figured I needed that much, just in case. College was not too interesting to me. The way I saw the educational system from an early age was that it taught you what to think, not how to think. There was no liberty, really, for free thinking. You were being trained to fit into a society where free thinking was a nuisance.

"I liked some of my teachers very much, but I had no interest in their subjects. So I would appease them – I think they perceived that I was not a dummy, although my report card didn't look like it. I would line the math room with ink drawings and portraits of the mathematicians. I did a tree of life for my biology teacher. I was always staying late at the school, down on my knees painting something." As she told Penny Valentine, in an intimate encounter: "I hardly ever read. As a result, I find difficulty in expressing myself – suddenly I find how limited my vocabulary is. I never was a reader, I always was a doer. To me, reading was a vicarious experience. But I have a hunger now, there are times when I'm among my friends and I feel like an illiterate. It's like I came through the school systems completely unscathed in a way, and completely unlearned in another way. Which makes me feel terribly ignorant. I find now that the most common phrase in my vocabulary is 'I don't know'."

33

It is a lack she is still doing her best to remedy, despite her constant need for self-reliance. "I love teaching myself things. In a way, that handicaps me because when someone tries to instruct me I can't be instructed. This is particularly painful to me in my music, because someone will say 'Oh, I like the way you play piano, will you play these key changes C to E?' And I can't do it. The only way I could is if they play the tapes and let me wander around and choose my own chords." This goes back to her earliest musical training. "I was constantly rapped on the knuckles at piano classes because I'd listen to what the teacher played and I'd remember it. So I never learned to sight-read properly and she'd bust me on it. I'd fake it – like I'd read the music and it wouldn't be quite right, there was a certain amount of improvisation in it. And she'd say, 'those notes aren't in there.' That kind of killed my interest in the piano for a good fifteen years or so. From the beginning, I really wanted to mess around and create, find the colours the piano had buried in it. You know, I always feel like such an irresponsible creature."

When Cameron Crowe asked Joni how she was viewed by other students, she came over as a tough, street-wise character, albeit one still trying to forge some kind of direction in her life. "I'm not sure I have a clear picture of myself. My identity, since it wasn't through the grade system, was that I was a good dancer and an artist. And also I was very well dressed. I made a lot of my own clothes. I worked in ladies' wear and I modelled. I had access to sample clothes that were too fashionable for our community, and I could buy them cheaply. I would go hang out on the streets dressed to the T, even in hat and gloves. I hung out downtown with the Ukrainians and the Indians; they were more emotionally honest, and they were better dancers." Here we see the first inklings of her later close connection with black culture, for its life-force and sexuality. We also observe the seeds of her 'apartness' and what has often been interpreted since (wrongly) as arrogance.

"When I went back to my own neighbourhood, I found that I had a provocative image. They thought I was loose because I always liked rowdies. I thought the way the kids danced at my school was kind of, you know, funny. I remember a recurring statement on my report card – 'Joan does not relate well.' I know that I was aloof. Perhaps some people thought that I was a snob. There came a split when I rejected sororities and that whole thing. I didn't go for that. But there also came a stage when my friends who were juvenile delinquents suddenly became criminals. They could go into very dull jobs or they could go into crime. Crime is very romantic in your youth. I suddenly thought, 'Here's where the romance ends. I don't see myself in jail...'."

Raised on robbery, indeed. There were no such inhibitions about her early attempts at creating art, largely self-motivated. "In high school, I was kind of like the school artist. I did backdrops for school plays, I was always involved in illustrating the yearbooks." This paid a spectacular – and quite unexpected – dividend. Joni designed a UNICEF Christmas card for the top dog at her school. He reimbursed her with a Miles Davis album. It was the start of another kind of love affair.

"Friends of mine who were older than me and in college began talking about Lambert, Hendricks and Ross. Their record flipped me out, but it was already out of print. I had to finally buy it off somebody and pay a lot, maybe fifteen dollars, which was unheard of at that time. But you couldn't get the record anywhere. Lambert, Hendricks and Ross were my Beatles. In high school, theirs was the record I wore thin, the one I knew all the words to." *The Hottest New Sound in Jazz* was characterised by *Q* as a "motormouth, avant-garde flare-up." It was also a record Joni would return to, for something previously unheard of on her albums: two cover versions. "I don't think there's another album I know every song on, including my own."

Rock 'n' roll and jazz were both interests which paid no dividends, at least for the moment. The first music that Joni found marketable was the hottest craze in town, and one that she would soon grow through, and out from: traditional folksong. It was the musical highlight of a dull, conformist era. "Folk music came in to fill the hole. At that point I had friends who'd have parties and sit around and sing Kingston Trio songs. That's when I started to sing again. That's why I bought an instrument. To sing at those parties. It was no more ambitious than that." Her interest began with a mistake.

As she told *Zigzag* (the first, and best, British rock fanzine), "One summer, I went to a coffee house to hear some jazz, and I was curious to find out what it was all about. I was still a rock and roller, teenybop, go-to-the-dances-on-Saturday-night-type. Anyway, that night there was

35

no jazz, there was this terrible folk singer. I didn't enjoy it at all, but I kept going down there... and I found some things I liked. I liked a group that was very Kingston Trio-ish; they were local and they were very amusing – it was really funny to hear comedy in music. I wanted the leader to teach me how to play the guitar, but he wouldn't, so I went out and bought myself a ukelele, because my mother thought that guitar music was associated with country and western, which was sort of hillbillyish – so she said 'No guitar'!"

Joni began playing a $36 baritone ukelele, bought with money from modelling. The uke was an instrument made famous by George Formby, and later by the thankfully totally unique Tiny Tim (the first a peddler of juvenile smut, the second a man who made innocence camp, and thus ridiculous). In both cases this small, tinny instrument-substitute was part of the joke. A ukelele cannot convey gravitas, or high passion! As Larry LeBlanc reports, as if something dragged painfully from his own memory, "At the Louis Riel, she began playing a baritone uke, taking it everywhere and going 'plink a plunk' every time she learned a new change." Joni hassled herself some gigs at a Saskatoon coffee house called the Louis Riel – named after a local folk hero, who led an insurrection against the Government. With the proceeds, she was able to buy a guitar, and a Pete Seeger instruction record. By the age of nineteen she had already appeared on local TV, an extraordinary achievement for an inexperienced performer, who was yet to write her own songs.

Too impatient to copy a style already current, Joni dumped Pete Seeger, and learned guitar by her own devices. She soon became impossible to imitate, with a weird and personal series of tunings. The downside of this was that she needed to retune her guitar after almost every song. Recently she has harnessed technology to enable her to programme her Stratocaster to find such tunings at the flick of a switch. In June 1996, *Mojo* chose the hot 100 of all-time guitarists, and there she is at number 77. 'Young pups' including David Wilcox, Ani Di Franco, Shawn Colvin, Michael Hedges and Stina Nordenstam admit their debt to her syncopated, melodic, chordal style, and the "dense poetic verse" she weaves into it. As Joni said, "I think of the guitar as an orchestra, the top three strings as muted trumpets, the mid range as French horn and viola. The thumb is a sparse, eccentric bass line."

Her vocal training was equally idiosyncratic. "I used to be a breathy little soprano. Then one day I found that I could sing low. At first I thought that I had lost my voice forever. I could sing either a breathy high part or a raspy low part. Then the two came together, by themselves. It was uncomfortable for a while, but I worked on it, and now I've got this voice." One early critic described her sounding as if she has just swallowed a mouse. More sensibly, she appears bang in the middle of Barney Hoskyns' list of the top 100 voices to have shaped rock. I suggest that people who believe the former quote should stop reading this book immediately! Mitchell's voice is a Rolls Royce, gliding effortlessly like the bird images which litter her early songs.

A reviewer in *Cue* magazine was perhaps chemically enhanced, but he expressed as well as anyone the way Mitchell's voice matches the grain of her music: "Richly modal, it is pervaded by an exotic calmness, reminding one of things like wind chimes or the glass globes Japanese fishermen use to float their nets. Against this delicate background, her reedy voice with its natural vibrato is free to discover its own paths of harmony. Suddenly, like a hawk on an updraft, she will carve a breathtaking harmonic arc and soar out over the landscape of her verse."

Like her contemporary Tim Buckley, she would develop from teenage folk purity to places where a human voice had never before dared to go.

I n 1963, Joni returned to Calgary to attend the Alberta College of Art. Folk music was still important, but something she had consciously put on the back burner. As she told Barney Hoskyns, "When I was nineteen, I went to art school. I had six months of playing baritone ukelele under my belt, so I was sort of a novice folkie when I got there. There was the one folk club, and some of the people from the art school frequented it. But it was just a hobby. Meanwhile, the art education was extremely disappointing to me, because all of the professors were fans of de Kooning and Barnett Newman and the Abstractionists, and I wanted classical knowledge." She left, disenchanted, after a year. "I wanted to sharpen my eye for a more realistic kind of painting, but it mis-timed. When I was there, all the professors were infatuated with abstract expressionism."

37

Her decision to abandon the course came as no surprise to her mother. "My childhood longing mostly was to be a painter, yet before I went to art college, my mother said to me that my stick-at-it-iveness in certain things was never that great, and 'you're going to art college and you're going to get distracted, you know.' Yet all I wanted to do was paint. When I got there, it seemed a lot of the courses were meaningless to me, and not particularly creative. So at the end of the year I said 'I'm going to Toronto to be a folk singer' and I fulfilled her prophecy – I went solo, and struggled for a while."

The role of the art school has been crucial. In Britain, Pete Brown even released an album called *Things May Come and Things May Go, but the Art School Dance Goes On Forever*. Its cover is a cartoon by Mal Dean, where Van Gogh mixes with the likes of Syd Barrett, the Yardbirds, Viv Stanshall, Pete Townshend and Charlie Watts – painters all – to whom art school gave the freedom to develop their musical careers. One could add figures as diverse as Eric Clapton, John Lennon, the Pretty Things, Ian Dury, and Adam Ant. From the late fifties onwards, Art School – which then required no formal qualifications to enter – provided an unstructured environment. Its students were free to experiment, to fail, to pursue obscure musics which would later colonise the world. And sometimes even to learn how to paint as well!

It was the impetus of attending art school that enabled Mitchell to develop herself both as an artist and musician, and – crucially – to begin to write her own material. Joni discussed her amazement at the consequences with Mick Brown. "I never thought that far ahead. I never expected to have this degree of success. It was a hobby that mushroomed. I was grateful to make one record. All I knew was, whatever it was that I felt was the weak link in my previous project gave me inspiration for the next one. I wrote poetry and I painted all my life. I always wanted to play music, and dabbled with it, but I never thought of putting them all together. It never occurred to me. It wasn't until Dylan began to write poetic songs that it occurred to me you could actually sing those poems."

As she told Barney Hoskyns, "I was always involved with music, not as a career direction, but as a spirit-lifter, so the irony of my becoming a confessional poet was very great to anyone who knew me in my teens. When I got to art college, there was a coffee house there and I went down to see if I could pick up some pin money, and it turned out they were willing to pay me fifteen dollars for a weekend." This was The Depression, a local coffee house. "She looked just tremendous, with all that blonde hair," its owner John Uren recalls. "I brought Peter Albing in from Toronto. And he listened to Joni and said she could sing. She met a lot of people. Will Millar was around, one of the Irish Rovers. It was a good scene in those days. And Joni was part of it." Albing later became 'Mycroft' of the Times Square Two: he moved to LA, where he now works the comedy circuit. He and Joni were the house acts, and it was here that she wrote and performed her first original composition. Even Joni's own memory of it is distressingly vague, as she told *Zigzag*: "I wrote one song in Calgary; I don't remember what it was about, but I wrote it for Peter. I don't remember how it went, and I'm sure he doesn't either." From small acorns...

Her first trip to the Mariposa Folk Festival proved to be a one-off affair. The return ticket remains uncashed, and in a real sense, she never came back. After the festival, she settled in the Yorktown district of Toronto, and started to make her way in the big city, as a professional folk singer.

This was not so much an abandonment of her chosen career as a painter, as its continuation in a different medium. As she said fifteen years later, "I was only a folk singer for about two years, and that was several years before I ever made a record. By that time, it wasn't really folk music anymore. It was some new American phenomenon. Later they called it singer/songwriters. Or art songs, which I liked the best. Some people get nervous about that word 'art'. They think it's a pretentious word from the giddyap. To me, words are only symbols, and the word 'art' has never lost its vitality. It still has meaning to me. Love lost its meaning to me. God lost its meaning to me. But art never lost its meaning. I always knew what I meant by art. Now I've got all three of them back."

Like Ladbroke Grove, Greenwich Village and Haight Ashbury, Toronto's Yorktown district had, by the early sixties, seen better days. Large and up-market townhouses were now largely broken up into run-down apartments, ripe for the 'boho dance'. Genteel poverty for the children of the middle classes. Here the Beats, and later prototype hippies, found a congenial environment for communal living: a network of cheap cafes and bars grew up to cater to their needs. Like London's Soho, folk music was associated with the former: licensed premises seemed better suited to rowdier music and patrons. Rock 'n' roll was catered for in raucous bars like Le Coq d'Or and The Colonial on Yonge Street: here the blowtorch lead guitar lines of an unknown sixteen-year old called Jaime 'Robbie' Robertson lit up the gutbucket vocals of Ronnie Hawkins. The acoustic music scene centred on Yorkville village, a self-contained, two-block stretch bounded by Avenue Road and Yonge Street – the rock zone – one way, and Davenport and Bloor Streets the other. More than a dozen coffee shops were packed tight together: bohemia on toast.

The coffee house has long been a crucible for cultural change. From its origins in the early 18th Century, when John Dryden and Alexander Pope would read their latest satiric verse, or magazines like *The Spectator* and *The Tatler* arose to convey the latest gossip, coffee houses were places for conversation and company. Pope even wrote a poem to the coffee bean:

As long as Mocha's happy tree shall grow
While berries crackle, or while mills shall go
While smoking streams from silver spouts shall glide
While coffee shall to British nymphs be dear
So long her honours, names and praise shall last.

It was in the coffee-houses of France that the Revolution was planned, and that a century later the Impressionists met and plotted a revolution in the visual arts. In London's Cafe Royale, Oscar Wilde polished his latest aphorism or swapped anecdotes with Aubrey Beardsley. In the same coffee houses of Vienna, Sigmund Freud would meet friends, and Schoenberg plan how to combine music and mathematics.

The coffee bar in post-war Britain fuelled a whole generation of Colin Wilson lookalikes, each carrying a copy of Sartre or Camus or Kerouac in their jacket pocket, and sometimes even trying to read it. It also played host to the first stirrings of British rock 'n' roll, which was certainly a mixed blessing. In the States, coffee houses flourished less

40

self-consciously. Usually based near a university campus, they acted as intellectual free zones, where a clientele of young people, eccentrics and outcasts could pass the time, converse, listen to folk music – not amplified, so easy to talk over or to listen to intently, as required – and generally put the world to rights. The coffee house acted as a rite of passage, something to be enjoyed then discarded. As Joni Mitchell herself wrote in 'The Last Time I Saw Richard', a song written to her ex-husband, it was "only a phase, these dark cafe days."

As that phrase suggests, it was a scene that came to life at night. The Toronto coffee houses were exactly that, two or three storey brick houses, once family homes, with folk-singers performing either in the front room or the basement. The audience were packed in like termites, infesting the stairs or hallway, even watching out in the street through the steamed-up windows. They were themselves part of the show, a kaleidoscope of colourful clothes and weird lifestyles. Fashion eddied between competing coffee shops, their very names redolent of the sixties: the Purple Onion, the Penny Farthing, the El Patio, and the Chez Monique. The Riverboat, on Yorkville Avenue and run by Bernie Fiedler, drew major visiting folk acts from the United States and beyond.

Toronto was at the crossroads of contemporary folk music. More European than New York, more American than Montreal, its coffee houses nurtured an extraordinary generation of native talent. The party was already in full swing when Joni arrived with an undeveloped, unfocused talent, and a few early songs, "love-lost pieces for a wandering Australian who really did me in." The pathfinders to this new musical frontier were Ian Tyson and Sylvia Fricker: they blended country and folk, topping the mixture with songs about their native country. In their wake, other local talent emerged, Gordon Lightfoot in particular. In a 1970 interview with *Melody Maker*, Tom Norcott identifies two groups between which his own career falls: "The old wave of Canadian singers such as Lightfoot and Ian Tyson, and the new wave which includes Joni Mitchell, Leonard Cohen and Bonnie Dobson."

Dobson, in particular, represents a school of folk protest which emerged post-Dylan. Her own 'Morning Dew' is a chilling evocation of nuclear holocaust, and was memorably covered by – among others –

41

Rod Stewart with the Jeff Beck group. David Clayton-Thomas began in Yorkville as a Barry McGuire figure, before he discovered fame and fortune fronting Blood Sweat and Tears. Indeed, others went on from coffee house obscurity to national fame. Zal Yanovsky went on to found the Lovin' Spoonful. Denny Doherty came from Halifax, Nova Scotia, and would eventually find fame with the Mamas and the Papas. And then there was Neil Young...

Bonnie Dobson also indicates the presence in the coffee houses of a new generation of female singer-songwriters, self-motivated and emotionally tough – role models for the young Joni Mitchell. Buffy Sainte-Marie had grown up on the Cree Indian's Piapot Reserve in Saskatchewan's Qu'Appele Valley. In the liner notes to her first LP, *Many Mile*, Peter LeFarge takes her to task for this very toughness: "I think Buffy has written very well for humanity, but loved it little... a soft Buffy would be a grand success internationally." Perhaps so, but the tough Buffy who actually emerged is still active, now a computer specialist who transmits her latest songs to the studio by means of satellite. A fearless fighter for her own people, and for anti-war causes in general, she wrote 'Universal Soldier' in Yorkville.

Phil Ochs wrote 'Changes' there too, and the Yorkville scene saw many American emigres take temporary refuge: Dave Van Ronk, Eric Andersen, Tom Rush, Odetta, and the barely known Chuck Mitchell. However, as John Einarson wrote in his book on Neil Young's apprentice years, folk music was already very much a part of native Canadian culture, drawing on cowboy laments and Celtic song. What turned Canadian songwriters on most was their own landscape. Einarson: "Just listen to Ian and Sylvia's 'Four Strong Winds' or 'Someday Soon', or Gordon Lightfoot's 'Canadian Railroad Trilogy' and you have a portrait of this land and its people. Drawing on the prairie yodels of Wilf Carter and Nova Scotia-born Hank Snow's 'I'm Moving On', Canadian folk music has never been very far from country music, and folk singers here often achieve cross-over success in both markets." Ian and Sylvia moved from folk to country in the late sixties: Marty Robbins took folkie Gordon Lightfoot's 'Ribbon of Darkness' to the top of the US country charts.

Although there were flourishing folk communities in Winnipeg – where Neil Young first saw Joni play – Vancouver, and Leonard Cohen's native Montreal, Toronto was where reputations were made, and careers established. As well as exposure in the coffee houses and folk festivals, Canadian television hosted popular shows like CBC's *Singalong Jubilee*, Oscar Brand's *Let's Sing Out* on CTV, and Malka and Joso's *World of Music*.

Thus it was that in August 1964 Joni Mitchell made the three-day trip by Canadian Pacific Railroad to the annual Mariposa Folk Festival. This was the event to which she was to return in triumph in 1970, like a visiting Queen. The ostensible reason for the trip was that she wanted to see Buffy Sainte-Marie: Mariposa was the biggest event of the Canadian folk year, a homely affair that was a home-grown copy of the Newport folk festival in the States. On the way, Joni wrote 'Day by Day', a bluesy number influenced by the rhythm of the train wheels.

Martin Onrot was one of the organisers at the event, held in Orillia – symbolically enough, as the birthplace of Gordon Lightfoot. He recalls having been forced by an injunction to change location, just as it was due to begin. With open air festivals, it was ever thus! He remembers that "Joni had come in with some people from the west, and she helped us load trucks and move the entire festival. She really chipped in."

Joni had found a whole new set of friends. Although she had intended to return to Alberta, she so enjoyed the Festival, and the people that she met, that she decided to stay on in Toronto. She started the hard way, playing unbilled and often unpaid in local coffee bars: "When I went East to hear the Mariposa Folk Festival I discovered the whole Yorkville coffee house scene and decided to stay. But Canada has a tendency to eat its young, and most of the coffee houses preferred to hire mediocre Americans over talented Canadians. That's the unfortunate mental sickness of my people." At the Penny Farthing, while she was playing in the basement, American singer Chuck Mitchell blew into town and played the main stage. In the light of subsequent events, this probably explains the uncharacteristic bitterness of her last remark.

As Larry LeBlanc remembers, "Joni was a strange young girl in those days – an all-around golden girl, running around discovering life for the first time. Playing and singing on Yorkville Avenue, she was part of the early scene." She was hardly an overnight success. Martin Onrot remembers "the first time I heard her sing was in a downtown Toronto rooming house. She had a soft, beautiful voice, and an easy, melodic style. It was nice, but I had no idea that she would become a superstar."

This small world was – as such tiny communities often are – itself prey to civil war. The folk style of the time divided itself into folk blues (like Dave Van Ronk), and pure traditional folk. Joni was very much in the second group, her material and vocal mannerisms heavily influenced by Joan Baez and Judy Collins. Joni Mitchell: "Even in the coffee houses, folk musicians were divided into two camps: those who played Gibsons and those who played Martins. And the Gibson players played the blues and the Martin players preferred more melodic English and Irish ballads. To tell you the truth, the blues never really registered for me at that point. Although I had great opportunities to see people like Mississippi John Hurt, it wasn't enough. I didn't get it. It didn't come out of my roots. I went for the Anglo-melodic."

What set Joni aside was the complexity of her unusual guitar tunings, and her melodious, lilting voice. She began to gain a small but loyal following, especially at coffee houses like the Penny Farthing and the Purple Onion. Living in a communal lodging house on Huron Street in the village, she worked during the day as a salesgirl at a Simpsons-Sears department store to pay the rent. With her wages, she also gradually raised the $140 union fee so she could perform. She began writing her own songs – about four new ones a week! – and honing her craft in front of late-night audiences (just like the Beatles in Hamburg a few years before, but that's a different story). "When I went to Toronto, I still didn't have an image of myself as a musician. I found I couldn't work, and I didn't have enough money to get into the union. So I worked in women's wear, in a department store. I could barely make ends meet. And then I finally found a scab club in Toronto that allowed me to play. I played for a couple of months."

She applied for a job at the Riverboat Club but Bernie Fiedler told her that the only vacancy at the time was as a dishwasher. Floor spots at upmarket venues like the Riverboat and The Bohemian Embassy followed. She was also becoming known for the quality of her songwriting. Joni revealed how this began in a fascinating interview with *Zigzag*. "I wrote 'What Will He Give Me' in November of 1964, and didn't write anything else until the following April, when I wrote a song called 'Here Today and Gone Tomorrow' and maybe one or two more; like I had one called 'The Student Song'. I guess I had written about five songs when I met Chuck."

Were there any common themes? "In the early ones, Love Lost. I met a wandering Australian who really did me in. As a matter of fact he continued to be the theme for a lot of songs that I wrote. I used to find it really difficult to write Love Found songs! My earliest 'real true love found' song was 'Dawntreader'... but Love Found songs were difficult to write, primarily because they really take a lot of confidence, not only that you are in love, but that the other person is in love with you. Otherwise you're afraid to say all the things that you want to say. It's a standard thing, so I didn't at that time have very much to write about. I was sort of relatively contented." She was a rising starlet in a scene already dying. Rising property prices and changing fashions would soon put an end to this cheap and potent lifestyle: Yorkville was later reclaimed by the well-to-do, and the energy level correspondingly plunged.

Meanwhile, Robbie Robertson and his fellow Hawks had swapped bosses. No longer were they backing Ronnie Hawkins in downtown Toronto bars. In late 1965, they joined Bob Dylan and toured America, Australia and Europe, giving an electric rock backing to folk songs. The resulting atomic cataclysm shook the world. Suddenly rock music – from the Beatles downward – learnt that it could accommodate poetry, surrealism, deep meanings, ambiguity, experiment: anything it wanted. And, correspondingly, the hermetically-sealed folk scene lost its leading singers to a wider world, and began to shrivel and die, like a flower after scattering its seed.

If Joni was to survive, she needed to be somewhere else. The Canadian rock journalist Ritchie Yorke knows as well as anyone the need to escape. "She left when it became obvious that the world would never have the chance to appreciate her unique abilities while she remained in Toronto, unknown, undiscovered and misunderstood." A decade later, she still felt the pull homewards: "I still feel a Canadian at heart and with the US being under such peculiar circumstances I may come back, perhaps to Vancouver. Most of my friends are in the US and that's why I'll stay a little longer." She is still there, with homes in Bel Air, New York and Florida, and a holiday home on the Canadian coast.

Joni was not the only native Canadian poised "on the edge of my feather," expecting to fly.

In late June 1965, Neil Young arrived at his father's house on Inglewood Drive in the posh Rosedale district of Toronto, still seeking his own secret alchemy to unite folk, rock and country into something new. Just as he arrived, Joni had left Toronto for good, again restlessly moving on.

Neil Young had first met Joni Mitchell in 1964 at the 4-D coffee house in Winnipeg, out near the the University of Manitoba. As John Einarson describes it, "With its drab tarpaper and snow fence decor, chequered table cloths, candles and expresso coffee and cinnamon tea, the 4-D was the stereotypical bohemian coffee house." He wrote an early song for her, 'Sweet Joni'. Sill unreleased, in its clumsy way it encapsulates both her air of beautiful mystery, and her essential restlessness.

Sweet Joni from Saskatoon
There's a ring for your fingers
It looks like the sun
But it feels like the moon.
Sweet Joni from Saskatoon
Don't go, don't go too soon

It could be an epigraph for later albums like *Hejira*.

Such a lifestyle has its pleasures and occasional ecstasy, but freedom is painful and has costs unknown to those who will or dare not embrace it. Dylan wrote a wonderful song about life on the road, addressed as much to himself as to anyone else. It was called 'Like a Rolling Stone', and turned rock music on its head.

Joni already knew about making difficult decisions, and casting adrift from family ties. She had given birth to an illegitimate daughter, named Kelly, who she had to give up for adoption. "I was late to lose my virginity. I was 20 and it was a crush with a fellow painter and I got pregnant immediately. To be pregnant and unmarried in 1964 was like you killed somebody. So what happened was I met Chuck Mitchell in trying to keep my child, and he was willing to take us both on." This was perhaps the biggest mistake of her life. Charles 'Chuck' Mitchell was a 29-year old American cabaret singer whom Joni met when he was playing upstairs at the Penny Farthing, and she was playing the basement. Chuck had dared to change the words of an as-yet unrecorded Bob Dylan song called 'Mr Tambourine Man', and Joni – fiery as ever – took him to task for sacrilege. Argument is often the first sign of sexual attraction, and he was immediately intrigued by her.

He must also have been taken aback by her talent, for this was to be a working relationship more than anything else. It also fits the whole archetype of the young woman learning what she can from an older man and then leaving him. However, it was Chuck who had, from the start, an emotional dependence. "He kinda latched onto me at this very vulnerable time, when I had no money, no work, and a child in a foster home, which was tearing me up." From his point of view, he was taking on a woman whose bearing of an illegitimate child stigmatised her in the society of the time. In those days, to have a child out of wedlock was still thought a thing of shame and a sign of ultimately loose morals. Nice girls didn't, or if they did and Nature caught them out, they either married the child's father, or had a secret (and illegal) abortion.

After a whirlwind 36-hour courtship, in June 1965, they were married in Chuck's parents' backyard in Rochester, Michigan, and took up residence in an apartment near the Detroit campus of Wayne State University. This was a pivotal moment in the young singer's life, leaving her homeland with memories of gigs in church basements and of having to wash dishes to earn enough money to eat. Chuck was perhaps what she secretly most desired: a prince arriving in town on his magic charger, kidnapping her heart and taking her off to his own far country. If so, then the folk song narrative was to go drastically wrong.

Mitchell updates the story in her song 'I had a King', whose villain "carried me off to his country for marriage too soon." And yet this was a move to be desired: "Many things took me to the States. For one thing, I married an American. I also went for recognition. The masses receive their information through American newspapers, magazines, radio and television. In Canada, there were only three major centres – Vancouver, Toronto and Montreal – and that's just not enough publicity. Exposure is vital to success. Nightclub owners wouldn't hire

47

you unless you had a name to guarantee a full house. So I packed my bags and went where I could get a name."

The change in Joni was profound, almost as if leaving Canada released something in her. The freedom to be herself. "Once I crossed the border, I began to write, and I began to find my real voice. From the first album, it was no longer really folk music. It was just a girl with a guitar, which made it look that way." These early songs, however, were written in code, and a great deal of self-censorship was involved. Joni told *Zigzag* that "I was limited in writing short stories, character sketches of people in love, for fear that people would say 'Listen to that song, there must be something wrong between them...' you know what I mean. You have to be very careful not to give the opinion that you're running around. At least, I always did... now I have no one to answer to, no one to be afraid of offending."

For the time being, Joni and Chuck were singing as a duo. Larry LeBlanc remembers their act as being pasted together like a collage. Chuck played heavy Brechtian material, while Joni "did her own thing." The two would come together for a few Gordon Lightfoot songs. The cocktail of hard work and poverty certainly helped Joni develop her skills as a public performer. "As a couple, I think we were making fifteen dollars a night." For all that, Joni had crossed that invisible divide between amateur and professional: however financially ill-rewarded, she was now very much part of the folk circuit, and was treated as such by her peers. There is a camaraderie among fellow performers – whether musicians, or actors, or poets – of those who have gone through the fire of live performance. It transcends critical success, or financial acclaim, and explains the 'luvvie' excesses of some actors, and the extraordinary atmosphere of Dylan's Rolling Thunder tour, in which Joni was to participate, which was almost a roll call of folk veterans. There is also, of course, terrible rivalry and jealousy buried beneath all the bonhomie and mutual congratulation.

Somehow immune to all this is the young girl of huge, as-yet untapped talent. Other women mother her, old men flatter and instruct, while young men fancy her, as anyone who reads JB Priestley's *The Good Companions* can verify. Joni was just this kind of golden girl, ripe with potential, whereas Chuck had already reached as high as he was ever going to get. She could discard her mentor, once she had (intellectually) squeezed him dry.

Joni told Cameron Crowe that "we were never a full-fledged duo. I'm a bad learner, see. I bypass the educational system. I learnt by a process more like osmosis. It's by inspiration and desire. So when we would work up songs together, we would bang into differences of opinion. Some people say 'Oh Joan, that's just because you're lazy.' But in a way, more than laziness, it's a kind of block that runs through my rebellious personality. If someone tries to teach me a part that I don't find particularly interesting, it won't stick. I'll end up doing what I wanted to do in the first place, and then they're annoyed. We had a difference of opinion in material. It was more like two people onstage at the same time, sometimes singing together. We had a difficult time." The marriage does not sound like a passport to heaven. But through her husband, Joni met fellow musicians who would help her begin her climb up the slippery ladder.

"In Detroit, we had a fifth-floor walk-up apartment with some extra rooms, and so when Eric Andersen and David Blue and Tom Rush and people like that passed through Detroit, they would stay with us." Meeting this new circle of friends – which also included Buffy Sainte-Marie, Gordon Lightfoot, and Rambling Jack Elliott – proved to be a vast learning experience for Joni. And she was more than keen to learn. "Eric Andersen started teaching me open tunings, an open G, a drop D. For some reason, once I got the open tunings I began to get the harmonic sophistication that my musical fountain inside was excited by. Once I got some interesting chords to play with, my writing began to come." It was not a development favoured by her husband, who seems to have felt only jealousy towards this cuckoo in his nest. It is oddly reminiscent – without the violent denouement – of the relationship between playwright Joe Orton and Halliwell.

"I was anti-intellectual to the max... my husband was different. He had an education, a degree in literature. Chuck always said that you couldn't write unless you read. He considered me an illiterate, and he didn't give me a great deal of encouragement regarding my writing." Perhaps unconsciously, as if to spite him, Joni worked at songwriting with a commitment and passion which at first met a blank wall of indifference among fellow performers, as well as from her own husband. A singer-songwriter faces an audience totally alone, with

49

nowhere to hide – not other people's songs, or other musicians, or someone else singing for her. She needs to painfully piece together her own imaginary suit of armour, and learn unquenchable self-belief, because if she doesn't have this belief, the audience sure as hell won't either. It is a baptism of fire.

The whole process was laid bare by Joni for Sankey Phillips and Dave Wilson of *Zigzag*. The first Mariposa festival, she went purely to watch, "but the second time I went, I was a performer. That was the first year I was married, and that was a very bad year. It seemed to be full of drunks and people looking for action rather than music – so I was pretty unprepared. I wanted to do all my own material. I didn't have much variety. I wasn't very good, and I had a lot of trouble with the audience booing and hissing and saying 'Take your clothes off, sweetheart.' Things like that really shook me up because I didn't know how to counter or how to act. I thought I'd bombed; I wanted to quit and I was really desperate."

On the way home, she wrote some odd lines in the car: "It's like running for a train that left the station hours ago/I've got the urge for going but there's no place left to go." Joni was really saying that "the folk movement had died at that point, and the music I loved had no audience left. It was futile and silly and I may as well quit. So then I forgot about the line, and then one day I was cleaning out my guitar case, which is usually full of scrap songs, lyrics I've started – and I came across that piece of paper. I used to clean the case out every so often, and read all the notes over – and I would sometimes find something where I couldn't even remember what the original thought was... but the line would stir up a whole fresh idea, completely new. That's what happened with 'Urge for Going'. I wrote that in August, and the next thing I knew it was September and then October. I was really cold, and I was saying 'I hate winter and I really have the urge for going someplace warm' and I remembered that line. So I wrote the song from that." Tom Rush was eventually to record the song, and it was this more than anything that helped Joni's breakthrough to a mass audience. But there were many false starts and disappointments on the way.

"I met Dave van Ronk and Patrick Sky that October. They were doing a Canadian television show called *Sing Out*. I was shaky and thought I was awful and amateurish and I wasn't growing fast enough. I could feel how good my peers were, and I wanted encouragement." Joni had come to the wrong place for that – this was already a contracting market, and the last thing they wanted was more competition from someone as young and photogenic as Joni. Male chauvinism – as then uncapped – also reared its ugly head. "They didn't give me any as far as I could see. Van Ronk was saying things like 'Joni, you've got groovy taste in clothes, why don't you become a fashion model?' And Patrick Sky was saying 'It sucks.' But David did like 'Urge for Going' and he asked me for it, I remember. I wondered what ulterior motive he had in mind, after saying all those dreadful things to me. 'He must just want to laugh at it or something.' I was that insecure about my writing. I really thought it was awful."

S he may say that now, but something drove her onward through such put-downs and public indifference. We'll rejoin Tom Rush and 'Urge for Going' later. Meanwhile, Rush also came to the rescue of Chuck and Joni's career as a folk duo, though not of their ailing marriage. *Zigzag* takes up the story: "Tom Rush encouraged us to get out of Michigan. So we went to New York and played the Gaslight; we didn't do all that well. We drew a few interesting people, but nothing really startling." This is rather an under-estimation: the occasion was actually the start of national recognition of Joni, and lit the blue touch paper for her eventual conflagration. It started a whisper about her talents which began to echo through the folk world.

Meanwhile, Joni and Chuck eked out a living on the Toronto-Philadelphia-Detroit circuit. "We got out of Michigan and went down to the Carolinas, and found out that South Carolina was too far south; I refused to work there any more. North Carolina was very nice; we met a lot of interesting people – very nice service people – which gave me a whole new point of view on the war. I know a lot of really nice, a lot of really tragic, and a lot of really gung-ho soldiers." It was from one of the former that she bought the instrument that was to ride her to success, like a witch's broom. "A captain who owned my guitar before me wanted to give it to me. He used to come in every night and get drunk, and say 'Oh, you're better than Peter, Paul and Mary.' So I bought the guitar from him at a very, very, very good price. Love it dearly." The guitar was stolen from an airport baggage carousel at Maui, Hawaii in the late 1970s, after which Joni's career began to decline. A magic charm, perhaps.

Chuck and Joni also began to feature original songs like Joni's 'The Circle Game', written for Neil Young. Joni felt the same sense of being trapped in adulthood – marriage and childbirth, while denied the pleasures of actually bringing up her daughter – and of having somehow missed out on a vital part of adolescence. Indeed, her future life and career could be seen as an endless quest for that lost freedom, and a determination to prolong it into middle age. Meanwhile, neither her marriage nor singing partnership was going anywhere.

Connoisseurs of the long, rich and strange career of Richard Thompson still talk with awe of the final tour with his (then) wife Linda in early 1982. Backing musicians reckoned the whole thing a battlefield, with the only ceasefire coming onstage, though even then Linda would occasionally kick out at Richard mid-song. Needless to say, their last LP together, *Shoot Out The Lights*, which itemises the coming break-up of a relationship, still sells steadily, and draws much of its tension from real life, whatever else Thompson himself might claim. In the same way, the final concerts by the Mitchell duo must have been a grisly but compelling spectacle. Joni's subsequent songs, which mercilessly pick at the marriage – and her ex-husband – are masterpieces of disdain and bile. The fact that Chuck Mitchell has yet to receive a recording contract, and at this point disappears forever after his brief appearance on the stage of rock history, means that we only get one side of the story.

With the Thompsons, Linda – a wonderful singer in her own right – put her own point of view on an LP, *One Clear Moment*, which has some of the icy beauty of Mitchell at her best. Meanwhile, it is said that Richard once referred to her in an unguarded moment at a folk club in Yorkshire as "the old slag." Some of us have never quite felt the same about a man who earlier could write songs as tender as 'A Heart Needs a Home' and 'For Shame of Doing Wrong', about her.

With the Mitchells, there is no such heritage of devastating love songs to overcome, and Chuck seems more like a millstone to fight free of than a musical and spiritual support to cruelly abandon. The differences in age and attitude proved insurmountable, and the couple soon separated, and later divorced. The marriage had fallen apart within two years. According to David Crosby, "Joni kept the last name and her half of an evenly-divided split of their furniture and fixtures." Although she was to later remarry, Joni seemed so emotionally burned by this experience – and the allied, part-buried one of previously giving birth to an illegitimate child – that she pursued a tentative attitude to relationships from now on, refusing to commit herself for long to anyone.

Part of Joni Mitchell's cultural importance is her iconic status as a free, rich and independent woman, living with whosoever she chooses, and without any written contract. It is one of the themes of 'My Old Man', her song of total love and commitment. This was a lifestyle choice of extreme bravery at the time, and if Chuck Mitchell has any lasting importance, it is that of helping in a small way towards the break-up of the nuclear family – indeed, the same kind of close-knit family unit which bore and cherished the young Joni.

She gave her own views on marriage to *Macleans*: "I've only had one experience with it, in the legal sense of the word. But there's a kind of marriage that occurs, which is almost more natural, through a bonding together – sometimes the piece of paper kills something. I've talked to so many people who said their relationship was beautiful until they got married. If I ever married again I would like to create a ceremony and a ritual that had more meaning than I feel our present-day ceremonies have. Just a declaration to a group of friends. If two people are in love, they declare to a room of people that they are in love, like a marriage vow. It tells everybody in the room, 'I'm no longer flirting with you' – I'm no longer available because I've declared my heart to this person."

Meanwhile, according to *Folk Roots* magazine, Joni stayed on in Motor City, wrote her heart out and developed her bent for open tunings. "The chords I heard in my head I couldn't get with my left hand so I just retuned the guitar. I have about fifty different tunings. If any of you are typists, imagine your typewriter letters, somebody comes in and puts them in a different place every day. It takes a lot of rehearsing to get your left hand accurate because some of the shapes are similar and your hand could go like a horse to the barn, you know, in the wrong direction at any moment. But, as a compensational tool, it coughs up very fresh, melodic movement. It seems to me that it's infinite. So musically, I'm as excited as I was as a kid, maybe more."

The hand that strums can also wield (metaphorically, at least) a knife. Chuck is the subject of Joni's two most bitter songs, 'I Had a King' – where even his drip-dry shirts provoke scorn – and 'The Last Time I Saw Richard', the portrait of a failed and soured romantic. Any sympathy for the man is immediately forfeited by his own bitter comments on his ex-wife to *Time* magazine. "She always had a strong visceral sense of what to do. She knew she was beginning to happen and needed out. She was into her magic princess trip. Her first LPs are for people who were frustrated, unhappy and also living in a fantasy world."

Well, include me in too, dumbo! Joni kept up her contacts with Neil Young, meeting him again when she appeared at a club in Toronto, playing solo. He also drove over to visit her in Detroit. Joni herself places the beginning of her career as a solo artist as "around the end of '66." She was already receiving attention in New York, as were other Canadian artists. Gordon Lightfoot had already been signed up by Dylan's forceful, not to say sinister, manager, Albert Grossman. Greenwich Village was where such contacts could be made, and contracts inked. It was really the only place that Joni could now logically go, unless she decided to abandon her career and skulk home in ignominy. One last heart-rending decision had to be taken first, though.

Joni allowed her daughter Kelly to be put up for adoption. "I've never seen the child since, although I've always thought of her. I know a lot of people who have looked for their parents, and parents who have looked for their children. The reactions to it could go either way. The foster parent who had her until she was adopted contacted me the last time I was in Toronto – she was an old woman by that time and ready to die; she said she recognised me on TV because of my bone structure – and gave me all of the child's early baby pictures. For years, I didn't talk about this because of my parents, although I did leak little things, little messages, into my songs for the child, just to let her know I was thinking about her."

Whether Joni's parents actually knew at the time that they had a grandchild is thrown into doubt by this answer. This lost child has come to haunt its mother's songs, and life. She did not talk publicly about her daughter for another twenty years. Barney Hoskyns, for *Mojo*, asked Mitchell if she ever regretted not having had children of her own. It was a motif for the feminist movement towards which Joni has otherwise been so lukewarm – if not at times hostile – that women were faced with an impossible dichotomy between career and home life. Much of the last two decades has been dedicated to proving how these can be united, albeit with the help of more nursery care, house-husbands, and part-time work. These are not options for a single musician, whose job forces her to tour the world. Joni makes a deeper point, that in some mysterious way her albums and paintings are children to her, and the process of creating them is analogous to the act of giving birth.

"I think the children of artists are frequently malformed. You can't really do justice to both. My grandmothers were both frustrated musicians in different ways. The creative gene then fell upon me, in a woman's form, and in a way you have to safeguard that and do it for them, because after 1965 it was really the first opportunity that women had had in history. There were the George Sands and Georgia O'Keefes, who ploughed against the grain. But even Georgia said to me, 'Well, I would like to have been a painter and a musician, but you can't do both.' I said 'Oh yes you can!' In the end, I'm happier and better off with cats and godchildren. I have a lot of godchildren." That's all very well as a philosophical position, but the hurt remains.

Meanwhile, Joni's career began to flourish – Bernie Fiedler booked her at the Riverboat coffee house (where he had once refused her), and other clubs followed. She now had her Musicians' Union card, and a growing reputation. Canadian Broadcast Corporation producer Ross McLean got her to compose the title theme of CBC's *The Way It Is*. As they do, other television and radio engagements soon followed. Joni had struggled enough for this not to go to her head. Cameron Crowe once asked her about the days before fame, when she had become totally self-sufficient, booking her own tours and handling her financial affairs. Was this already part of her nature, or something forced on her by the end of her marriage?

"Both. At that point, I didn't know how far it was going to carry me. I had a little circuit of clubs that I could go in and say, 'Okay, your capacity is such and such. I've got you up to full capacity now. Last time I made this much; this time, why don't you pay me this much more, and you can still make a profit. Let's be fair.'

"People were starting to record my songs, I drew audiences even though I didn't have a record out. I really felt self-sufficient. I was working constantly, every night, and I was trying to build up a bank account because I didn't think it was going to last too long. I thought I was going to have to go back into what I knew, which was women's wear. Become a buyer for a department store. But I was going to go on with it as long as I could. Or maybe into commercial art. Whatever." The idea that she could make a long-term living from folk singing was as fanciful as – well, some of her own imagery. She had about as much chance of becoming a millionaire from this as of marrying a fairy prince.

"None of us have any grandiose ideas about the kind of success we received. In those days it was really a long shot. Especially for a Canadian. I remember my mother talking to a neighbour who asked, 'Where is Joan living?' And she said, 'In New York, she's a musician.' And they went 'Ohhh, you poor woman.' It was hard for them to relate." Joni was ever suspicious, however successful she eventually became, of anyone who took an interest in her merely because she was fashionable. Indeed, she later expressed some bitterness about sudden acceptance by those who had previously ignored her work.

"I don't like receiving things that don't mean anything. I couldn't get work in these little piddling clubs, and then I couldn't believe that suddenly overnight all these people loved me for the same songs. These same people sat in clubs where I was the opening act and talked through my show. Now suddenly they were rapt? I wanted to see where they were at. I wanted to show them where I was at."

And show them she certainly did.

In 1966, Joni had been asked to do a guest spot at the Checkmate Club in Detroit, where Tom Rush and his band were featured artists. Rush was so impressed with the spot that he asked to add 'Urge for Going' to his set, and later recorded it as a single, which became an unexpected hit, going Top Ten in New England. Rush re-recorded it, adding another of Mitchell's verses, and included two more songs by her on his next LP, one of which provided its title. *The Circle Game* enjoyed a healthy run in the US album charts in 1967, and brought Mitchell's songwriting talents to a mass audience. As Joni herself gratefully related to *Zigzag*: "Tom took my song 'Urge for Going' to Judy Collins, and she apparently didn't like it – it just didn't excite her enough to do it. He learned it in the meantime, and one day I got a letter from him saying 'I'm going to do 'Urge for Going' – I don't think it's my sort of song but I'm going to try it anyway.' And he had beautiful success with it."

Her debt to Rush does not end there. It's to this Harvard-educated folk singer that she really owes her artistic breakthrough, and she has always been glad to acknowledge the debt. "My husband didn't give me a great deal of encouragement regarding my writing. But Tom Rush did. Tom would say, 'Do you have any new songs?' I'd play him a batch and he'd say 'Any more?' I always held the ones out that I felt were too sensitive or too feminine, and those would always be the ones he chose. Because of Tom, I began to get noticed."

It was Rush who persuaded her to get out of Michigan, and try New York as a solo act. She played the Gaslight but the concert did not match up to her own high expectations. That's where a highly paid eighties-style consultant would quietly slide out of the door, but Rush taught the two secret ingredients in any career: hard work and persistence. That, and the odd lucky break. *Zigzag* again: "Tom really started it. He opened doors. I was running out of clubs to play, and there wasn't very much money where I was playing. And the only way I got work was through Tom. He'd go into a club and he'd stand up there and sing my song, and build me up and people would get curious, you see. So he really opened up a whole circuit for me. That's where I grew and through experience got some other ideas, and lived some other things."

Rush's most precious gift, though, was to give self-confidence to the young songwriter. As an established artist, already recording with Elektra records, and noted for his good taste in choosing other people's songs to cover, his words carried real weight. "Tom really helped me because at that time I was terribly insecure about my writing – I really thought it was awful." Such insecurity stretched further. Joni's move from country to city – Toronto was only one step on the way –

was traumatic, and was to form the main theme of her first album.

"I was raised in a country town in Saskatchewan and I thought the city was a glamorous, glittering place. But I discovered that it's vulgar, plastic, in a rush for a dollar." The cover of her first LP says it all, a swirling child-like drawing of paradise – peacocks, sailing ships and exotic flowers – half-concealing a small photo of Joni in a filthy back alley in the rain, apparently menaced by dalek-like trash cans and a parked van. On the back cover, the photo has expanded, and Joni has taken a few steps forward. She looks lost and threatened, overburdened by her umbrella, suitcase and guitars. Whether by chance or accident, she is walking towards the shelter of a transparent umbrella, presumably held by the photographer. A peacock looks on in amazement, as if inhabiting the truer reality, that held inside the singer's skull. Half-hidden in the swirling design is her name – and the injunction to "love life". Birds in the sky spell out, less certainly, *Song to a Seagull*. The photo of the 'real' Joni is enclosed in what looks suspiciously like an opium poppy.

Joni relocated to a one-bedroom apartment in Manhattan's Chelsea district, between 5th and 6th Avenue on 16th Street. Here she lined one bedroom wall with silver foil, festooned the door-jambs with crepe paper, and draped Old Glory in the window. It was the start of bedsitter music, whose other exponents included Leonard Cohen – with the archetypal *Songs from a Room* – and Al Stewart, copying the trend in England with *Bedsitter Images*. Joni was also a devotee of Tolkien, the subject of a vast underground cult. (For such reasons, Marc Bolan was later nicknamed the bopping elf!) She even toyed with writing a children's book about mythical kingdoms. Her ex-husband's princess taunt was coming vibrantly to life – but only in that she was finding a new kind of freedom, not indulging in sad escapism. Joni's new apartment, with its brick wall and fireplace, faced the street. Somehow she managed to convert city bustle and dirt into lyrical jewels: one masterstroke was to describe the morning light, tinged with smog and soot, pouring into her home "like butterscotch." A curse was thus transformed into a blessing.

Given the opportunities of living in a great city, for a time Joni intended to create and sell art nouveau clothes and designs, but her growing success on the New York folk circuit soon took over. Dave

Crosby remembers her "planning a career in retail clothing, sales and design and had already begun accumulating (at bargain prices) the art nouveau and Tiffany antiques that would come into vogue years later." These were the "second-hand trappings" that *Time* magazine sneered about when describing her Laurel Canyon home. Meanwhile, she worried that her chosen career was on a downward curve. The folk-rock boom – now literally electrified by the likes of the Byrds – seemed to be wiping out the established folk clubs, from which she earned a precarious living. Folk-rock had floated away from its roots, and inhabited instead theatres, sports grounds, and upmarket drinking venues. It was later to spawn a whole new circuit of psychedelic clubs. The answer for the moment was to plunge herself into live gigs with an even greater commitment. Joni "worked for forty-some weeks on the Eastern seaboard, just getting this nest egg so that when the whole thing collapsed I could afford to go back into women's wear."

In his autobiography, *Long Time Gone*, Dave Crosby remembers (with surprising accuracy, considering how he abused his nervous system ever after) his own career, and those of his friends and rivals. Joni "moved to New York on her own to continue singing her songs on the folk circuit, counting herself a lucky woman because she could work forty weeks a year, kept her rent paid through the end of the next month, and had $400 in the bank. Her audience was the hipsters and progressive folkies in little coffee houses and clubs around the dying folk circuit." Joni was not unduly dismayed: a true child of the sixties, she always had the clear hope that something else would turn up. In those optimistic times something usually did, though the freedoms of the era are derided by devotees of the kind of economic brutalism that destroys the hopes and dreams of ordinary people. Joni knew how to avoid disappointment, by never expecting too much at once.

"I always kept my goals very short. Like I would like to play in a coffee house, so I did. I would like to play in the United States, you know, the States, the magic of crossing the border. So I did. I would like to make a certain amount of money a year, which I thought would give me the freedom to buy the clothes that I wanted and the antiques and some women trips, a nice apartment in New York that I wouldn't have to be working continuously to support. But I came to folk music when it was already dying. The year Dylan went electric, the folk clubs started closing all over the country. It was an epidemic. The only people being hired were those who had records out. I was always bringing up the rear. In those days, if you played acoustic guitar, club owners treated you as if you were a dinosaur." Joni stored up the slights of these times as one does however rich and famous one later becomes. The cruellest blows came from those whom she regarded as heroes or friends.

"I went to the Newport Festival. Judy Collins called me up. She was supposed to take me. Well, Judy stood me up, and she was my hero. It was kind of heartbreaking. I waited and waited and waited and she never came to pick me up to take me to Newport. A day went by and I got a phone call from her, and she sounded kind of sheepish. She said somebody had sung one of my songs in a workshop. It was a terrible rendition, she said, but people went crazy. Judy really felt I should be at Newport, so she gave me instructions on how to get there."

All's well that ends well, except that it isn't. Joni was now to know at first hand what it was like being at the cutting edge of the hit-making machine, and quite how miserable fame could be. "When I played there I got that large roar and it made me incredibly nervous. That night my girlfriend Jane, who was road managing for me, and I went to a party at one of those old mansions. Standing at the gate was like being at Studio 54 in New York. People all over the place who couldn't get in." A guard asked us for credentials. I kind of waxed passive and backed down. Jane, who was always trying to get me to use my existential edge, said 'Do you know who she is?' Well, she said my name and these kids standing at the gate went 'Aaah' and sucked their breath in. My heart started to beat like crazy, I turned around and ran in the other direction like some crazed animal. I ran, and I ran, and I ran. I must've run about five blocks before I realised how strange my reaction was."

In another interview, Joni elaborates. "My eyes bulged out of my head. I bolted like a deer. I came back to Janie and said 'I'm so embarrassed, why did I do that? It's a mystery to me.' Well, she had lived with retarded children. And a retard is smart in a lot of ways. They're simplified down to a kind of intelligence that a more complex mind is not hip to." Her friend told her it was one of the smartest things she had ever seen. It was not unique. Leonard Cohen ran off stage after one song at his first important solo concert, although fortunately (in my eyes at least) he was later persuaded back, and completed his set to wild applause. Psychologists say that the most powerful response to stress is 'fight or flight': take on your audience, or run away from it. Joni was to do the latter immediately after the Rolling Thunder tour, but that story must wait.

She certainly had no intention of running away from her new celebrity as a songwriter, and the growing income that it was soon bringing in. Royalties for her songs flowed back into her newly instituted publishing company, a BMI-administrated entity she christened 'Siquomb'. Its strange title derived from an acronym – 'She Is Queen Undisputedly Of Mind Beauty' – from a list of characters for her projected children's fantasy. This conceit (in both senses) also yielded the name of a song – 'Sisotowbell Lane' – on her first album, which stands for 'Somehow In Spite Of Trouble Ours Will Be Everlasting Love'. Nice.

Indeed, much of Joni's material was covered before she had an opportunity to record it herself. She need never have sung or performed a note to become rich and famous. Joni as songwriter had already attracted the attention of singers like Buffy Saint-Marie, who recorded 'The Circle Game' and 'Song to a Seagull', and Dave Van Ronk, who put early reservations aside, and cut 'Both Sides Now', under its original title, 'Clouds'. Al Kooper – who had seen her at the Cafe a GoGo – recommended her to Judy Collins, who recorded 'Michael from Mountains' and 'Both Sides Now' on her great LP for Elektra, *Wildflowers*. 'Both Sides Now' gave Collins a million-selling single and a Top Ten hit.

Some of her greatest songs – 'Urge for Going' and 'Eastern Rain' spring immediately to mind – were never actually recorded by Mitchell herself, and thus only appear on bootleg vinyl, if at all. A songbook officially published in 1969, includes compositions like 'Jeremy' and 'Winter Lady'. Other unrecorded songs from the period include 'Just Like Me', 'Brandy Eyes', 'Mr Blue', 'London Bridge', 'Drummer Man', and 'Carnival in Kenora'. A long-lost bootleg called *The Posall and the Mosalm* contains priceless tapes of broadcasts and live performances from 1966-7. I have been unable to locate it – these things are illegal, you know – but the most intriguing titles are 'Joni's Coke Commercial',

'Queen Siquomb', and a radio broadcast entitled 'Approximately Sugar Mountain', presumably a version of Neil Young's song, on which 'Circle Game' was based.

The song 'Winter Lady', which gives its name to another bootleg, recorded in Canada in 1967, is exquisite, and very much a self-portrait in the manner of similar haunting mood-pieces by Sandy Denny, Mitchell's spiritual sister across the Atlantic. It is written as if by a man addressing a woman, but the imagery and longing are prime Joni:

Staring out your winter window
At a silver sky you know you've been to
In a kiss, upon a day
Before a spring

No wonder that, as early as 1967, a reviewer was writing that "she plays Yang to Bob Dylan's Yin, equalling him in richness and profusion of imagery, and surpassing him in conciseness and direction." On the other hand, classical music critic Fritz Spiegl wrote that artists like Dylan and Joni offer "instant bliss without mental effort." But then so do the likes of Keats, Tennyson and Shakespeare. What is important is that, on later readings, there is a mental as well as a verbal structure (which there isn't always in the work of, say, Swinburne!).

Joni passes that test conclusively. Underlying her verbal pyrotechnics is a precision and clarity of thought which Dylan – for all his greatness – often lacks. Less controversially, Mitchell was also rapidly gaining the reputation of being an engaging live performer, singing solo backed by her own acoustic guitar and dulcimer. In some ways this was the happiest time of her life. As she later told Cameron Crowe: "I was outspoken. I enjoyed performing. I loved the compliments I received when I came off stage. Everything seemed to be proportionate to me. I had $400 in the bank. I thought I was filthy rich. I liked the liberty of it all. I liked the idea that I was going to North Carolina, visiting all these mysterious states. I used to tell long, rambling tales onstage. It was very casual."

The problem was, it all became too much of a good thing. "Then it began to get really disproportionate. I couldn't really enjoy it after that. I knew it was good, but the adoration seemed out of line. People are attracted to you because you smell of success. And they're simultaneously saying to you, 'Don't change.' But as soon as you have so many hangers-on, you have to change, and then you go through the pains of hearing that you 'changed, man.' It goes to your head. There's a whole lot of levels of adjustment. There are no books written on it; nobody tells you what to expect. Some people get all puffed up and say 'I deserved it.' I thought it was too much to live to. I thought, 'You don't even know who I am. You want to worship me?' That's why I became a confessional poet. I thought, 'You better know who you're applauding up here.' It was a compulsion to be honest with my audience."

It was that kind of intimacy that Joni managed to conjure up, even in front of around half a million people on the Isle of Wight. "I liked playing in small clubs the best, still do. I really like holding the attention of thirty or forty people. I never liked the roar of the big crowd. I could never adjust to the sound of people gasping at the mere mention of my name. It horrified me. And I also knew how fickle people could be. I knew they were buying an illusion, and I thought 'Maybe I should know a little more about who I am.' I wanted to believe that the attention I was getting was for me. I didn't want there to be such a gulf between who I presented and who I was. David Geffen used to tell me that I was the only star he ever met who wanted to be ordinary. I never wanted to be a star. I didn't like entering a room with all eyes on me. I still don't like the attention of a birthday party. I prefer Christmas, which is everybody's holiday." In career terms, Joni was about to have all her Christmases and birthdays at once.

The period of Joni's first public triumph was neatly topped and tailed by two visits to England, mysterious events now, half covered by the sands of time. The first visit was probably sometime in 1967, or early the following year, and she brought back to America a taste of swinging London. Her host was an American in exile, the legendary Joe Boyd, who had been involved backstage when Dylan first went electric, at the 1965 Newport Festival. He became a mainstay of the burgeoning English underground, producing the first Pink Floyd single, and helping to manage the UFO club, where English psychedelia had its strange birth.

Boyd went on to run Witchseason, a company specialising in the first vintage of British psychedelic folk: the Incredible String Band, Fairport Convention and – later – Nick Drake. These were people who were taking folk roots and twisting them into another dimension. Boyd immediately recognised Joni's talent in New York, and brought her over to London, though whether he was ever actually her manager remains a matter of conjecture. "Joe Boyd had taken me to England with the Incredible String Band, and I'd done some work in some little coffee houses there. I'd come back all Carnaby Street, with false eyelashes, sequinned belts, flashed out."

Joni added in another interview, "that was during the Twiggy-Viva era, and I remember I wore a lot of makeup." She played some low-key gigs, and there is a wonderful photograph extant of her sitting outside the Revolution Club, all innocence and impossibly long legs, cradling her guitar. The trip produced several new songs, including a parody of 'London Bridge is Falling Down' ("London Bridge is falling up/save the tea leaves in my cup"). Boyd helped Joni obtain a publishing deal with Essex music in the UK, long before her own first album was released. After her visit, she left a tape of ten or so songs, which led directly to cover versions of her work by the likes of fellow American exile Julie Felix. "She was doing quite a few of my songs, not very common ones, but peculiar ones I'd forgotten. She got them off old lead sheets and tapes."

Fairport Convention, the English counterpart to Jefferson Airplane and the Grateful Dead, recorded sparkling versions of 'I Don't Know Where I Stand' and 'Chelsea Morning' on their first album. Kingsley Abbot recalls the band puzzling over exactly what the "incense owl" mentioned in 'Chelsea Morning' actually was! The lyrics are tossed between singers Judy Dyble and Iain Matthews, like a beach-ball. Matthews would later have a Number One single with his own version of 'Woodstock'. Early Fairport were also regularly performing 'Marcie' and 'Night in the City': both appear on a recent bootleg drawn from radio sessions of the time (and subsequently have been poached back by Ashley Hutchings, in his *Scrapbook* series of CDs). Uncredited on the bootleg is a rough and ready version of 'Both Sides Now', notable for Richard Thompson's sensitive transposing of Mitchell's open chording on his Gibson Les Paul.

When Sandy Denny joined Fairport in place of Dyble, the band continued to mine the Joni Mitchell songbook, her lyrical delicacy and delight in melody fitting their own bouncy optimism. Fairport could always pick a good new song, as they can to this day. Sandy made 'I Don't Know Where I Stand' her own on a radio session, collected on *Heyday*, and their second album *What We Did On Our Holidays* features a version of 'Eastern Rain' which glistens with plucked electric guitars imitating rain drops. Fairport later made a full-time move into traditional folk, but when a highly nervous Judy Dyble reappeared at Cropredy for their 25th anniversary, it's no coincidence that the song she chose to perform was 'Both Sides Now'.

Shortly after the release of her first album, on 28th September, 1968, Joni joined Fairport on the bill of a one-night Festival of Contemporary Song at London's Festival Hall. Tickets were priced between 7s 6d and £1. It was this concert that really established her as a major artist in Britain; she was billed as a 'special guest star from America.' Few details of her set survive, but Mark Cooper – who was there – remembers Fairport performing long, supercharged versions of Leonard Cohen's 'Suzanne' and Richard Farina's 'Reno, Nevada'. The other artists – and for once that overdone word means something – to appear were Al Stewart, the Johnstons (with a young Paul Brady), and Jackson C Frank, a mysterious figure whose songs were legendary in Soho coffee houses of the time, and who had a love affair with Sandy Denny. Joni still remembers the event with great nostalgia, remarking "I'd sure like to meet the Johnstons again."

The following evening, a session by Joni was broadcast on John Peel's *Top Gear*. No tapes are known to exist, but Ken Garner's *In Session Tonight* – a work of deranged scholarship – lists the songs as 'Chelsea Morning', 'Gallery', 'Night in the City' and 'Cactus Tree', only the last of which was then available on record. Of special interest, in view of later projects, is the fact that she is backed by the John Cameron Group, a jazz combo. The line-up of this early fusion group was Cameron on piano, Harold McNair on saxophone, Danny Thompson on string bass, and Tony Carr on drums. McNair died young, having provided some beautiful flute accompaniments to Donovan's magic garden period. Thompson joined Pentangle, another group at the epicentre of jazz-folk fusion, and has since played with just about everyone, from Tim Buckley to his namesake Richard Thompson. According to Garner, Joni Mitchell was booked for various other Radio One sessions during tours in 1968 and 1969, but all were cancelled for some reason or other.

She gave one of her first major interviews – a rare thing then as now – for Karl Dallas of *Melody Maker*, and it gives a particular insight into the mind of a woman just emerging into fame. "Since I started writing songs, the range of my voice has extended downwards something like two octaves, which gives me a lot more freedom in the sort of melodies I'm writing."

Joni also reveals a hitherto unknown political dimension to her work. She was not doing too much writing at the time: "I'm too hung up about what's going on in America politically. I keep thinking, how can I sing 'night in the city looks pretty to me', when I know it's not pretty at all, with people living in slums and being beaten up by police? It was what happened in Chicago during the Democratic Convention that really got me thinking. All those kids being clubbed. If I'd been wearing these Levis, they'd have clubbed me – not for doing anything, but because this is the uniform of the enemy. That's what they are beginning to call the kids today, the enemy. I keep trying to put what I feel into words, but it's all being said so much better by other people. Strangely enough, a song I wrote at the end of last year, 'The Fiddle and the Drum', expresses what I feel now, though I wasn't conscious of feeling that way then."

That song was to appear on her next album, *Clouds*. Dallas makes a very sharp comment, when he says that these songs are the work of a visual artist, "the things that stick in the mind are all visual." Meanwhile, we must return to what had happened to Joni herself between these two London visits. In the space of a few months she had acquired herself a hotshot manager, a recording contract, and a producer (and boyfriend) who had just left one of the greatest rock bands of all time, the Byrds. The 'seagull from Saskatoon' was herself about to take flight.

J oni looked after her own bookings and finances until, in autumn 1967, she met Elliot Roberts, an up-and-coming agent/manager, born Elliot Rabinowitz in the Bronx. Buffy Sainte-Marie brought him to see

Mitchell opening (for fifteen dollars a night) for Richie Havens at the Cafe a GoGo in Greenwich Village. Roberts: "I told her I'd kill for her." He immediately quit his job – just after his friend and rival David Geffen – at the William Morris agency in New York, to become her full-time manager.

He described Joni at the time as "a jumble of creative clutter," her guitar case stuffed with napkins, road maps, and scraps of paper, all covered with lyrics. Dave Crosby described Roberts as "a good dude. And he is not a fairweather friend, and he is not a bullshitter. However, he is, in his managerial capacity, capable of lying straight-faced to anyone, anytime, ever. But he's really a beautiful cat, he really has a heart. You just naturally get to love him, unless you gotta contract with him. He's armed robbery in a business deal." As to his future business partner, if "he doesn't rob you blind, he'll send David Geffen over; *he'll* take your whole company." Roberts set up a tiny office on West 57th Street, but he was initially trying to push water back uphill. Roberts: "Everything about her was unique and original, but we couldn't get a deal. The folk period had died, so she was totally against the grain."

Not for long. By 1969, Mitchell owned a music publishing corporation worth at least $1.5 million, and by 1973 she owned two such corporations, as well as a good deal of valuable real estate. This for somebody who had once, literally, starved for her art. Roberts helped polish her act – as Epstein once had with the Beatles, and nobody had ever dared to with Bob Dylan. He also provided a managerial umbrella, perhaps as symbolised on that first LP cover. Mitchell: "I was very sheltered by Elliot Roberts and Crosby, Stills and Nash when I entered the business. I was in the industry for a long time before I had any idea of what drugs people were doing. I mean, I'd say 'Geez, he looks awfully skinny. Why doesn't he have an appetite?'"

The idea of such legendary drugs dabblers as Crosby, Stills, and later Neil Young providing protection is touching, if not farcical. Indeed, Roberts seemed more of a stern father-figure. As Roberts himself told it, "when I first met David Crosby he was going with Joni Mitchell; Joni was my only client. The day after I first saw her play we left on tour. We did a month of clubs. Joni went to Coconut Grove and met David Crosby, and I went to California alone to meet with Mo Ostin at Warner Brothers to get Joni a record deal." Crosby advised Roberts to talk to

Andy Wickham at Reprise. Wickham was English, and had worked for Lou Adler at Dunhill. Roberts recalled years later that "Andy was a folkie at heart," his best friend being Phil Ochs, with whom he roomed. Ochs was once thrown out of a taxi by Dylan, who then wrote 'Positively 4th Street' about him. Ochs hung himself in 1976 after being 'uninvited' to the Rolling Thunder tour. Even his greatest fans (like me) are turned off by the whiny nature of his voice, which has the timbre of an electric drill.

Roberts was knocking at an open door. Reprise records, originally Frank Sinatra's label, was by 1967 in radical need of some hip credibility. Other signings that year included Jimi Hendrix, Randy Newman, and Arlo Guthrie. Mitchell had already turned down an approach from the folk stalwarts' record label Vanguard as "a slave labour deal." On her return from her first trip to England, she appeared at the Gaslight South folk club in Coconut Grove, Florida, which is where Crosby 'discovered' her. With Wickham as Mitchell's first record company supporter, Reprise supremo Mo Ostin paid for a David Crosby-produced demo, to be recorded at Sunset Sound (with Buffalo Springfield, boasting two other future members of Crosby, Stills, Nash and Young, recording across the hall in Studio B). It was certainly a mutual appreciation society.

Joni said of her mentor that "Crosby is the most into my music of any outsider I've ever met. He also has very good judgement, and gets a very good sound out of me in the studio. He's taught me a lot of things about recording, and he's managed to get that stage presence on the album." She later added "David was very enthusiastic. He was twinkly about it." At the end of the 'summer of love', Crosby was technically unemployed, literally a Byrd dropping. On *The Notorious Byrd Brothers* LP, his place on the front cover is taken by a horse, which seems to sum up the way his ex-colleagues now felt about him. Jefferson Airplane had recorded his song 'Triad', about a *menage-a-trois*, and Crosby was hanging out in San Francisco (the Byrds were far more LA), with the Airplane and the Grateful Dead.

That winter, he returned to Coconut Grove, where he had once been a struggling folk artist, before fame and Roger McGuinn beckoned. With money loaned by Peter Tork, a veteran both of the Monkees and of LSD, Crosby bought a schooner, The Mayan, on which to live, for the bargain basement price of $22,500. On board, he wrote the song destined to become his masterpiece, 'Wooden Ships', with Paul Kantner and Stephen Stills. It was, and is, a terrifying movie in sound about post-holocaust survival, with odd parallels to a long poem, 'Misanthropos', written at about the same time by SF-based English poet Thom Gunn.

It was here, equally apocalyptically, that he also met Joni Mitchell. Crosby tells the story himself in his extraordinary autobiography, *Long Time Gone*, the portrait of a man going to hell and back. "Her original material was complicated and jazz tinged and fell into no currently popular category. If anyone labelled it at all it was 'art folk' and unique to Joni. It was the dawning of the age of electric guitar technique, where the only realistic limit to the total wattage would be the electrical capacity of the power lines feeding the auditorium. A willowy blonde with big blue eyes and high cheekbones, singing art songs in a bell-like soprano with a Canadian accent, and accompanying herself on acoustic guitar and dulcimer was not anyone's idea of the next big thing."

Over to Joni: "I used to secretly call him Yosemite Sam in my mind. I don't think I ever called him that to his face. He mistakenly thought I wrote a song called 'Dawntreader' for him, and was thinking of naming his boat the same. I guess people identify with songs that you write and think that you wrote them just for them. David was delightful company and a great appreciator. His eyes were star sapphires to me. When he laughed they seemed to twinkle like no one else's and so I fell into his merry company and we rode bikes around Coconut Grove, and the winds were warm, and at night we'd go down and listen to the masts clinking on the pier. It was a lovely period, and soon we became romantically involved." She added to this picture for Cameron Crowe, suggesting the personal magnetism Crosby then possessed, which he was later to burn out of his system, free-basing crack cocaine.

"He was tanned. He was straight. He was paranoid about his hair, having long hair in a short-hair society. He had a wonderful sense of humour. Crosby has enthusiasm like no one else. He can make you feel a million bucks. Or he can bring you down with the same force." Elliot Roberts now re-enters the picture, no slouch himself at getting his own way when required, but here he had met his match, twice. "She called

69

to say that she was coming back with David Crosby, and David was going to produce her first album. He showed up at my office in New York; he had long hair flowing to his shoulder, he had the trademark moustache. He was the first hippie that I met in that era. He didn't talk very much. The three of us went to California. I slept on the floor in the basement on a mattress, and David slept in the big bed with the little woman. The very first day in the studio at Sunset Sound, about an hour into the session, an engineer comes in and tells David that the Buffalo Springfield were in the room next door. Joni says 'You've got to meet Neil Young. I know him from Canada. He's so funny. You're going to love this guy'."

Crosby's effect on Joni was to rob her of her inhibitions, and of her makeup, too artificial for this brave new world. In this communal oneness, even somebody as conventionally 'ugly' as Janis Joplin, or Pigpen of the Dead, attained their own beauty, just by being themselves. Joni was beautiful by any measurement, but Crosby wanted her to be natural, not man-made. A surprisingly feminist move. Back to Joni: "I think I even had on false eyelashes at the time. And Crosby was from his scrub-faced Californian culture, so one of his first projects in our relationship was to encourage me to let go of all this elaborate war paint. It was a great liberation to get up in the morning and wash your face... and not have to do anything else."

In the spirit of the new togetherness, Joni and David lived together while they worked on the album. Elliot moved first to take up the offer of a bed in Stephen Stills' house, then stayed with Neil Young, who he ended up managing. Within a few months, Roberts was renting his own house in Laurel Canyon, just up the road from Joni's modest wooden bungalow. If anyone thought, however, that Mitchell was going to be a pushover when it came to determining her own career, they were soon to be rudely awakened. She was too busy actively 'being free.'

"When it came time to make my record, David did me a solid favour for which I am eternally grateful, because the way you enter the game in this business is usually the way you stay. David helped me keep control of my work, which I do to this day. The record company was going to 'folk rock' me up and David thought that would be a tragedy, that my music should be recorded the way I wrote it. Since he had been in the premier folk rock group, he could go to the record company with some authority and say 'I'm going to produce her' and the trick was he was not going to 'produce' me at all. He said: 'It's like you're sitting on the patio of the Old World Restaurant, and a girl goes by in blue jeans and after she goes by you think 'Did she have a little lace down the seams of her blue jeans?' Anything we added would be minimal; that's the way we proceeded."

Joni updated this account for Timothy White. "I didn't work with another producer for thirteen projects – except for one cut ('Tin Angel', produced by Paul Rothchild). I found that all the producers were men, and if I stood in defiance of them, then somebody would call me a 'ballbuster.' There were a lot of good things David did in producing that record, but mainly his theory was: [here she approximates Crosby's high-pitched, fast talking earnestness] 'I'm going to pretend to produce this record, but I'm not going to do a damn thing – but because I'm folk rock and that's happening and you look like a folkie, in order to make you commercial we have to rock you up and I don't want to hear you rocked up, so I'm going to pretend to rock you but I'm not going to do it.' So that was the ruse we perpetrated in making that first record. There wasn't even much overdubbing, because I couldn't overdub, really, in the beginning. I couldn't separate my playing from my singing sense, it was locked together from so much touring."

As she later told *Folk Roots*, "Mozart didn't have a producer. I don't need an interior decorator for my music. All the mistakes, the things you like about it, and don't like about it are on me... there are things I would like to change. But a lot of it holds up. I think I got it right the first time. Thirteen albums without a producer is unheard of. I don't think there's anybody else in the business that ever did that." Joni also noted, "I'm not lettuce, what do I need a producer for?" This, of course, flies in the face of corporate wisdom, that everything has to be produced, managed, and packaged for mass consumption. Even the ornery Bob Dylan had a decent (ish) LP butchered by an Arthur Baker remix, which squeezed all the life out, like a man choking a rat. Patrick McGoohan predicted all this in *The Prisoner*: increasingly we are numbers, our destinies in the hands of others. By which reckoning, Joni Mitchell is definitely a Number Six!

Back then, though, Crosby and Mitchell were writing the rule book, making things up as they went along. Their discoveries are now codified as the dull strictures of corporate rock. To an age of PR experts and company spin doctors, the way her friends went about 'breaking' Joni to a wider public now seems touchingly naive, and brilliantly successful. Crosby took particular delight in showing off Joni like a rare orchid, valuable and strange. One night, he brought back to his pad the now forgotten SF satirical group, the Committee. At 4am, everyone now presumably flying high, he announced "I want you to hear someone." Like an angel previously hidden from sight, Joni appeared and sang a half-dozen songs. One of the stunned audience later declared, "We thought we had hallucinated her." Joni nodded, said little, and disappeared upstairs. Crosby simply grinned. Peter Fonda was also bowled over by the essence of newness.

"She was brand new, hadn't been heard by any of us. David comes strolling in one day. 'I've got one for you.' I thought he had some groupie or something, so I said 'This is my house, David. My wife...' He says 'No, no, come on. Serious, man. Listen to this.' And Joni, kind of shy, appears. Staring at the ground for something to do, she sees my twelve-string guitar leaning against the wall and asks 'Can I use that?' She grabs hold of my guitar and detunes the fucker and then plays thirteen or fourteen songs, warbling like the best thing I'd ever heard in my life. David's so proud and he says 'That song's about me, and that song's about so-and-so and isn't this great.' Joni was fabulous, with a wonderful voice and a great style. Lovely."

Elliot Roberts could only watch in amazement. "David invited some people over one day. I remember Mama Cass, John Sebastian, Michelle Phillips, about seven or eight people, all heavy players. David says 'Joan' and calls Joni out. She was upstairs and came down with her guitar and she played eight or nine of the best songs ever written. The next day B Mitchell Reed talked about it on the radio, how there was this girl in town that's recording this album and whenever this album comes out, it's going to be one of the great albums of all time. When the album finally came out, everyone in LA was aware of Joni Mitchell. The first club date we played, at the Troubadour, was standing room only for four nights, two shows per night." That is pure show-biz. Worthy indeed of 'Talky' Malcom McLaren – an archetypal old hippie – and the way he broke the Sex Pistols, first making them the property of a small clique, then spreading the story to media barons like John Peel.

At least Joni never turned around and asked her audience if they felt as if they'd just been swindled! Because they never were.

I f Joni seemed at times to have been transported direct from another planet, there were identifiable influences on her work, which time has made clearer. Just like the Sex Pistols, in fact. She once told Timothy White that her song 'Ladies' Man' is "a song Aretha Franklin could have sung. In fact, there's two little catches in my vocal that are out of admiration for her. I also have at least one note I got from Tony Bennett, who I liked as a kid. And there's a lot of the Andrews Sisters in my choral work, although my harmony is different from the harmony of that era."

A more obvious musical inheritance was the folk purity of Joan Baez – soon discarded – and a certain freshness learnt from Judy Collins. The French critic Jacques Vassal noted (in translation) that both shared "the same fire, the same passionate ardour, even though modified by an admirable reserve." Collins herself noticed a distinct Canadian feel, that of an old-fashioned bouquet, in her former pupil. "I sing Joni's songs because I like them immensely. There doesn't seem to be anyone quite as good. She finds words that unthread the confusion and paints scenes as vivid and direct as her watercolours. When she sings, the circle is completed. Joni takes you on trips interwoven with magic and the secret of what it feels like to be a woman." As to the original influence, Joni is wholehearted, telling *Broadside* that "for the first year and a half of my career I memorised her albums. And that's what I sang, my sets were her sets."

Joan Baez is a different proposition: "Oh, she was horrible. She was always supercompetitive and threatened by me." This must have made backstage chat at the 1970 Isle of Wight Festival a joy and delight. There is also an element of matricide here. Joni herself once appeared to be "a spin-off of something that was going out of vogue, which was like a poor man's Baez or Judy Collins." Fortunately, "musicians could see I was a musician," from the start. Perhaps as a result, Joni has been peculiarly sensitive ever since about attempts to categorise or belittle her, especially in gender terms.

"For a while it was assumed that I was writing women's songs. Then men began to notice that they saw themselves in the songs too. I'm not a feminist. That's too divisional for me. This guy came up to me at some public event once, and said 'Joni, you're the best woman songwriter in the world.' And I went 'Ha' and kind of snickered. And he insisted 'No, you are the greatest female singer-songwriter ever.' And I walked off. And he thought it was because I was being modest. But this whole female singer-songwriter tag is strange. You know, my peers are not Carly Simon and these other women." In 1971, just such an article, in *Disc*, placed Mitchell among a whole phalanx of female singer-songwriters, most of them artistically not fit to cobble her boots, as if this were some kind of new movement. You know, the kind that journalists love to invent. Besides the likes of Carole King, Priscilla Coolidge, Carly Simon and Melanie, *Disc* targets the figure of Laura Nyro, now almost forgotten outside a small coterie of admirers.

King is a fine songwriter, with little of Joni's vocal range, Simon is featherlight in comparison, and Melanie an endearing but one-dimensional figure. Nyro came out flying at the start of her career, her strange songs fuelled by early LSD overload. Like Mitchell, her songs were immediately covered by all kinds of rock bands. Her singing style was more confrontational, and her roots were in soul and doo-wop rather than folk, but both had swooping voices, and inner complexity. Cameron Crowe reminds Joni that the two were once considered equals but that it is now "all but taken for granted that Laura Nyro wasn't tough enough to survive in the business." Her reply fascinates, as Nyro is Joni's mirror image, exchanging fame for domestic peace.

"Inspiration can run out, you know. Laura Nyro made a choice that has tempted me on many occasions. And that was to lead an ordinary life. She married a carpenter, as I understand, and turned her back on it all. Which is brave and tough in its own way. Many, many times as a writer, I've come to a day where I say 'None of this has any meaning.' If you maintain that point of view, if you hold onto it and possess it, that's it for you. There's a possibility that you can come firmly to that conclusion, as Rimbaud did, and give it up. I've always managed to move out of those pockets."

Mitchell was also an early admirer of, and friend to, Buffy Sainte-Marie. From her, she learnt about stage presence (some call it dignity) and self-belief in her songwriting. Joni has at times herself claimed native roots – like Neil Young, she has been called a Hollywood Indian – but unlike Jimi Hendrix, Cher, Robbie Robertson, or Sainte-Marie herself, this is metaphorical, not actual. I can certainly find no evidence otherwise in Mitchell's family tree. Still, the two women share a sense of the Canadian landscape which is nostalgic and angry, proprietorial and dispossessed, at the same time.

Neil Young was like a kid brother, someone to encourage and look after. Their careers intertwine, like braids twisted into a rope. It has been a mutual support system, rather than a direct musical influence, one of the few times she actually appeared on stage with Young being at the Band's 'Last Waltz'. They first met when Joni and Chuck came to Winnipeg, playing the 4-D folk circuit. Mitchell: "I remember putting up this Christmas tree in our hotel room. Neil was this rock 'n' roller who was coming around to folk music through Bob Dylan. He came out to the club, and was the same way he is now – this off-handed, dry wit. And you know what his ambition was at the time? He wanted a hearse, and a chicken farm. And when you think of it, what he's done with his dream is not that far off. He just added a few buffalo. And a fleet of antique cars. He's always been pretty true to his vision. It was years later, when I got to California – Elliot Roberts and I came out as strangers to a strange land – and we went to a Buffalo Springfield session to see Neil. He was the only other person I knew. That's where I met everybody else. And the scene started to come together."

Both Mitchell and Young remain free spirits, doggedly following their own direction, sometimes to the cost of those around them. Both contain within themselves an essential 'do not touch' solitude. If Joni's artistic vision has darkened over the years, Young's was bible-black from the very start. Joni's greatest tribute to him is her early song 'The Circle Game': in concert in 1970 she introduced it with her usual breathless urgency, and with tender affection.

"There was a friend of mine who had just left a rock 'n' roll band in Manitoba, near where I come from on the prairies. He had just turned twenty-one, and that meant in Winnipeg he was no longer allowed into his favourite haunt, which was a kind of teenybopper club, and once you were over twenty-one you weren't allowed in there any more, and he was really feeling terrible, because his girlfriends and everybody that he wanted to hang out with, and his band, could not go there... that

75

was about the same time that *Esquire* magazine was doing photographs of girls in trash bins, you knew that once you were over twenty-one you'd had it. There was a very strange philosophy going around at that time, so he wrote this song called 'Oh to Live on Sugar Mountain', which was a lament for lost youth, and I thought God if we get to twenty-one and there's nothing after that, that's a pretty bleak future, so I wrote a song for him and for myself, to just sort of give him some hope, and for all of you, and it's got a chorus we can all join in... now I'm losing my voice."

Bob Dylan is a more problematic figure for Mitchell. His sprawling muse is the exact opposite of her careful, precise word-play. In *Zigzag*, Joni reveals that "I was what was known as a 'late Dylan fan.' At one time I was almost anti-Dylan, and I made a lot of enemies... I thought he was putting me on, I couldn't accept him. The thing was, I shared no experience with Dylan at the time, I thought a lot of his stuff was ambiguous, and not written honestly. It's like I always thought Shakespeare was really wordy and weird, right until I went to Stratford and saw a man who recited Shakespeare like it was really 20th century. It lost all of that super-drama stuff that really turned me off, and it flowed, and I understood it. So it's the same thing with Dylan; now every time I listen to him, the things I thought were just words for words' sake make sense to me."

Elsewhere, she makes almost the same point about Dylan, but differently. "My enthusiasm is growing the more I live in urban places. The last two years have made me a very strong fan, but before I lived in cities I couldn't see what he meant. I was sheltered, I hadn't seen the injustices. Now I can understand him." Once this lesson was learned, Joni turned full circle, though she had always done a particularly mean Dylan impression, of both his speaking and singing voice (which are much the same).

"I wrote a song called 'Cactus Tree', which is Dylan-influenced in its melody and even its style. I even lengthen my 'A's when I sing it because it sings better. It's all sort of in a monotone – I wrote it after I saw *Don't Look Back*, which I think left a big impression on me." In *Folk Roots*, Joni elaborates: "Bob Dylan's 'Positively 4th Street', that particular song showed me. I remember thinking 'the American pop song has finally grown up.' You can sing about anything now. 'You've got a lot of nerve to be my friend.' Just in that statement was a different song than any I had ever heard." Of the same song, she also said it was as if "a lightbulb went on in my head." She told Danny Wild what this light illuminated.

"Just a simple thing like being a singer-songwriter – that was a new idea. It used to take three people to do that job. And when I heard 'Positively 4th Street', I realised that this was a whole new ballgame; now you could make your songs literature. The potential for the song had never occurred to me – I loved 'Tutti-Frutti', you know. But it occurred to Dylan. I said 'Oh God, look at this.' And I began to write. So Dylan sparked me." 'Positively 4th Street' was Dylan's brutal kiss-off to the kind of folk scene that had nurtured Joni herself. 4th Street is in Greenwich Village, metaphorically and just about literally across the block from the setting of 'Chelsea Morning'.

In an interview with Barney Hoskyns, the rivalry between the two comes into the open. Dylan once implied that Mitchell wasn't really a woman, which has not gone un-remembered by Joni. "They asked him about women in the business and he said 'Oh, they all tart themselves up,' and the interviewer said 'Even Joni Mitchell?' And he said 'I love Joni Mitchell, but she's' – how did he put it? – 'kinda like a man,' or something. It was a backhanded compliment, I think, because I'm probably one of Bobby's best pace-runners as a poet. There aren't that many good writers. There are a lot that are touted as good, but they're not literature, they're just pretty good for a songwriter."

Joni herself presents Dylan's taunt as a source of strength. "The thing is, I came into this business quite feminine. But nobody has had so many battles to wage as me. I remember early in my career somebody wrote that my work was 'effeminate', which I thought was pretty odd. So over the years, I think I've gotten more androgynous – and maybe become an honorary male, according to Bobby." She immediately gets in a counter-thrust, about his birthday, of all things. "But he's born on the 24th of May. My mother, Queen Victoria and Dylan were all born on that date. I always think that birth date is the day of the extreme moralist."

Dylan's own work is itself deeply androgynous, as is much great art. Tiresias, the narrator of TS Eliot's *The Waste Land* contains all ages and all sexes within himself. Renaissance literature is full of cross-dressing: Shakespeare's comedies, Sidney's *Arcadia*. The critic Camille Paglia has written brilliantly of this (as a riposte to the gender apartheid of some of the more simple-minded 'women's studies' courses). Dylan was possibly writing about himself – or a male lover, or Joan Baez – in 'Just Like a Woman.' Similarly, Joni can use a gruff, male bass voice – as at the end of 'Big Yellow Taxi' – and has gone to parties dressed as a black man. It's all relative.

Joni and Dylan's intense rivalry continued until the mid-nineties, when the two were reunited on stage at the Great Music Experience in Tokyo. "On the third night they stuck Bob at the mic with me and that's the one that went out on tape. And if you look closely at it, you can see the little brat, he's up in my face – and he never brushes his teeth, so his breath was like... right in my face – and he's mouthing the words at me like a prompter, and he's pushing me off the mic. It's like he's basically dipping my pigtail in ink. The press picked up on it and said 'Bobby Smiles!' Yeah sure, because he was having a go at me out there."

The two go back a long way together, way before the Last Waltz, or the Rolling Thunder Revue. Cameron Crowe asked her when they first met. "The first official meeting was the Johnny Cash Show in 1969. We played that together. Afterward Johnny had a party at his house. So we met briefly there. Over the years there were a series of brief encounters. Tests. Little art games. I always had an affection for him." Both are also painters – Joni, it has to be said, with more artistic success. Both have designed their own LP sleeves. Even here, the rivalry is palpable.

"At one point we're backstage at this concert. I knew he was discovering painting. At that point, I'd just come from New Mexico, and I'd seen colour combinations that had never occurred to me before. Lavender and wheat, like old fashioned licorice, you know, when you bite into it and there's this peculiar, rich green and brown colour? The soil was like that, and the foliage coming out of it was vivid in the context of this colour earth. Anyway, I was really getting carried away, and Bobby says to me 'When you paint, do you use white?' And I said 'Of course.' He said ''Cause if you don't use white, your paint gets muddy.' I thought 'Aha, the boy's been taking art lessons.' The next time we had a conversation was when Paul McCartney had a party on the Queen Mary. After a long silence, he said 'If you were gonna paint this room, what would you paint?' I said 'I'd paint the mirrored ball spinning, I'd paint the women in the washroom, the band...' Later, all the stuff came back to me as part of a dream that became the song 'Paprika Plains'. I said 'What would you paint?'. He said 'I'd paint this coffee cup.' Later he wrote 'One More Cup of Coffee'."

Dylan's most notorious point-scoring came when he pretended to fall asleep as she played him an acetate of one of her finest albums. Joni has neither forgotten nor forgiven. It was late at night, with Louis Kemp, Asylum boss David Geffen, and Dylan. "There was all this fussing over Bobby's project, 'cause he was new to the label, and *Court and Spark*, which was a big breakthrough for me, was being entirely and almost rudely dismissed. Geffen's excuse was, since I was living in a room in his house at the time, that he had heard it through all of its stages, and it was no longer any surprise to him." Joni finishes the story (and Dylan) off. One of the women present takes her aside, and tells her not to pay any attention: "Those boys have no ears."

Like Neil Young, Leonard Cohen is a companion – and compatriot – and not a threat. The two did not really meet until both had left Canada. Both are famed for their restlessness, geographically and in matters of the heart. Cohen appears in three of Joni's songs: in 'That Song About the Midway' – about their brief affair – he is a devil wearing wings. In 'The Gallery' he is a saint, though a tainted one. 'Rainy Day House' is said to be a tender farewell from her to him, though he was the one who instigated the parting. He left his melancholy spell on her music: "I think I'm rather Cohen influenced. I wrote 'Marcie' and afterwards thought that it wouldn't have happened if it hadn't been for 'Suzanne'."

Cohen's influence has been verbal rather than musical, showing her how poetry can be integrated into the popular song. "My lyrics are influenced by Leonard. After we met at Newport last year (1967) we saw a lot of each other. Some of Leonard's religious imagery, which comes from being a Jew in a predominately Catholic part of Canada, seems to have rubbed off on me too." Elsewhere, she described Cohen and Dylan as points of departure. "Leonard didn't really explore music. He's a word man first. Leonard's economical, he never wastes a word. I can go through Leonard's work and it's just like silk. Dylan is coarse and beautiful in a rougher way."

Her greatest influences, however, have been way outside the range of rock 'n' roll. A brief review of her favourite listening revealed a love for Lady Day and Piaf, and a shot of Stravinsky ("a real rock 'n' roller"). "Most of my heroes are monsters, unfortunately. Miles Davis and Picasso have always been my major heroes because we have this one thing in common. They were restless. I don't know any women role models for that. But Picasso was constantly searching and changing and changing. Even I have favourite periods of Miles, but I would always go to see him in any incarnation. Because he's managed to keep alive. I thrive on change. That's probably why my chord changes are weird, because chords depict emotions. They'll be going along on one key and I'll drop off a cliff, and suddenly they will go into a whole other key signature. That will drive some people crazy, but that's how my life is."

Joni has learnt from all these influences how to distance herself as an artist. "Even if I'm writing about myself I try to stand back... as if I was writing about another person. From a perspective." As Geoffrey Cannon found, her work avoids sentimentality, while exploring "the emotional meaning of memory." Discuss, without writing on both sides of the paper at once! Joni put it more simply: "If you are sad, you should feel sad. The French are good at that. They show what they feel and in that way purge themselves of it. My songs are very honest, they are very personal, extremely personal. Sometimes they really hurt to sing." She rejects, however, any valuation of her lyrics as poetry. It is as if Chuck's intellectual put-downs still resonate somewhere at the back of her mind.

"I never liked poetry at school, a lot of it was archaic. 'Ode to a Daffodil' didn't mean that much to me, you know. The only time I read at school was when it was compulsory, like for a book report." Her teacher, Mr Kratzman, to whom her first album is dedicated, taught her to "love words," and how to unlock her childhood. He taught her to value the simple things in life, "like gathering tadpoles in an empty mayonnaise jar after the rain. I still remember playing dress-up in the attic of the house in Saskatoon with trunks of old clothes in a world of make-believe." This sense of wonder has provided an endless source of images for Joni's work ever since. As Steve Winwood, of Traffic, sang,

"Heaven is in your Mind."

Kratzman remembers the young Joni as "a blonde, bright-eyed kid. Very receptive to ideas. I can see her now, in the back seat of the seventh grade." It is a mutual admiration society. "I had a very good teacher in the seventh grade who marked me as a college student, in terms of writing poetry, and insisted on me writing in my own blood. He encouraged us to write in any form we liked. Even at that age, I enjoyed poetry, the structure of it, the dance of it... he'd just tell us to write something, not criticising our spelling or grammar."

Poetry merged with her early love of rock 'n' roll. She told Rod Campbell, "I never thought of songs as poetry. To me they were apples and oranges. I loved 'Tutti Frutti' – the lyrics weren't important. I was a dancer. If you could dance to it I didn't care if the words were any good." Her own work was different. As she told *Zigzag*, "my songs are very honest, they are extremely personal. Sometimes they really hurt to sing. Some nights you really get into them, and they really take a lot out of me." As to her sources of inspiration, "I use dreams a lot; I thought I could say certain things in dream images that I couldn't say in factual things. I went through a period when I got into stories – like, I remember I wrote a song called 'The Gift of the Magi', which was just one of O'Henry's short stories, done as a poem and set to music... and 'The Pirate of Penance' was just a story."

Should one write about one's own life at the time, or after the event? It's a question that reduces Joni to silence. Her eventual reply maps out her entire future career. "You spend any time with a person and you soak up some of them – but generally it doesn't come out until after you've left them... it's a sort of delayed reaction. Often I don't feel their presence or what they've given me until a long while later... until all the confusion of leaving them is gone.". John Keats described the same process as "emotion recollected in tranquillity." Another definition which seems to connect with Joni's work is the preface to *Lyrical Ballads*, first published in 1798 by those two young rockers 'Willi' Wordsworth and Samuel Taylor Coleridge: "It is the honourable characteristic of Poetry that its materials are to be found in every subject which can interest the human mind." Wordsworth, too, had sired and then had to abandon, an illegitimate daughter. With his sister Dorothy, he retreated from North Devon – where he and Coleridge were the hippies of the day, and regarded with great suspicion by the locals – to the Lake District. There he would live simply in the hills, and dedicate himself to his art. Like Joni, there too he was at the centre of a circle of devoted new friends.

By late 1968, Joni Mitchell had finally found herself a home, and a new direction. At least temporarily, her 'urge for going' was quenched. Settled in Laurel Canyon, she parted from Crosby to begin a love affair with Graham Nash. With him she would pioneer – and sing about – a new lifestyle, one based on equality and sharing. Behind her lay a broken marriage, a lost daughter, and an abandoned homeland. In front was the blank screen of the future. The trip was just beginning.

chapter 2:

Laurel Canyon Days

In September 1968, Karl Dallas interviewed Joni for *Melody Maker*. The feature was tucked away in the 'Focus on folk' page. Mitchell: "Marcie is a real girl, she lives in London. I used her name because I wanted a two-syllable name. But I'm the girl in all these songs. And the first song, 'I Had a King', is about the break-up of my marriage." Dallas is quick to note that *Song for a Seagull* hangs together as a complete whole, like *Sergeant Pepper*, or Frank Zappa's conceptual works for the Mothers of Invention. Joni confirms this, with reservations. "The album does tell a story, though not necessarily in chronological order. Certainly, the songs aren't placed in the order that I wrote them. As we were working on it, songs came up that would fit in. And since it was finished, I've written others that could go into the sequence too."

Like Van Morrison's *Astral Weeks*, issued a few months later, the two sides of the album are separately named, two sides of the same coin. Both records explore innocence through the eyes of experience. Mitchell symbolises this by contrasting the city – dirt, excitement, betrayal, non-communication – with the sea: escape, mystery, dreams, death. Even now, this is a startling debut, timeless and self-assured. The first impression is of the gorgeousness of Joni's voice, and its range from intimate soprano to gliding tenor. Overdubbing ensures that Joni's background vocals can be used either as a chorus or a counter-argument. The acoustic guitar work is startling, as inventive and fresh as the work of a maestro like John Fahey. Dave Crosby's subtle production adds Steve Stills on bass and Joni herself on overdubbed piano on 'Night in the City'. The one psychedelic sound effect is the banshee wail of a police car in 'Nathan La Franeer'.

Melodies swoop and loop like the seagulls on the cover, spelling out their own name. Lyrically, each word is chiselled into place, the songs chock-full of internal rhymes – "the city looks pretty" – and alliteration: "with gangs and girly shows/the ghostly garden grows." Karl Dallas comments on the visual sparkle of these songs: "the taffeta patterns of an oil slick," neon signs which seem to waltz in time, the reds and greens of 'Marcie'. The overall impression is one of a musical and lyrical richness which can be quite overwhelming. Just like the cover, in fact, a generous spill of technicolour paint, Van Gogh's sunflowers as if seen on LSD. It is actually a visual counterpart to side two; the cactus tree, the Dawn Treader, seagulls, they're all there. Whatever its title – Joni usually refers to it as *Song for a Seagull*, official guides and rockologies as *Joni Mitchell* – the album made the US Top 200, reaching 189, a solid achievement for a virtual unknown. Mitchell won the instant respect of her songwriting peers with this album, selling 70,000 copies at the time. (It remained a steady seller, and by 1981 had reached the 400,000 mark.)

There is certainly little trace of Joni's love, as since proclaimed, for early rock 'n' roll or blues: this is very 'white' music. On the other hand, it is not folk music in any conventional sense: although some songs refer to folk motifs and narratives – pirates, kings, sea voyages – these are embellished in a very knowing way. In the same way, the music embraces classical and Broadway, with a hint of jazz. Like *Sergeant Pepper*, and little else at the time, the lyrics are printed on the inside of the gatefold sleeve, next to a black-and-white photo of the young artist, in a herring-bone coat, with enigmatic smile, and bright eyes rather like an, um, seagull. No wonder Karl Dallas headlined his interview 'Joni, the Seagull from Saskatoon'! Joni has invented a new genre, a seamless mix of words, music, and their creator's singing voice and instrumental expertise. It crosses the gender divide. Women respond to its picture of a role-model for a new kind of girl "so busy being free," romantic, a dreamer. Men find the singer's freedom alluring, and wish secretly to be the one male sensitive and brave enough to be able to match it.

Nothing is quite what it seems. The girl "so busy being free" resembles a cactus tree because her heart is not just full, but hollow with a tough outer skin to match. The songs have a surprising range, from peridots to Marcie's faucet, which needs a plumber (startlingly, this also doubles as a sexual metaphor, immediately followed by her need for a man). They also encode all kinds of secret meanings: 'I Had a King' is obviously autobiographical, but emblematic. Joni, a modern woman in "leather and lace," fails to live up to his stereotype of femininity, where "ladies in gingham still blush," just like in *Gone with the Wind*. Ironically, this is just the kind of romantic fantasy that Lou Reed conjured up in 'Sweet Jane' – when "the ladies rolled their eyes." Male fantasies die hard. An adventuring and untrustworthy male is also at the centre of 'The Pirate of Penance', a strange *menage a trois* which seems to end with his murder. By which of the two women is never made clear.

Gilbert and Sullivan, with a twist. This is not as bizarre an influence as at first seems: Mitchell's old friends, the Incredible String Band, did much the same in their 'Minotaur's Song'. 'Michael from Mountains' also has a transatlantic counterpart, Ralph McTell's 'Michael in the Garden'. His Michael is emotionally retarded, while Joni's hero is all-knowing, acting simple, child-like only in his sense of wonder. The song ends with a hinted seduction. Michael is also in part a portrait of the singer – a musician who can reinvent the natural world – as is Marcie, alone in the city and, unlike, Joni retreating back home to Saskatoon, "west again." Largely unremarked now is the significance of these songs to denizens of the drug culture of the late sixties, which is to say a majority of the 'baby boomers' generation. The opening of 'Night in the City' – "light up, light up" – could be coincidental, or it could be in code, but the search for visual disarrangements is of its era: "Colours go waltzing in time." 'The Dawntreader' is pure marijuana whimsy. Not that there is any evidence that Joni herself was taking such substances at the time, or that Lewis Carroll or Hieronymus Bosch had either. It was the effects that counted.

In just the same way, the underlying contrast between city and country, seen best here in 'Sisotowbell Lane', was part of a generation's wish to return to Eden. Woodstock was the crystallisation of this wish to "get back to the garden," as was the trend of moving from inner city collectives to communes way out in the countryside. Mitchell had made the move in the other direction, fighting her way from country to city, to find fame and anonymity. She is honest enough in her art to also convey the charms of big city life, its night-time excitements. She also predicts some kind of apocalypse. 'Sisotowbell Lane' opens with hints of this: "Noah is fixing the pump in the rain." One could compare here Joni's greatest spiritual counterpart as musician, Sandy Denny, and songs like 'The Sea', where the streets of London town are subject to a great flood. Doubtless the authors of that brave but bizarre book, *The Sex Revolts: Gender, Rebellion and Rock 'n' Roll*, would derive some hidden message here about trapped female sexuality.

What Mitchell is doing is far more subtle. *Song for a Seagull* is an extraordinary conceit, in which Joni sees herself as re-creating the seaside in the city in a flawed and false way. Concrete becomes sand, electric lights the stars. The singer so apparently innocent in her ivory tower sees humankind pretty exactly. When humans find Eden, they immediately destroy it: "humans are hungry/for worlds they can't share." This vision of an untouched shore, along which the singer dances, is like the hymn-like epiphany at the end of Roy Harper's epic song 'McGoohan's Blues'. That, too, dissolves into ashes, Cinderella flees the ball, finds herself once more scrubbing pots and pans. The dreams here fade: Marcie leaves without saying goodbye, the king goes back on the road. The fairy coach becomes, literally, a taxi driven by Nathan La Franeer, a bad-tempered and misanthropic man soured by life who tries to cheat her, and leaves with a curse. They travel through a New York as if seen by Fellini, where an ageing cripple sells Superman balloons, and she is met at the airport by disembodied, grasping hands. "I filled it full of silver/and left the fingers counting." So much for the modern highwayman.

Like the hypnotic fictions of Angela Carter, Joni Mitchell's first LP is a modern take on the (not so secret) terror of fairy tales, masking an extremely adult sensibility in child-like clothing. The only comparison in musical terms is the debut album by Kevin Ayers, *Joy of a Toy*, which is an equal mix of childhood, bright daylight and horror, effortlessly tuneful and self-aware. Each song sounds as fresh, and odd, as the day it was first laid down.

Critical response to Mitchell's first album was largely positive, among those prepared to notice this obscure folk singer, whose song-writing was becoming a minor cult. As Janet Maslin later remarked, at the time it would have been difficult to peg her as anything more promising than "an obviously gifted but dour and arty poet, more comfortable behind the scenes, supplying material to Judy Collins, Tom Rush, or Ian and Sylvia, than she might ever become in the limelight."

In retrospect, the album has an uneasy feel, exemplified in the opening track. Apparently a dainty account of the break-up of a marriage, it is astonishingly snide, right down to noting her ex-husband's predilection for drip-dry shirts. Maslin notices a conflict between the lyrics, quietly resigned, and the voice in which they are transmitted, "baleful, scathing, charged with an anger she cannot bring herself to express directly." I hear only resigned sadness myself. Maslin further charges that the album has a "glum, thin-lipped sound." Apparently the master tapes were accidentally damaged, and when they were restored the high notes had lost their clarity: Joni later said it sounded "like we recorded it under a bell jar." A double-edged remark, with its echoes of Sylvia Plath's novel of the same name, a chronicle of madness and self-absorption. My own vinyl copy shares this airless sound, but the remastered CD is clear as a bell.

Joni does add that "I liked the sound of my voice and my guitar on that first record, because I wasn't influenced by anything. Ninety per cent of the singers in this business pretend they're Southern blacks, and I didn't want to fall into that pitfall of losing my natural song-speech." Bob Sarlin considers that this LP establishes Mitchell "as the epitome of a certain kind of folk preciousness, an almost ultrafemininity in both her imagery and her vocals." If so, it was largely due to the marketing rather than the music. Warner Bros ran an advert that referred to their new star as "99% virgin." Joni herself complained that a man in the promotions department had criticised her music for "its lack of masculinity." In fact, she put it rather more graphically. "They said I didn't have any balls. Since when do women have balls anyway? Why do I have to be like that?" For precious, read idealistic. An anonymous critic later wrote that "this vision of people sitting in rocking chairs and making pretty things may now seem rather facile, but only because its better side is now almost taken for granted. It is hard to realise how much of a breakthrough it represented at the time."

For Nick Kent, feyness impaired much of the album. Her exotic open tunings often produced sublime melodies, but could also relegate her songs into the realm of "doll's house music." His comments sound closer to a restaurant report than a record review, with a sting at the end: "A vivid triumph, as intricate watercolour/patchwork quilt imagery, garnished around themes that overcame an almost brittle prissiness." Crosby's production made the whole thing sound "like it was recorded on a frozen pond." Paul Gambaccini is perhaps closer to the mark in noting the confessional mode here – drawn from poets like Sylvia Plath and Anne Sexton, both later to commit suicide. From the start, she "was always painfully open about her private life, selling ringside seats to her heart for the mere price of an LP."

The album certainly brought Joni's work to a wider audience, and she continued her hectic gigging, but now with a higher public profile. She participated in the December 1968 Miami Pop Festival, with Peter Green's Fleetwood Mac, Marvin Gaye, Three Dog Night and Canned Heat. In the following February, she made a memorable appearance at New York's Carnegie Hall. From then, it was forty weeks solidly on the road, playing festivals in Atlanta, Newport, Big Sur, New York – she shared a stage with doomed troubadour Tim Hardin at the Schaefer Folk Festival – and Monterey, the year after it would have really counted. Reports from the time are entrancing. At the Schaefer Festival, "dressed in a long sea-green gown that brought out the colour of her long flowing hair, she sang songs about this city." At the Newport Folk Festival, we see her through the photo-studded book *Festival*, "pursing her lips, eyes closed, hands clasping, shoulders hunched, bent into the stand microphone." One moment she looks like a young widow, the next she breaks her anguished stance and runs her voice up an octave or two, "looking like a woman seeing her lover come into view after an absence of a month."

This was not coincidental. Meanwhile, there had been a crucial change in her domestic arrangements. Joni had fallen in love.

The story is told in David Crosby's biography, *Long Time Gone*. Joni was now an industry legend, ready for breakout success: "That followed, as did romantic complications between Joni, David Crosby and Graham Nash. Three people's lives were braided together, and others would join a tangled skein that would finally drive every one of the artists involved to write a song about the experience." Joni wrote

'Willy' as a love song to Nash; he, in turn, wrote 'Our House' as a picture of domestic harmony with Joni. Also recorded by CSN, Crosby's Arthurian saga 'Guinnevere' was in part about Joni, and their days sailing together on his ocean-going schooner, her gaze turning "to the harbour where I lay, anchored for a day." In a direct reference to the album he produced, Crosby notes how "seagulls circle endlessly," and he claims that Mitchell's 'Dawntreader' was also about those days, though Joni has been less specific. One day, Hollywood will film the ensuing complications. Crosby had in fact written about a threesome in 'Triad', though that song was about his idea of sharing his bed with two women.

Reality took a different course. Joni Mitchell: "I was living with David. Graham and I had a kind of ill-fated beginning of a romance. I was playing one club in Ottowa and the Hollies were playing another. We finally got together in Winnipeg. He ended up at David's place and I was staying with David until my house was ready. Graham came down sick, and I took him home to my new house to play Florence Nightingale. At first it wasn't for romance's sake – he was sick, and I still had some domestic chops because I hadn't been trained to be a celebrity. I had been trained to be a regular Frau. I took him home, and was looking after him and I got attached – here was a mess. What was I going to say? I'm kind of going with David and we sort of staked claims, but I'd written all these songs, trying to explain my position to him, that I'm still in an independent mode. But I really got attached to Graham and I guess that's the first time I harboured the illusion of forever. I really felt for the first time in my life that I could pair bond."

Graham Nash fills in the details: "I camped out with Crosby and then I rekindled my relationship with Joan, whom I'd met a couple of years earlier in Canada. There was a party at David's house and Joni was there. I was already totally intrigued and in love with this woman and she invited me home. I went with her and I didn't leave for a couple of years. It was a cute little house. That was an incredible time for me, probably the most intensely creative, free and special time I've ever experienced. Not only was I in love with Joni but I was in love with David and Stephen and I was in love with the music and I'd taken a giant choice." As in life, Crosby completes the story. "At that time in particular I subscribed to the hippie ethic of non-ownership. The thing with Joni and Graham was that I felt great about it. I wanted to be with Christine. I know I was happy with her and Joan was a very turbulent girl and not an easy person to be in a relationship with, particularly then. I was very happy for them. They were in love and it was cool. Graham was then – and is now – my best friend: I loved him and I loved her and I couldn't be angry at two people I loved for loving one another. That just didn't make a lot of sense to me."

The sad afternote is that Christine Gale Hinton was later killed in a head-on car crash, driving their cats to the vet in Crosby's souped-up VW bus. The love affair between Mitchell and Nash was also but a brief interlude – one that lives on in song, however, and in the memories of all concerned. In the CSN box set, Nash reveals that 'Our House' was "written for Joni, about her house that we shared in Laurel Canyon, on Lookout Mountain. It was written on her piano. Such a charming house. She had a collection of multi-coloured glass in a window that would catch the light – the 'fiery gems.' There was a fireplace, and two cats in the yard. It was like a family snapshot, a portrait of our life together." The love for coloured glass goes right back to Joni's childhood. Twenty years on, a niche high on the wall in Larry and Joni Klein's kitchen held the art deco vase "that you bought today" celebrated in Nash's song, listening to her singing "all night long/for me, only for me." And then for the world.

With inferior words, the song is currently being used to advertise a building society on British TV, with people climbing up on each other's shoulders to form a living house. The real thing appeared on CSN's second album, *Deja Vu*. Their first album had featured Crosby's song 'Guinnevere', partly about Joni – he said, cryptically, that "it's a love song, an answer to some other love songs, and part of a conversation" – and another song by Nash, 'My Lady of the Island'. "It's a song for two ladies. The Islands in question are Ibiza and Long Island. Warm, gentle feelings." In 'Our House', the fire is a symbol for contentment and a cosy coupledom: in the earlier song, it is a metaphor for sexual frenzy, and its aftermath: "Our bodies were a perfect fit, in afterglow we lay." Such is the progress of love.

Joni also stoked the fires of creativity, and in David Crosby's own account was directly responsible for the creation of Crosby, Stills and Nash (and later, Young) as a working musical entity. "We started singing together and one night we were at Joni Mitchell's house; Mama Cass was there, Stephen Stills was there, me and Willie, just us five hanging out. You know how it is at that time of night, so we were singing as you would imagine, we sang a lot." One presumes from this circumlocution that all concerned were in a suitably 'mellow' condition. Stills and Crosby started to sing a new song, 'Helplessly Hoping'. Nash looked at the rafters for about ten seconds, listened, and "started singin' the other part like he'd been singin' it all his life. It was like havin' somebody give you head all of a sudden in a sound sleep. It was like waking up on acid." Well, Crosby certainly has a way with words. Stephen Stills remembers the same evening, but places it elsewhere, in Mama Cass's dining room, looking out at the pool, where John Sebastian was swimming, presumably without his tie-dies for once. "We went to Joni's from there."

It is poetically apt that the ultimate 'supergroup' of the late sixties be formed at the house which Joni had bought with her royalties, and was now sharing with Nash. It was a log cabin, a pine-panelled, two-bedroom property nestling on the foothills of Laurel Canyon, and only three miles north of Hollywood's Sunset Strip. It made up in homely charm what it lacked in elegance, and was "filled with the easy-going good spirit of the Laurel Canyon music scene." Neighbours included Steve Stills, Dave Crosby, and Mama Cass. As she later told Phil Sutcliffe, her love affairs centred around this musical community. "They usually began as friendships, burst into flame (laughs) and continued after the fact as friendships." As Sly Stone was to write, it was a "family affair." It was not, as Joni carefully pointed out, a commune, like the San Francisco household of the Dead, or the Airplane. "There was a community of musicians but we didn't all live under the same roof and alternate duties, or anything like that. I'm too much of a loner."

One account has Joni sitting at the grand piano in the oak-beamed, wooden-floored lounge, composing the songs that were to appear on *Clouds*, and apparently living on one. *Time* magazine was less charitable, describing her home as "a ramshackle house in a canyon, with second hand trappings" – trappings which are now highly valuable antiques. Coincidentally, it also printed Joni's sarcastic poem about her own growing wealth and business acumen:

91

Zsa Zsa's got her jewels
Minnie's got her chickens to go
I've got my corporation
I'm a capitalistic so and so

It was a long way from Saskatoon, though Graham Nash added that she baked better pies than her mother.

Rolling Stone painted a more intriguing – and sympathetic – portrait of Joni, in "her isolated, wood-hewed home, surrounded by stained Tiffany glass windows, oak-beam wooden floors, a Priestly piano, a grandfather clock, and a black cat named Hunter, a nine-year old tom." It was like an episode of *Through the Keyhole*. The grandfather clock, which didn't work, was a gift from Leonard Cohen. If there had been an auction sale, other contents would have listed as follows:

Item: one turkey made out of pine-cones.
Item: one 'Souvenir of Saskatoon' ornamental plate.
Item: one Art Nouveau lamp in the shape of a frog on a lily pad.
Item: one hand-carved hat rack.
Item: one giant antique wooden pig.
Item: several brown velvet rocking chairs.

Talking years later to *Q*, Joni elaborated. "You have to put it in the context of those times. Back then, we, the musical heroes, for lack of a better word, didn't feel very separated from our audiences. We were all hippies. It's not like now, where the musical stars have become like the movie stars of the era before us – transformed by luminous images. We felt we were all in this together. I didn't feel separate from the press, which was a mistake. You must maintain some privacy. I mean, I like my place to be cosy. I like cats. They give the home a heartbeat – in lieu of children. I see home as a sanctuary with a tea kettle rocking and good conversation." It was an attempt at a new lifestyle, as democratic and down-home as the later emphasis on style in the eighties was exclusive and aggressive, city based. It's all oddly reminiscent of the Bloomsbury group of the 1920s, who left London for rural retreats in Sussex, where they worked endlessly, evolved a lifestyle based on feelings, art and home design, and engaged in free love. Bloomsbury had the Omega workshops, and Laurel Canyon its knitting circle.

One reporter conveyed the priceless insight that Joni "sees her friends in shades of colours, and has made for them appropriate mufflers." Mama Cass was fitted out in bright, gypsy colours, Graham Nash's in darker tones: purple, black and green, while Elliot Roberts' was dusty: brown, navy, rust and grey." Sandra Shevey enlarged on these talents: "Joni is a wholly creative person. If she is not writing, she is painting, weaving, working in enamel. She makes lovely jewellery. She's finished a wardrobe of simple A-line dresses, and she has begun to knit scarves on planes to keep from smoking." The freshest account of those days is by Allan McDougall, writing for the *New Musical Express* in 1970. A picture of the hippie dream. "One of Joni's favourite subjects is the preservation of wildlife and plants and flowers and rivers. All of which, in America, are in great jeopardy from ever-increasing pollution. Joni drives a Mercedes sports car but still feels a bit guilty about all the money she earns. She explained to me once 'I want to spend more time just living and relaxing. I'm not really into the big showbiz bit. I want to write a lot, and get on with some painting.' Joni gave me a painting of Willie Nash, sleeping like an angelic devil alongside Joni's cat, Calico. A very simple lady, she used to do my sewing and darning for me. And provided a sympathetic shoulder for me to cry on when the pressures of America's paranoia closed in on me too much."

Perversely, Mitchell later denied that she had ever been at home in the hippie daze. "It was a style, you know. Lay off the scissors and you were a hippie." The lifestyle produced more than its fair share of casualties; those who didn't burn out, blanded out. "Back in the drug worshipping era, everybody threw caution to the winds, but there was a spirit of adventure, of being on the verge of something. Then in the seventies we kinda retreated into drugs, because the dream died away."

Fellow musician Happy Traum interviewed Joni for *Rolling Stone* in Laurel Canyon in early 1969, as part of a supplement on the new singer-songwriters arising from the old folk scene. Traum's article, complete with a front-cover photo of Joni, her hands spread in front of her face like wings, first brought her to a mass audience. He concludes his article apocalyptically: "Joni Mitchell has arrived in America." Her music is an "aural backlash to ps-ky-delic rock and to the all-hell-has-broken-loose styles of Aretha Franklin and Janis Joplin.." Joni sits through all this on an antique sofa, shrugging her shoulders in disbelief at an offer from Hollywood to write a movie – "on any theme I want to" – for a huge amount of money. She talks about her newly written book of poetry, which never appeared, as "just an eclectic collection of all kinds of things I've done that I don't know what else to do with them. I'm putting them into a book because I don't like to lose anything."

Joni is also catching up on her reading. The mystical narratives of Herman Hesse, Leonard Cohen – "her favourite poet" – and Rod McKuen. The whole thing is like a rehearsal for *Hello* magazine, the rich at home and at play – but this is no exercise in glitzy excess. Stardom is being deconstructed in front of our eyes: a symphony in simple living, setting the taste of a new generation. Traum breathlessly describes the house, filled with the things she loves. Antique pieces crowd tables, mantelpieces and shelves. Antique handbags hang on a bathroom wall. A hand-carved hat rack stands by the castle-style oak front door. Graham Nash perches on an English church chair, while Joni emerges from the kitchen, using the only electric lights in the house. She has been making the crust for a rhubarb pie.

In this homespun Eden, all is not as it seems. "Lately, life has been constantly filled with interruptions. I don't have five hours in a row to myself. In New York the street adventures are incredible. You see the stories in the people's faces. You hear the songs immediately. Here in Los Angeles, there are less characters because they are all inside automobiles. You don't see them on park benches or peeing in the gutter or any of that." She has consciously withdrawn from the world. "It's good to be exposed to politics, but it does damage to me too. Too much of it can cripple me." It's more than a throwaway metaphor, given Joni's medical history. She is seeking freedom, not in a national context but in her own life. Like Neil Young, she resists any attempt to commercialise or manipulate her career, and has recently turned down a bid of $1.5 million for Siquomb Music. Like the Clash later, Joni wants "complete control."

Perhaps because of this, a live album recorded at Berkeley and Carnegie Hall never actually emerged – which is a great shame, as in concert, a looser, more intimate Joni emerges, and the aural purity of her work at that time came over best in a live setting. The flip-side of Mitchell's 'You Turn Me On, I'm a Radio' single is a live, acoustic version of 'Urge for Going' which, although copyrighted in 1972, sounds very much like a 1968 or 1969 performance. If so, it might well be a track from this missing album, the only one to emerge officially. So far.

For Free, a bootleg of a 1969 NET TV broadcast, contains an interesting mix of songs: neither 'Blue Boy' nor her cover version of Dino Valente's 'Get Together' have ever been given an official release. As Traum describes it, the freshness of her stage persona then came shockingly close to the real person. "She can charm the applause out of the audience by breaking a guitar string, then apologising by singing her next number acappella, wounded guitar at a limp parade rest. When she talks, words stumble out to form candid little quasi-anecdotes that are completely antithetical to her carefully constructed, contrived songs. But they knock the audience out every time." For those lucky enough to have seen Sandy Denny, this is close to how she was on stage, right up to the final 1977 tour, though all that clumsiness and letting down of too many barriers were steps on the way to her early death. Joni learned much better how to keep her distance, even from her most devoted admirers. An audience can be your best friend: it can also snatch your very soul.

In 1969, Joni became involved in a national tour, opening for Crosby, Stills, Nash, and Young, then the hottest new band in America. She earned standing ovations and encores nearly every night. Joni's professional involvement both cemented and put a huge strain on her relationship with Graham Nash. It was at this time, just before she and CSNY played a sell-out week at the Greek Theatre in LA, that she wrote 'Willy'. It reveals Nash's sadness and loneliness, and captures a relationship doomed from the start, like something out of Greek tragedy. Willie is both child and father, unable to fully love her because of an "ancient injury/that has not healed" – an ominous song. In 'I Had a King', Joni warned "beware of the power of moons." Here the moon is conquered, just as Willy says that "I gave my heart too soon." Nash's old band, The Hollies, were similarly spurned. They wrote and recorded a song, 'Hey Willy', to Nash, a single release in 1971. Compared to Joni's ambivalent masterpiece, it was a piece of pop fluff.

The end of the affair also preceded an important concert, and Nash himself tells the tale, poignantly, on the CSN box set. "The day before the Fillmore East show in June 1970, I broke up with Joni and my whole world fell apart. The afternoon of that show I wrote this song ('Simple Man'), and that evening I performed it for the first time, with Joni sitting in the audience. I don't know how I got through that." They remain firm friends, to this day, as old lovers often do.

The summer of 1969 wrote itself into rock history because of an open air event near Bob Dylan's home in upstate New York. Dylan himself had escaped to England, to play the second Isle of Wight festival. Another notable absentee was Joni Mitchell, but she became famous for writing its theme tune, after the event. As she told *Folk Roots*, "Woodstock was just a concert, and I wrote a song which glorified the event and probably made more of a legend of it than it would have been. I was supposed to play Sunday night, but I had to play Dick Cavett on Monday morning. When we got to the airport, it was a national disaster; it was mucky. There was no way in, so David Geffen and I went back into Manhattan. The boys rented some kind of plane and got in and out because they showed up on my TV show the next day. I was the girl that couldn't go to the party. It was from that perspective that the song was written."

She also explains the song's most symbolic moment. "There was some beauty in it too. When the bombers were going over at the Woodstock event – they did it out of curiosity, apparently – they just kind of veered off to look at this big crowd. The contrast of the two camps – America's youth divided into the gung-hos and all these kids that popped acid – that was a striking image." Looking back, she discovers a strange irony. "I was apolitical, but I would say my generation was intrigued by anarchy. We had some valid arguments but we had no plan to correct anything, so when the older generation said 'You do it' everybody went 'Oh, oh' and started sucking their thumbs. Which led to apathy in the seventies, which led to yuppiedom, and then yuppiedom spawned Generation X, which is a generation of nihilists. So I don't know what is going to happen next." It's as if Johnny Rotten now felt that the punk movement he spawned led to Thatcher's Britain. Both are probably right.

In the rarely seen movie of *Big Sur*, an open air festival held that summer at the Esalen Institute, Joni perches prettily on a stage which is little more than a strip of tiles, facing an open swimming pool, and backing onto a sheer drop into the Pacific ocean, which twinkles behind. The rocky coast of California stretches away to her right. It is a kind of metaphor for hippiedom, continuing its bright show on the edge of a precipice. Joan Baez joins in with everyone. Later in the film, Stephen Stills loses the plot during a CSNY run-through, and lunges out at a member of the audience, in a kind of flash forward to Altamont. A sultry Neil Young hunches behind his organ, as if part of another band. Joni is a young princess, a goddess of the sun. What else should she be singing, but 'Woodstock'. The camera pans to a man in a leather cape and a huge, hippie grin. David Crosby. A perfect moment to encapsulate those times, on the cusp of the age of Aquarius.

In Nick Kent's *The Dark Stuff* – the reading equivalent of stuffing yourself with a whole box of Black Magic – David Geffen reveals the business machinations behind the film which turned the Woodstock festival into a myth. He managed to make CSNY appear to be the central act, though originally they had been a humble thirteenth on the bill. "I would not allow them to use the footage of Crosby, Stills and Nash in the movie unless they used [fellow client] Joni Mitchell's song, with CSNY singing it as the theme of the movie. That's how it happened. The producers were simply going to give me what I wanted or that was it. And since I represented a lot of important acts on Warner Bros, Atlantic and Elektra, they weren't going to fuck with me."

CSNY had actually played so badly and sung so out of tune at Woodstock that they had subsequently to redub their set for the film and soundtrack album. Furthermore, just prior to taking the stage, Neil Young had kicked up a huge fuss about not being filmed, or even named, at the event which was to catapult CSN (and Y) to international superstardom. "Listen, if you look through every frame of the movie, I'm not in the film. If you listen to the introduction, it's been edited down so it sounds like 'Crosby... Stills... Nash' 'cause they had to cut my name out. We were pretty bad at Woodstock. Nothing jelled, not for me anyway." An ornery cuss, even then, which is why his career has survived.

In the CSN box set, Joni reveals an even better kept secret, that prior to writing 'Woodstock' she had undergone a brief religious conversion, much the same as that which Bob Dylan later experienced – far more publicly – in the late seventies. This explains why the song remains timeless, and survives its period and direct subject matter. The "child of God" is more than just a poetic conceit. The sense of deprivation she felt at missing the event, and watching it on TV in a New York hotel room, made her "one of the fans. I was put in the position of being a kid who couldn't make it. So I was glued to the media. And at the time I was going through a born-again Christian trip – not that I went to church. I'd given up Christianity at a very early age in Sunday school. But suddenly, as performers, we were in the position of having so many people look to us for leadership. For some unknown reason I took it seriously, and decided I needed a guide and leaned on God. So I was a little 'God mad' at the time. Woodstock, for some reason, impressed me as being a modern miracle, like a modern-day fishes and loaves story. For a herd of people that large to cooperate so well it was pretty remarkable, and there was tremendous optimism. So I wrote the song 'Woodstock' out of these feelings." Joni was to turn her devotions away, towards her own inner fulfilment, while retaining this other-worldliness. She continued to believe that it was possible to build heaven on earth.

Joni's second LP, *Clouds*, sold 100,000 copies in advance of its release in October 1969. It reached Number Thirty-One on the US album charts. 'Clouds' was the original title of 'Both Sides Now': Judy Collins' version of this song had reached Number Eight in the singles chart, and she also had a hit with 'Chelsea Morning', another song from the new LP. Dedicated to Sadie McKee, Joni's mother, the album contains no outside musicians, which gives it rather a hermetic, closed-in quality. To add to the (literal) self-control, the whole album, with the exception of the opening track, 'Tin Angel', was self-produced, with the help of engineer Henry Lewy, and recorded at the tiny, almost old-fashioned A&M Studios in Hollywood. This set the pattern for her next eight studio outings, as does her front-cover painting, a self-portrait this time.

The original idea had been to show the progress of the seasons with a castle and a moat. Joni had become depressed with the picture, left it, and only finished it with Graham Nash's encouragement. The result is dominated by Joni's face, more specifically her sky-blue eyes and freckled nose. She grasps a red flower in one hand. The effect is of straightforwardness, looking direct at the viewer without flinching. The whole thing reminds me of the work of the Victorian photographer Julia Margaret Cameron, the same amalgam of beauty and sexuality, staring out the viewer. The background is of clouds – what else? – dyed red by the setting sun, above purple hills and a rippled river. This landscape carries over to the back cover, an effect rather spoilt on the CD, which overlays it with a list of the songs, and chops out the menacing, dark forest in the foreground, a fir tree silhouetted against the evening light.

To the right of Joni appear the outskirts of a city, a modern white building nestling against a taller and older structure, half castle, half tower block. The overall feel is more Canada than Los Angeles. The album inside contains a more assured vocal performance than her debut, though Joni still has her reservations. "On the second album, I'd been singing a lot with CSN – I introduced those guys to each other – because we used to jam when they were in the throes of their musical courtship. You've got an Englishman and a Southerner and a Californian boy and a Canadian trying to get an accent blend, and they ended up with this twang and a nasal thing. I ended up singing the album in it." In fact, she seems to sing each song in a slightly different voice. Joni also later described this album as her "artistic nadir." Many performers would give their whole careers in exchange for such an album, but it is a flawed masterpiece, as some perceptive reviewers noticed among the general rush of praise.

The great lost British rock critic Mark Williams was on the spot as usual, for *International Times*. The album is not as immediately impressive as her debut, "despite her gorgeous voice, which she knows how to control and to apply to her own compositions to maximum effect." *Disc* mentions "extra accompaniment from an orchestra," so must have been sent a different album to everyone else! It does praise the "brilliant poignancy" of her writing, though. *Melody Maker* has moved her from the folk pages to the main review section: Joni "is a great talent, and this album more than confirms it" On the page opposite, in the jazz section, is a review of Wayne Shorter's LP *Schizophrenia*, a harbinger of things to come.

As a record, *Clouds* doesn't quite hang together, although as its basic theme is paradox, this is all part of its conception. There might even be a subtle clue in the flower which Mitchell seems to be presenting on the front cover. With the leaves and shape of a lily, but the colour and stamens of a poppy, it is either some kind of Canadian hybrid, or a plant invented by Mitchell herself, playing God. *Clouds* is a transitional work, halfway between romance – where crickets court their ladies – and reality, where people are at heart unknowable, and which entails fear, danger and ageing. This is Mitchell's *Songs of Experience*.

The opening song, 'Tin Angel', is a deliberate smashing of illusion, but she finds reality with a lover himself like something from a fairy story, a toy with no heart. Also set in New York, 'Chelsea Morning' is a love song to a city, but there is hidden desperation in her attempt to hang on to romance – "pretty baby won't you stay." 'I Don't Know Where I Stand', set in California, captures that delicious moment of being newly in love, but with a matching uncertainty about whether such tender feelings are reciprocated. The singer cannot quite commit herself, by letter or on the phone. The lover in 'That Song about the Midway' is mysterious, slightly threatening. As mentioned earlier, rumour has it to be a portrait of Leonard Cohen. Side one of the vinyl release concludes with 'Roses Blue', a portrait of a proto-hippie, a girl obsessed with the occult. Paradox again: roses are never blue, except perhaps this Rose. The song is brooding, not quite focused, filled with images of drowning. The previous song dealt with a gambler – like Richard Farina's 'Reno, Nevada' or Dylan's 'Jack of Diamonds'. The game here – "can you win?" – is for real, gambling with her very soul.

Side two opens with an extremely sinister item, 'The Gallery', supposedly about Leonard Cohen, and portraying a man as manipulative as the narrator of, say, Robert Browning's poem 'My Last Duchess'. This lover collects women: like the traditional song 'Reynardine', there is the suggestion he might kill them. Like Rose, he appears brainwashed. After these songs of terror, 'I Think I Understand' is reassuring. As in the picture on the album cover, dark forests fail to "block the light" of inner certainty. The narrator has walked through the valley of the shadow of death, and lives to tell the tale. 'Songs to Ageing Children Come' is even weirder, its opening verse virtually meaningless, except as a string of images. What exactly is "the throbbing light machine," for example? "Crows and ravens" come, like so much else on this album, from the wellspring of traditional song, where they pick at the corpses of knights lying dead on the battlefield.

'The Fiddle and the Drum' provides some kind of key. Lightly disguised, it is about a country going to war, the looming quicksand of Vietnam. Its original title was 'Song for America'. Mitchell's voice – otherwise so flexible – does not quite have the strength to carry this unaccompanied lament; June Tabor's later rendition invests it with the proper terror. Finally, 'Both Sides Now' picks out reassurance from a time of change, but ends in failure: "It's love's illusions I recall/I really don't know life at all." Again, the song conveys a hermetic sense of being shut in, duped, locked in the dark. Triple rhymes resonate like drum beats, partially resolved by a second set of rhymes – "way", "away", "day" – and the repeated couplets of the chorus. Everything is in flux. Clouds are nice, clouds threaten. Love is a fairy tale, illusions shatter. Friendship is everything, old friendships die. Dylan's 'Tangled Up in Blue' inhabits the same territory: things and people change: the only thing to do is "keep on keeping on."

Of 'Both Sides Now', Joni later commented "this is probably the song that's been the most gregarious of my children. I saw a translation of it come back through the Chinese. It had gone to China, been translated into Chinese calligraphy, then been translated back out into English. And it came out 'Joni's Theory of Relativity'. There's another comic footnote to the album. In concert with James Taylor, Joni prefaced 'The Gallery' with the following aside: "This next song is a little play, a little soliloquy. It's about an artist's old lady. I play the part of that old lady. There's one thing that kind of holds true about artists, and that is they're connoisseurs of beauty, you know, and that's what this song is about, it's about an artist who runs around the countryside connoisseuring lots of beauties." Nick Kent, never an easy man to impress, wrote of the same song that it demonstrated a wit and insight that "came like a breath of fresh air in the wake of all the brooding self pity, fast establishing itself as the singer-songwriter's only calling card."

Later writers have tended to revalue *Clouds* downwards. Dave Marsh describes the way it captures "the emotional conclusions of weakening romanticism," a hangover from the first album. For Bob Sarlin, *Clouds* is weighed down with a number of melodramatic attempts at complicated narrative poetry, which bog down in "words and more words." For Mike Allen, *Clouds* is "so completely inert as to be but half-alive. Was she sinking into 'post-highschool narcissism'?" He then spoils things by admitting that he loved the album when he was younger. Maybe that's the answer. If her first album was a picture of a prolonged adolescence, this is Mitchell fighting her way into emotional adulthood, while scared about losing her youth and innocence, forever. She confirms this in her interview with Cameron Crowe. At the time of the first album, she was "still very concerned with childhood." Her paintings and songs were both "full of the remnants of fairy tales and fantasia." She had, painfully, to grow up. "Suddenly I realised that I was preoccupied with the things of my girlhood and I was twenty-four years old. I remember being at the Philadelphia Folk Festival and having this sensation. It was like falling to earth. It was about the time of my second album. It felt almost as if I'd had my head in the clouds long enough. And then there was a plummeting into the earth, tinged with a little bit of apprehension and fear. Shortly after that, everything began to change. There were fewer adjectives to my poetry. Fewer curlicues to my drawing. Everything began to get more bold. And solid, in a way." This gives her title of *Clouds* for this album a whole new meaning.

Paul Gambaccini refers to the way 'Songs to Ageing Children Come'. is used at a climactic point in the film *Alice's Restaurant*, also about (avoiding) the Vietnam war. A young friend of Arlo Guthrie dies: in the calm that follows the tragedy, we hear the song performed by another artist. "These days it seems absurd that people in their teens and twenties should be obsessed with their own ageing. But in the late sixties the American generation which opposed the war in Vietnam, resisted racism, and constructed a counter culture were almost by definition narcissistic. In a world where you could "never trust anyone over thirty" a birthday was a disaster. 'Songs' is touching today. Then, it was shattering."

The sixties had passed away, just like they do at the end of the movie *Withnail and I*. The greatest decade in the history of the world was over, and it was time to either shape up, grow up, or fade away. Bang at the start of the new decade, in early January 1970, Joni flew into London with her friends CSNY, to do what she planned to be her last concert for a long, long time. Caroline Boucher interviewed her at a record company reception: in a long green skirt, with green velvet top and long fair hair in pigtails, Joni looked about sixteen. She wore a collection of cameo rings on her left hand, twisting them as she spoke. "I always smile when I'm nervous," she admitted.

"I would like the luxury of a day with nothing to do, so I could wake up and say 'what shall I do today?' It's been years since I could do that. I need a rest. I'm going through a change as an artist. I'm beginning to write on the piano, which is a much freer instrument, and I want to learn the concertina and the violin. When you know you're going back on the road there's so many things to do – every minute becomes vital – and my writing suffers. As a woman, I have a responsibility to my home, and it takes me a week to get the house reperking." Joni's hippie, free love image is just that, a mask for a deeper loneliness and insecurity. Today, such soul-baring is commonplace, and wearying. Then, it was virtually unique. "My personal life is a shambles, and it's hard on me knowing I'm not giving anything to people I love. Most of my friends are musicians – I'm not very social. I'm a very solitary person, even in a room full of people. I feel completely alone. You need solitude to make anything artistic. You need the focus which you can't have surrounded by people."

As to her music, "I'm very possessive about my own art. It's expanding now and I can see other instruments. I can't write music, though. I sing different parts into a tape recorder. If I had two years off, I'd probably go back and learn composition." Joni announced to Jerry Gilbert that she had postponed all bookings indefinitely, "just to catch my breath." She was not so much resting, as redefining her career. "I've got a hard core of fans who follow me around from one concert to another, and it's for them I feel I ought to produce some new songs. I want my music to get more involved and more sophisticated. I've a feeling that America may suddenly get very strange." Joni emphasised that she would not be playing any folk clubs while in Britain. Those days had long gone. Apart from her London concert, and an appearance on – of all things – the Tom Jones Show, she was here to rest. "I want to get out into the country, in particular to Scotland."

On February 10th, CSNY played a two-hour show, which included 'Our House', at the Royal Albert Hall. The cracks in their music were already starting to show. Chris Welch hit the nail bang on the head: "They could improve themselves by being a little less self-indulgent and knowing when to stop." A week later, Joni shocked a sell-out audience at London's Festival Hall by announcing that she was to quit live performances, though she would break this resolution later that year by appearing at the Mariposa Folk Festival and the Isle of Wight.

She had spent her time in London profitably, visiting the Victoria and Albert Museum, and rummaging through the Chelsea antique market. When she walked out to enthusiastic applause from a particularly young and receptive audience Mitchell seemed very much at home. Wearing a plain, red maxi-length dress, she radiated warmth, opening with 'Chelsea Morning.' This she encored later, as one transfixed man kept crying out "Oh Joni please do it again, please." After two more songs on acoustic guitar, she switched to piano for 'He Played Real Good For Free' which, she told the audience, had been inspired by a street musician on the Kings Road. She closed the first set with 'Both Sides, Now'.

After the interval, Joni returned in a dark blue dress to play a much longer set, including her 'Galleries', 'Michael from Mountains' and 'Marcie'. She also premiered what she called "the only rock and roll song I've ever written," then entitled 'They Paved Paradise and Put Up a Parking Lot'. Joni went back to the piano for 'The Arrangement' a song she had written for the Elia Kazan movie, and which had been turned down! Still at the piano, she sang another new song, 'Woodstock', which had just been recorded by CSNY, as their new single. "I wanted to join the group," she laughed, with a wink to the wings where Graham Nash was unobtrusively standing throughout the evening, "but they wouldn't let me." The audience wouldn't let her go and screamed and stamped for more. After doing 'Chelsea Morning' again, for its persistent fan, she ended with Dino Valente's anthem 'Get Together' and again left the audience standing and cheering for ten minutes. She had been on stage, solo, for over two hours.

Ticket prices for this extravaganza, billed as her only concert appearance in Great Britain, ranged from 8/- to 25/-. It was to be her last appearance in a concert hall for almost a year. She cancelled two important US gigs, at Carnegie Hall, and Constitution Hall in Washington. We now enter the most mysterious phase of Joni Mitchell's life. It was a less dramatic version of Agatha Christie's disappearance (and reappearance at a seaside hotel) at the height of her career, or Dylan's supposed motorbike crash in late 1966. Part escape, part broken heart. At the time of her London visit, Joni told an interviewer that she and Nash had been talking about getting married. It was not to be, and the relationship collapsed soon afterwards.

In the midst of all this fame and fortune, Joni's personal life was suffering. She had little privacy. The confessional nature of her work provoked endless upsetting speculation about romantic liaisons with other famous artists. *Rolling Stone* later voted her 'Old Lady of the Year' and 'Queen of El Lay' – unfair when the promiscuous antics of male counterparts attracted little or no comment. Indeed, she was becoming a counter-culture pin-up. The same magazine published 'Natural History', a poem by MG Stephens, in April 1970. It is a kind of secular hymn, beginning thus:

My lady, Joni Mitchell
I dance twice a week at
the right hours, I'm home from
work after midnight, all is forgiven.
Come back to Monet
my dungarees love you
I work nights as a clerk in the
Eighth Street bookshop
you bought you hung out for
half an hour
by the art books

The young art lover suggests an assignation between "Paul Klee & the New York Art Scene," and compares Joni favourably with Jane Fonda.

The gossip, the break with Nash, and the extra strain of spending about forty weeks a year on the road, led Joni to go into semi-retirement for the next two years.

Depressed, doubting her motivation about performing, and in a quandary about her new-found wealth, Joni travelled extensively and continued writing. In March, she won Best Folk Performance of 1969 for *Clouds* at the twelfth Grammy awards in New York. Her third LP, *Ladies of the Canyon*, was released in May 1970. It reached Number Twenty-Seven in the US album charts, and Number Eight in the UK, earning Joni her first gold record, selling over a million copies. CSNY reached Number Eleven in the US singles chart with their version of her song 'Woodstock'. Joni herself got onto Top Forty radio with 'Big Yellow Taxi', a single taken from the LP, which reached Number Eleven in the British singles charts.

The album contained some outside musicians: Teressa Adams on cello, Milt Holland on percussion, Paul Horn on clarinet and flute, and Jim Horn on baritone sax. Bop vocal was by the 'Saskatunes' – a multi-tracked Joni – and the chorus on 'The Circle Game' was provided by the 'Lookout Mountain United Downstairs Choir', a thin disguise for CSNY. This time around, the lyrics were scripted on the inner sleeve in Mitchell's own clear handwriting. The cover was minimalist, a half-composed line drawing partially filled in with a watercolour depicting houses, parked cars and trees. The seagull and peacock on the first LP are here transformed to farmyard ducks. Talking to Larry LeBlanc, Joni declared that "the drawings, the music and the words are very much tied together. The kind of material I want to write – I want it to be brighter, to get people up, to grab people. So I'm stifling my feelings of solitude."

She agreed that she had deliberately tried to simplify her work, to make it more accessible. To make things appear easy, she had had to work extremely hard. "In order to be simplified it has to be honed down more. It takes a lot more polishing for that simplicity than it did for anything complicated. I do a lot of night-writing. I need solitude to write. I used to be able to write under almost any condition, but not any more, 'cause I have to go inside myself so far, to search through a theme. When I finish a new song, I take it and play it for my friends who are fine musicians and writers. If they like it, I'm knocked out. I guess I write for those people. They're really my audience. My music now is becoming more rhythmic. It's because I'm in Los Angeles and my friends are mostly rock 'n' roll people, and being influenced by that rhythm. I've always liked it. When I was in Saskatchewan, I loved to dance."

This new communality and rhythmic freshness inspire the whole album. She continued to use the A&M Records Studios – built on Charlie Chaplin's movie lot – because "the piano at A&M is the best in the whole world," and this is very much a piano-led album. It hangs together as a suite of songs, as do all of Joni's best records. 'Morning Morgantown' opens with a new richness of sound, over which Joni's vocals hover like a hummingbird, filled with hope and new potential. The song is an invitation to a new lover, and the final verse is half a sexual come-on. Her voice almost literally smiles with pleasure. The kind of music that brings eyesight to the blind. 'For Free' is more stately, though the way Joni intones "two gentlemen" would make a monk twitch. The piano rings like a bell, and a cello comes in subliminally under Joni's vocal for the last verse: her voice rises up on the last "free" as if taking flight. Ragtime clarinet ends the track, giving weight to the rumour that the unnamed street musician was Lol Coxhill, a legendary player who would busk long, wild improvisations in the street, as well as playing r&b – he is seen on an early *Ready Steady Go* backing Rufus Thomas – punk with the Damned, and free jazz. Free as in unfettered, not unpaid, which gives an extra dimension to this track, as Joni's first foray into the world of modern jazz. The lights change, and Joni walks away. Of course, the man isn't playing for free, he is playing for small change, a kind of precursor of a 'downsized' economy, in which everyone fills in with odd jobs and short-term contracts to make ends meet.

'Conversation' is also addressed to a fellow musician, and is Joni's first rock performance, with percussion driving things along. It also alternates her two voices, angelic glide and low, sexy growl – but you need to listen to that, not analyse it. The alliteration which seems clumsy on the first album is by now masterful – "comes", "conversation", "comfort", "consultation" – world-class poetry by any definition. The title track is more ambiguous than it first seems, as is Joni's marvellous vocal, celebratory with a hint of irony. Structurally, this track is very cunning – the way in which each verse turns back on itself midway, the way in which all three characters are gathered up at the end. It is a picture of three women finding a way to express

107

themselves – through art, playing at earth mother, through music and mystery – but surely all three are aspects of Joni herself. And not a man in sight!

The man in 'Willy' is also far from the macho stereotype, a male counterpart of the new women in the previous song, but one wounded and incomplete. What is almost beyond description is Joni's marvellous vocal here, each line subtly different: hopeful, sad, yearning, ethereal, tender. The way the melody dips, the symmetry between voice and piano – soaring high, plunging low together – reveals an artist at the very height of her powers. 'The Arrangement' is ironically just that, with lyrics which never quite match the sheer gorgeousness of piano and vocals, which is probably why at one point – like Van Morrison at his best – she leaves behind words altogether, substituting a kind of feral howl. And that's just side one of the original album.

Side two divides into three songs in the old style, slightly fuzzy round the edges, and three masterpieces. 'Rainy Night House' is a strange song, quietly underpinned by cello. Joni becomes a whole choir at one point. It's a gentle farewell to Leonard Cohen – a boy who gave up his inheritance to become a "holy man on the FM radio" – who is gently parodied in the religious imagery she calls up. The way "called" is used twice, in two different senses, is pure Joni. 'The Priest' is also Cohen territory, an agnostic age's nostalgia for faith, but given a sexual charge. The guitar accompaniment is old Joni; the drums and the way her voice lingers on "time" are something totally new. 'Blue Boy' is a hymn to love, Joni's astonishingly intimate vocal conjuring up a man who "comes" and can "give his seed to her." Her wordless "ohs" seem too private for public consumption. The story is straight from fairy tale, but filtered through a modern sensibility. The narrator looks out through a window's pain, not pane: the song is ambiguous, the lyric sheet clear.

Mitchell told Ray Coleman where she got the inspiration for 'Big Yellow Taxi': "When I was in Hawaii, I arrived at the hotel at night, and went straight to bed. When I woke up next day, I looked out of the window and it was so beautiful, everything was so green and there were white birds flying around, and then I looked down and there was a great big parking lot. That's what Americans do. They take the most beautiful parts of the continent and build hotels and put up posters and all of that and ruin it completely." She described the song itself as "Ecology rock 'n' roll." Humour carries the message, like a sweet to help down the medicine. Joni now likes the "life that it has," its re-emergence as a children's song. As she later told *Music Now*: "I don't believe protest songs have any great significance. These songs are being listened to by the converted, those who already agree. Perhaps if a song was written that Mr Nixon would listen to!" Maybe he tapped his toes to this tune! Being written by Joni, there's a hidden meaning in the song. It is not just Nature that is being betrayed – the big yellow taxi is used by her lover for a moonlit flit. Joni's vocal is innocent, childlike, a swanlike glide which ends with a throaty laugh.

'Woodstock' is performed with the accompaniment of a lone Fender Rhodes, and a heavenly chorus of herself. Joni delays the word "band" just a fraction. Her voice almost breaks on "smog" and floats on "butterfly": it ends in wordless evocation. You feel, at this point in her career, that vocally she can do anything she pleases. Michael Watts commented that CSNY's version whipped up her "lovely, floating" song into something fierce and pounding, almost a new entity. She replied, "I liked their performance, too, in its way. They were seeing Woodstock from the point of view of the performers." Iain Matthews' rendition is different again, gentle and almost bland, sweetened with steel guitar. 'The Circle Game' concludes this near-perfect album – for which it would have provided a more appropriate title, if Tom Rush hadn't beaten her to it. Crosby, Stills and Nash are somewhere in the backing chorus, but I can't hear Neil Young's unique prairie-dog howl, which is strange, as he inspired the song in the first place. A set of lyrics performed in Joni's sweetest voice, totally without anger at time's ravages. A children's song for adults.

Later critics have, as usual, failed to get the point. Bob Sarlin, while noting that Joni's vocals were starting to loosen up, considered that "she still spends too much time trying to send her voice to the moon or beyond with high and most unnecessary howlings." Jacques Vassal thought that "the title track describes the quiet decay of the dilettante upper middle classes." Steve Clarke, more sensibly, saw 'The Circle Game' as "Mitchell breathing new life into the traditional folk metaphor of the seasons as a symbol for ageing." The most vicious – and unfair – response to the album was by Nick Kent, writing at the cusp of punk. It "billowed forth," like some hippie vestment, "draped in all the fey paraphernalia of the whole loathsome Laurel Canyon tradition – all sanforized denim, dippy children with toenails hard as walnuts, astrological obsessions, the whole utterly useless, sun drenched existence." This is particularly unfair, as Mitchell was always sharply aware of the self-contradictions of hippiedom. But he continues: "Mitchell's ailing chipmunk timbre had become fairly annoying, with its squeamish pitch impairing many a tweeter of the more sensitive hi-fi system." Not mine, squire.

Paul Gambaccini thought that the lyrics on *Ladies of the Canyon* read as marvellous poems. "In the words of 'Woodstock', one can find all the optimism of that courageous if self-indulgent culture, the desire to free one's soul from material encumbrances." The song which set off all kinds of resonances in her later work, 'For Free', was on a similar theme. Talking later to fellow Canadian folk singer Malka, Joni explained that "I had no idea that I would be this successful. I had difficulty accepting my affluence, and my success, and even the expression of it seemed to me distasteful. I had a lot of soul searching to do." She was also searching for new subjects, and new ways to express herself. This constant quest is the sign of a great artist, in whatever medium, although it also meant that some experiments would prove to be in hopelessly wrong directions. Just look at the career of David Bowie, for an extraordinary succession of highs and lows (no pun intended!). A lesser artist would simply have repeated the *Ladies of the Canyon* formula, now perfected, for the rest of her or his career.

Not Joni, though. She would take the fragile insights of a song like 'Willy' and put them at the heart of her next project. First, though, came a period of restlessness and pain, a premature retirement. Richard Thompson did the same, twice, leaving Fairport just as they were breaking through commercially, and abandoning music altogether for a year after his apocalyptic 1975 tour. In both cases, he came back with something rich and strange, and so did Joni, with *Blue*. "I really don't think I've scratched the surface of my music. I'm not at all that confident about my words. Thematically I think I'm running out of things which I feel are important enough to describe verbally... most things that I would once dwell on and explore for an hour I would shrug my shoulders to now." In which case, *Ladies of the Canyon* was the most majestic and beautiful of leave-takings.

In the summer of 1970, Joni arrived back home in Canada at the Mariposa Folk Festival. During an afternoon workshop she freely doodled a dulcimer, smiled, and hummed in rhythm with her hands. In the evening, she talked with Larry LeBlanc. The sun was gone, and a small cloud of insects hovered over. A few feet away, Gordon Lightfoot sat on a park bench; 'Rambling' Jack Elliott pulled his broad-brimmed cowboy hat over his forehead. Joni's comments are disjointed, alienated, like an internal monologue, briefly overheard.

"In January I did my last concert, with the idea I'd take this year off. I don't know what the balance is – how much good and how much damage there is in my position. From where I stand it sometimes gets absurd, and yet, I must remain smiles, come out of a mood where maybe I don't feel very pleasant and say 'smile.' Inside, I'm thinking 'You're being phony. You're being a star." I was very frightened last year, but if you're watching yourself over your own shoulder all of the time, and if you're too critical of what you're doing you can make yourself so unhappy. As a human you're always messing up, always hurting people's feelings quite innocently. I find it difficult, even here. There's a lot of people you want to talk to all at once. I get confused and maybe I'll turn away and leave someone standing and I'll think – 'oh dear.' I've changed a lot. I'm getting very defensive. I feel like I'm going to be an ornery old lady."

Joni took a flight to Matala, where she went back to Nature in a big way. In a 1971 concert, she relived her experiences in Crete before singing 'Carey', which looks back to that experience: "This is a mountain dulcimer from the Appalachian mountains in America. I'm going into a tuning now which I call Matala tuning, because I found it there. There were two big walls of cave on each side of a flat plain: at night they looked like big tenement buildings, because people had little fires going in their caves and all the different levels would be lit up, with spots of light all over them. Last spring, there were a whole lot of people living there, about 150 freaks, from France and Canada and the United States of America and England, everywhere. They used to

111

eat at the Mermaid cafe, and they also did most of their drinking there 'cause the guy who ran the place, Stelios, really liked the freaks, he really encouraged their business, not like other people in the town who smiled and took your dracs from you.

"At Easter there was a family who came down the beach who were going to blend in with the freaks. They came in wearing headbands they'd made out of cloth, that they'd ripped off their pillowcases or something, and round his neck one man had a string with old curlers on it, for his beads, and another guy had zucchini squash threaded onto a spring painted bright red. And they gave us red easter eggs and little breads with kind of egg paste in the middle, and they were really nice, and the girl played guitar, and we sat around and had a really good Easter. But this is a song about a friend of mine from Matala, a friend of mine from London and Los Angeles and North Carolina." James Taylor, no less.

In subsequent interviews, Joni affectionately revisited her time in Greece. She met a man on the plane who invited Joni and her travelling companion – "a poetess from Ottawa" – back home for supper. "They had a maid who brought the dinner and prepared all the national dishes of Greece kinda in our honour. From the peasant on up, when they have guests in the house they're hospitable and lay on their best feed. Then they took us to a couple of nightclubs. It was a very sophisticated introduction to Athens. He would always say that we must be spontaneous. The Greek is spontaneous. Let us dance, drink some wine, throw the gardenia to the singer." She giggles here, bringing a smile to her tanned and freckled face that almost closes her eyes with pleasure. "I hiked in boots through the fields. It's very rugged, very simple, very basic. People live from the land much more. Peasants walked donkeys. There were very few cars. Even the poorest people seem to eat well: cucumbers and tomatoes, oranges and potatoes and bread. They lived in concrete huts with maybe one or two chairs, a bed where the family slept, and a couple of chickens. To me it was a lovely life, far better than being middle class in America. I lived for five weeks in a cave there."

Matala itself was as near to Eden as this earth allows. It was just like her first album, escaping from city to seaside. "It was between the two cliffs, on the beach. The caves were on high sedimentary cliffs, sandstone, a lot of seashells in it. Carved out by the Minoans hundreds of years ago, they were used later for leper caves. Then after that the Romans came and they used them for burial crypts. Then some of them were filled in and sealed up for a long time. People began living there, beatniks, in the fifties. Kids gradually dug out more rooms. There were some people who were wearing human teeth necklaces around their necks. We all put on a lot of weight. We were eating a lot of apple pies, good bacon. We were eating really well, good wholesome food. There were a couple of fishing boats that went out, that got enough fish to supply the two restaurants there. The bakery lady who had the grocery store there had fresh bread, fresh rice pudding, made nice yoghurt every day, did a thriving business, and just before I left, she installed a fridge. She had the only cold drinks in town. It was all chrome and glass. It was a symbol of her success."

This Eden was already doomed: perhaps in this experience we can see the embryo of the idea that later became *The Hissing of Summer Lawns*. Talking to Penny Valentine, Joni elaborated: it was the paradox of 'Big Yellow Taxi' all over again. "You tailor-make your dreams, then inevitably it can't live up to your hopes. Hawaii had so many really beautiful parts to it, and the island of Kuwaii is still agricultural. I guess I had thought of it from all those movies I had seen – sacrificing the maidens to the volcano, rivers running with blood and lava, guava trees and Esther Williams, you know, swimming through the lagoon. And you get there and have to sort through the stucco and the pink hotels. Crete was for the most part pretty virgin and if you walked to the market you'd find farmers with burros and oranges on the side, it was wonderful. Matala was full of kids from all over the world who were seeking the same kind of thing I was, but they may as well have been in an apartment in Berkeley as in a cave there, because the lifestyle continued the same wherever they were."

Joni only came to live here by chance. "After my initial plans to be accepted into the home of a Greek family fell apart we came to this very scene – the scene we were trying to escape from – and it seemed very attractive to us. There were so many contradictions. Like the kids couldn't get used to seeing all the slaughtered meat hanging in the shops – they'd only ever seen bits of meat wrapped in cellophane, and to see it there on its frame turned their stomachs." It was a fantasy world, that couldn't last, much like the Woodstock spirit, and its aftermath. "Then the cops came and kicked everyone out of the caves, but it was getting a little crazy there. Everybody was getting more and more into open nudity. They were really getting back to the caveman. They were wearing little loin cloths. The Greeks couldn't understand what was happening. When I first got there I found I was carrying around a sketch pad, pens, paper. I was all prepared, should inspiration strike in any shape or form. I'm going to do something with my time."

But inspiration did not arrive on time, like a train. Instead, she felt intrusive as an artist, so simply enjoyed things as they happened. "Well, I somehow felt like I do sometimes about photographers. When I was in Jamaica with my friends, we went up into the mountains. Suddenly we stopped in this village. It was beautiful and primitive. We all got out, I jumped around, cameras up to our eyes. I thought from their point of view we must've looked like creatures from outer space, real monsters. I got into capturing the moment like a kind of rape. Even with a pencil or a brush. It was just an attitude I had at that time. I couldn't do anything, really, until I got away from Crete. When I got to Paris and back into the city, with time to reflect, I began to realise differently." Mitchell retreated back to Laurel Canyon, to sift through these experiences, and begin work on her next album. Meanwhile, there were further adventures to come.

Joni was emblematic of a generation of young travellers – inspired by Kerouac's *On the Road* – undertaking vast geographical pilgrimages in search of some kind of fulfilment. The hippie trail to Katmandu was just one of the delights on offer: this was travelling, not tourism. And yet, as Mike Allen acidly observed: "The vision of her on the world's dusty roads is an interesting one. On one hand, it's a paradigm for the quest which her music so obviously is, and yet on the other hand there's something incongruous about that lofty, sophisticated and intuitively aristocratic face catching dust and stuff in its eyes, sleeping and travelling rough."

Joni's search next took her to the Caribbean. "I've been to Greece, Spain, France, and from Jamaica to Panama, through the canal. Some of my friends were moving their boat from Fort Lauderdale up to San

Francisco. I joined them in Jamaica and sailed down through the canal. It was really an experience." David Crosby's girlfriend, Christine Hinton, had died in a car crash. He decided on the romantic notion of scattering her ashes at sea. Graham Nash had been in constant attendance, afraid that Crosby was set on committing suicide. The only true sailor in the group, Barry Cuda, attended to the serious navigation, while hired hands were taken on to actually sail the Mayan. Joni came along for the trip. Crosby takes up the story in *Long Time Gone*.

"We sailed off down through the Bahamas and then the Windward Passage, between Cuba and Haiti, and went to Jamaica. Had a wonderful, crazy week. From Jamaica we sailed to Panama. Going through the Panama canal was a total thrill, absolutely amazing, sailing through a three-tiered rain forest, a jungle two hundred feet high with parrots and monkeys and alligators and all that shit." Joni flew home, while the others sailed up the west coast of Central America, and home to San Francisco. Christine's ashes were cast into the Pacific, outside the Golden Gate bridge. Then a grief-stricken Crosby went back to finish recording *Deja Vu*.

Joni's state of mind at this time is hard to discern. Jacona Atlas sees her as poised between the dying of the hippie dream and the beginnings of the women's movement. "All too seldom in music is the female view set down," but Mitchell pins it exactly. She agrees. "I think there's a lack of romance in everything today. I think that women are getting a bum deal. I think we are being misguided. There's the fear of the big hurt, we're taught to be very cool. And to be non-committal. Anything that's repressed and goes underground really gets distorted." Mitchell admitted that she had herself visited a psychiatrist just before she made the decision to come off the road.

The shadow of Joni's former husband still looms large in her mind, like a stain. "I used to be in a duo and that was the last time I played with anyone else except for my friends." Joni now sings with the likes of Graham Nash and Judy Collins, but purely for fun. "I flat-pick my music and I know there are places to be filled in. There could be more texture to it. When I finger pick, I play the melody line and in many cases that's the way it stays. When I've finished a song, I've honed it to a point where it's a completed song to me. And anything that is added might, to other people, sound better and more complete, but to me it sounds extraneous." She reveals that "I sing all the instrumental parts onto a tape and my arranger transcribes them." The problem is that, when she has settled down to write, friends often suddenly drop by. "I have to socialise, but then my concentration and enthusiasm is disturbed." The same thing happened to Coleridge, when he was halfway through 'Kubla Khan'.

Joni talked these problems over with a sympathetic woman journalist, Penny Valentine of *Sounds*. "A couple of years ago I got very depressed – to the point where I thought it was no longer a problem for burdening my friends with. But I needed to talk to someone who was very indifferent, so I thought I'd pay a guy to listen to me. I just started to rap from the time I came in through the door – which turned out to be forty minutes of everything I thought was bothering me. Which included a description of myself as a person who never spoke, which naturally he found hard to understand. But in day to day life I was practically catatonic." His response is to hand Joni his card, and suggest that she call him when she feels suicidal. This works, though presumably not in the way he intended: "I went out into the street – I'd come in completely deadpan, my face immobile even when I talked – and I just felt this grin breaking over my face at the irony of it all. I wanted some wisdom, some kind of counsel and direction. He didn't know. He only knew the way to his office in the morning and the way to the bar afterwards."

The thing that Joni most fears is losing her creativity. "You come to dry periods as an artist and you get really panicky. I've known people that haven't written for maybe a year and they're chewing their fingernails right down to the wrist. Their record company is beginning to withdraw from them, the spark is going out. Or maybe it's the fact that at seventeen they were so pretty, and all of a sudden in the morning they have bags under their eyes. My creativity, in one form or another is very strong, and will continue. I say to Elliot 'Oh I haven't written anything for three weeks' and he's always laughing at me because I'm very prolific." Indeed, Roberts confirmed that Joni's career worked in cycles. When she had written five or six new songs that she

116

enjoyed playing, she would tour again: "She doesn't like to when she feels she's just being repetitious." Joni's lifestyle brought other fears and complications. "I'm also very lonely – which is one of the dues you pay. I don't have a very large circle of friends. I have a few very close friends and then there's a whole lot of people I'm sort of indifferent to. I used to be nice to anyone who was nice to me – I had this obligation to be nice back. But that's a discrimination I've learned. I'm older and wiser now." What Joni seems to be undergoing during her enforced retirement is a form of nervous breakdown. "It's like driving out your devils – do you drive out your angels as well? An artist needs a certain amount of turmoil and confusion, and I've created out of that. It's been like part of the creative force – even out of the severe depression comes insight. I think analysis did me a lot of good." This self-searching sparked off the most profound music of her whole career, only coming to rest when she eventually remarried. Meanwhile, her greatest emotional challenge was about to hit her, in front of half a million sightseers.

In July 1970, Joni sang backing vocals on James Taylor's number 1 single, 'You've Got a Friend', and on their friend Carole King's *Tapestry*. In late August she flew to England, to play the third Isle of Wight Festival. Ian Samwell, head of Artist Liaison for Warner Bros, went ahead to check that things were correctly set up. On his way back to the quay, he saw a red, vintage Rolls Royce coming off the ferry. Neil Young had hired it, and he was coming along with Joni and Elliot Roberts to see the show. As Joni told *Q*, "the driver had to sit outside, a real horseless carriage." Suddenly, a plain-clothes policeman pulled them over, a spliff was found in Elliot's shirt pocket, and he was hauled off to jail. Neil Young was so disturbed by this that he just turned the Rolls round and went straight back to the mainland. This was a precursor of worse things to come, for Joni was to be plunged, unsuspecting, into a virtual war zone. It proved to be a kind of public initiation under fire, a 'learning experience' and a half.

"The first time I stood my ground was in front of half a million people at the Isle of Wight. It was a hostile audience to begin with. A handful of French rabble-rousers had stirred the people up to feel that we, the performers, had sold out because we arrived in fancy cars."

Which, of course, she had. "Backstage there was all this international capital – bowls of money, open coffers. Some acts cancelled, so there was a dead space of about an hour. No one would go on. But in a spirit of co-operation, knowing it was death, I said 'OK I'll go out there'." Looking like a buttercup in her yellow dress, Joni emerged into brilliant sunshine onstage. It was Saturday afternoon, midway through the three-day Festival. She was obviously nervous about performing to such a huge crowd, which stretched as far as the eye could see. Halfway through 'Chelsea Morning' she stopped, declared "I don't feel like singing that song very much," moved over to the piano, and announced that she'd sing 'Woodstock', which this festival was so obviously trying to recreate. The opening act that day had been John Sebastian, still tie-dyed and still high. Islander Mike Plumbley remembers to this day the clear notes of the piano as Joni started 'Woodstock': "it sounded timeless, floating in the air out to the perimeter fence where I was walking."

Joni's own memories are slightly less idyllic, as she told *Q*: "A guy in about the fifth row, flipped out on acid, comes squirting up and lets out a banshee yell, guttural, demented, devils at his heels. It's as if a whale came out of the water, the energy from him spreads to the back so fast. Now the whole thing is undulating." Jan Hodenfield of *Rolling Stone* reported that an obviously up-tight Joni looked everywhere but where it was happening, her concentration locked firm on the stage floor. All other eyes swung towards a swaying, puppet-like figure obviously on the worst of bad trips. In an instant the stage was full of frightened eyes and everyone was standing, staring at the ghastly figure, who was madly resisting all attempts to drag him away. Joni went back to the piano stool, picked out the opening chords of 'Woodstock' and began the song. She could not have made a worse choice. At that moment, with terror in the air, the garden isle had become a place of squalor.

She announced "this is a song about another festival. I didn't actually go there, I only got as far as New York airport, but I saw it all on television and wrote a song about it." The atmosphere settled slightly, but was still charged with tension when suddenly a small, bearded American, chillingly reminiscent of Charles Manson, seized the microphone and started to recite "a very important message for the people of Desolation Hill. I have an announcement that I have to make.

I believe that this is my festival." This was all too much for Joni's retinue, who pinioned his arms and forced him off, as the crowd began to bay "Let him speak... let him speak." In Murray Lerner's film of the event, he does. What the audience missed is a backstage rant. "I was coming to talk to an old friend of mine, Joni Mitchell. Rikki Farr came to me on Wednesday: he gave me a hundred tickets and named me the head of the official committee to paint the fence invisible." Laurie Say, of the organisers Fiery Creations remembers a funny little ragged hippie. "He told me that he went there to give a message to the earth and he left his drum on stage." Laurie went out on stage with him after the set to collect it. "He was alright, quite a nice bloke, intelligent." DJ Jeff Dexter confirms that he had been officially sanctioned to go on stage, to make an announcement to people sitting on Desolation Hill, who had not bought tickets, and were therefore literally watching Joni "for free." Elliot Roberts and Ian Samwell hauled him off. Bizarrely enough, his claim to know Joni also turns out to be true, as Joni confirms.

"I go and sit at the piano and this guy I know from the caves at Matala, Yogi Joe, he taught me my first yoga lesson, he leaps up on stage. He gives me the Victory sign, he sits at my feet and starts to play the congas with terrible time. He looks up at me and says 'Spirit of Matala, Joni.' I bend down off-mike and say 'This is *entirely* inappropriate, Joe.' It was 'Woodstock', of all songs to be singing, because this was so different, it was a war zone out there. At the end of 'Woodstock', Yogi Joe springs up, grabs the microphone and yells 'It's desolation row and we're all doomed!' or something to this effect. A couple of guards grab him. The crowd then stand up and scream 'They've got one of ours!' And they're moving forward." Meanwhile, she is playing disjointed chords on the piano, a kind of improvisation of 'For Free', until things quiet down. Obviously shaken, and in tears, Joni struggles to compose herself. For her, this is obviously a 'near death' experience. Talking to Q some twenty years on, the memory of it still bites deep.

"Now what would you do? I've run for much less than that. But I thought, I can't. I have to stand up. The place I drew my strength from was very bizarre. I had been to a Hopi snake dance ceremony – it's a very high ceremony to bring rain to their runty corn crops. They dance

119

with live snakes and there was one that stood up on the end of its tail, and launched itself like a javelin right into the audience. The people scattered but the musicians, the antelope-priest drummers, never missed a beat. Their earnestness, their sincerity, their need to bring rain, was unaffected. They kept the groove. So, with my chin quivering, fighting back tears and the impulse to run, I said 'I was at a Hopi snake dance a couple of weeks ago and there were tourists who acted like Indians and Indians who acted like tourists – you're just a bunch of tourists. Some of us have our lives involved in this music. Show us some respect.' And the beast lay down. The beast lay down."

She lightened the atmosphere with 'Willy', and a new song, 'California', her ballad about homesickness – particularly appropriate in the circumstances – on which she played dulcimer. One line, "We asked for peace, but they wouldn't give us a chance" was particularly apt. She was called back for four encores, including a supercharged 'Big Yellow Taxi', a new song, 'Good Samaritan', and 'Both Sides Now.' By the time she finally left the stage, she had defused a potentially dangerous situation, simply through the sheer beauty of her songs. The ovation which greeted her final item was tremendous, almost as if the multitude was offering an apology for the misbehaviour of an unwelcome majority. As she left the stage, Rikki Farr announced "Miss Joni Mitchell. I think you will all agree that despite the interruption, she did a beautiful job." "My heart is just going thump – thump – thump," she confessed at the end of her mangled set.

On the *Message to Love* CD, Joni sings 'Big Yellow Taxi' and 'Woodstock', while the matching video shows some of the confrontation with the stage invader/audience. Mignon Jones remembers that those who shouted at her from the auditorium were not quarrelling with Joni, but trying to warn her, for her own safety. A man had climbed the sound/lighting rig, and was in danger of toppling over onto the stage. But I remember coke cans arcing towards her in the afternoon sunlight, lobbed by members of the audience who reckoned that they deserved some respect too. It all gives added irony to the programme note: "Her voice and her acoustic guitar are free, pure instruments in themselves. There is an additional beauty in the way she uses them to convey such a full range of idea-emotions. But if she looked like your grandmother, and her voice cracked and she only knew three chords, her performance would be justified by the songs alone."

The organisers were by now aware of the calming effect she could create. Joni was brought back the next day to address and attempt to pacify the audience. Whatever fee she was paid for that weekend – and estimates wildly differ – she was worth every cent.

As if to confirm her status, *Melody Maker* readers voted Joni the world's top female singer in their 1970 poll. Sandy Denny was voted best in Britain, and fifth in the world. Joni's other runners-up were Grace Slick, Janis Joplin, Aretha Franklin, Christine Perfect, Judy Collins, Laura Nyro, Joan Baez, and Julie Driscoll. The same rock paper sent Michael Watts to watch Joni record a BBC TV special, in September 1970. Dressed in a long pink shift, which catches at her ankles, she hesitantly picks out a few bars on the piano, then asks for a glass of something hot, tea perhaps. She chats to the audience, sitting out in the darkness of the television theatre, and tells them that she must have picked up a cold. She always gets colds when she is in England; does everybody get colds when they go to America? She giggles nervously, then resumes the song, unfolding it "like a love letter written on the finest paper, pouring out its lines with a peculiar little sob in her voice, as if she cannot bear to let the words slip away."

She plucks at a dulcimer, then picks up her guitar and sings 'Big Yellow Taxi', which gets a good reaction, as does 'Both Sides Now'. She falters a bit on the latter song, not quite able to reach the pitch, but it is the last number, and she has made it through all right. A short pause, "while she stands timidly in the centre of the stage, looking vulnerable and dreamy," then the lights fade down. Backstage, she looks slightly severe, but "in an attractive sort of way, with her fine blonde hair scraped back from her tanned face, which has large bones around the cheeks and forehead, and a wide, generous mouth. It's a pleasant, open face, that sits on top of a body whose seeming fragility inspires a feeling of instinctive protectiveness." She speaks softly, telling Watts about her broken marriage, and that as a result "there is a certain amount of my life" in all her songs. "They are honest and personal, and based on truth, but I exercise a writer's licence to change details. Honesty is important to me. If I have any personal philosophy it is that

I like the truth. I like to be straight with people, and them with me. But it is not easy to do this all the time, especially in this business where there is so much falsity."

Always one for a memorable quote, she concludes her interview with laughter, and her philosophy of existence: "Clean linen and funk is my idea of a good life."

In October 1970, Matthews Southern Comfort topped the UK charts with 'Woodstock'. It acted as a taster for Joni's visit to London in late November, as did a BBC2 broadcast earlier that month of her *In Concert* appearance. She appeared at the Festival Hall on Saturday, November 28th, for a solo concert. Failing to project her voice, then allowing it to fly out of control, forgetting the occasional song and completely unable to tune up for one number, it seems as if Joni's nervousness will defeat her. A frail, vulnerable figure on stage, she somehow keeps going, with the support of a sell-out audience who will her on. As she settles down, the concert develops into an intimate, friendly occasion. Joni sings and plays as if she is sitting at home, not performing to a thousand strangers. Switching from guitar to piano to dulcimer and back again, she draws on her three albums, even delving back to the first for 'Nathan La Franeer', 'Michael from Mountains', and 'Marcie', whose namesake was in the audience. There were also new songs: 'California', 'Carey', and the achingly intense 'I Wish I Had a River', written the previous Christmas.

The second set ends with 'Woodstock'. As Nick Logan reported for the *NME*, "hearing her emotionally shrilling about getting back to the garden, you realise that no other interpreter will ever convey what she means by the phrase." For an encore – and what else could it be but 'Circle Game'? – she calls on her manager Elliot Roberts and a self-conscious Graham Nash to help out with the chorus. *Sounds* ended their report of the concert as follows: "Few other performers today can strike such a rapport with an audience, yet few others are prepared to expose themselves, their private loves and fears, to the public gaze. Unlike her countryman Leonard Cohen and other contemporaries who enact their emotions against a background of human desperation, Joni sings of hope, of love and joy. Of dignity in despair."

Elliot Roberts had turned down flat the idea of Joni recording a live concert for the BBC so soon after her TV show. After he had flown back to the States, Joni slipped into the Paris studios to lay down an hour of live material for broadcast on Radio One that Christmas. So short was the notice she gave that she had to be brought in after a recording date by Jon Hiseman's Colosseum. When the audience was asked if they could endure an unexpected concert by Joni Mitchell on top – for free, of course – very few declined to stay. She surprised even the BBC by bringing along an unbilled James Taylor, whom she was "stepping out with at the time," as the show's producer gracefully put it. On the other hand, she was still on obviously good terms with Graham Nash the previous week at the Festival Hall. No wonder *Blue* – recorded as soon as she returned to the States – proved to be such a rich and confusing album.

The BBC Broadcast has turned up illicitly as the bootleg *For Free* (a particularly ironic title, as artists get no royalties from such recordings), with almost perfect sound quality. Of course, one finds the bootlegging mentality reprehensible, and strongly condemns it, just as a tape of this concert is often on my own hi-fi. In the absence of any official live recording from this time, it is a priceless document, capturing the intimacy and vocal flow of an artist totally in command of her material, and her audience. The breathless introductions are worth the price of admission alone. The CD credits 'Circle Games' as well as 'Rainy Day Man' as both written by James Taylor. He should be so lucky.

Accompanying herself on guitar, Joni runs through 'That Song about the Midway' and 'The Gallery', then moves to the piano for 'The River', topping and tailing it with a brief burst of 'Jingle Bells', and introducing it thus: "It's a very sad song. Get yourselves in a melancholy, just-before-Christmas spirit." Still at the piano, she sings 'My Old Man', back to guitar for 'The Priest', then for 'Carey' she accompanies a new song with a new instrument. Both are unfamiliar to the audience, so she gives a short lesson in musicology. "This is a mountain dulcimer from the Appalachian mountains in America. It was made for me by a girl named Joellen who's from California. She does beautiful work, she's used all kinds of wood, purple heart for the sides, and cocoburra, which is a kind of ripply orange wood, for the back, and for the soundhole she's carved little stylised swallows and on the tuning head there's a hawk. This is the twelfth one that she's built, and everybody's waiting for the next one."

James Taylor is brought onstage. Unlike the embarrassed Graham Nash, he is happy to be in attendance. "I'm not going to be singing right away, but I love being here." He provides acoustic guitar on 'A Case of You', then himself introduces 'California': "Joni wrote it; she wrote it partially in Paris and partially in Ibiza..." "And partially in Los Angeles" she butts in, then adds "There's a tribute there for you." Taylor, his usual phlegmatic self, ignores this completely, and concentrates instead on the job in hand. "You just start and I'll catch up with you." He introduces the next song too, 'For Free'. "First time that I ever heard this tune, we were at Newport, doing some workshops in the middle of a field and it was raining a little bit; and the mikes were shorting on and off, it was a kind of a weird day, but I'd never heard this tune before, it is a kind of cowboy-type tune, and I've never played it with her before either, but I play a little too, maybe we can make it work."

Joni adds "it's sort of on the order of 'Happy Trails to you, until we meet again'," though whether this is targeted at Taylor or the audience is not quite clear. The combination of his gentle guitar lines and her piano – ringing clear as a bell – is heart-stopping. Taylor actually sings on the final song, joining in the chorus of 'The Circle Game'. Joni tells the audience they must join in too, as her voice is going, then gives a loving, unhurried rendition. It all ends in giggles.

The relationship with Taylor was nowhere near as cosy as the on-stage banter suggested. One of the first rock journalists to get right under the skin of his victims was Jules Siegel. He published the true state of affairs in *Rolling Stone* early in 1971, in one of the articles which led to a ten-year feud between singer and magazine. Siegel was in all the right – or wrong – places, and he was busy taking notes. James Taylor looked a lot leaner and sharper than the photograph on his album. With him was one of the most beautiful women Siegel had ever seen, and she turned out to be James Taylor's current 'old lady'. "A joint was lighted and passed around. Joni strummed his guitar. She was wearing a grey woollen knitted long dress and a hand-knitted scarf. 'I spend a lot of time on planes. It's a good time to knit.' The drummer brought out a small vial that looked like a miniature sweet cream bottle and contained cocaine. He horned the white powder from a tiny silver spoon. The room became crystal sharp. Joni was even more beautiful and desirable than she had been before, her eyes crisp and glistening as she stroked the guitar. It was time for James to go onstage. He picked up the guitar and ran his fingers lightly over the strings and frowned. 'Joni, did you re-tune my guitar?' She blushed, made a small 'O' and put her hand to her mouth."

Taylor relaxed onstage, but Siegel could still not bring himself to like him. His upbringing as a rich kid, and the much-publicised battles with mental breakdown and heroin addiction, had made Taylor a selfish and haughty man, who seemed to crave total attention. His album had established a whole new genre: the self-absorbed singer-songwriter, consumed by his own psyche. On another night, Siegel had brought a book of his own drawings for Joni to look at. Lacking Taylor's cool, she was taking a real interest, and this infuriated her lover. "Taylor sulked and pouted. Joni handed me back my book and stretched out her foot to touch his. He smiled reluctantly." The Woodstock spirit is fading fast; here are the seventies in all their flash and insincerity, their notions of a rock aristocracy. Siegel aptly titles his piece 'Midnight in Babylon'.

CSNY themselves were fast disintegrating: Nash would often find himself bursting into tears from the frustrations keeping all four of them so distant from each other: the drugs and sexual politics which had brought them together were now driving them apart. Nash ran off with a girl who Stills had wanted for himself, and that was that for a few years. After this temporary break-up, Crosby and Nash began a project of their own. Both tremendous admirers of Joni's songwriting, they decided to record her early song 'Urge for Going' as a pop single. In June 1971, Joel Bernstein came to the studio with Nash, just in time to witness a heated argument, as a result of which the song was never completed. It would finally appear some twenty years later, on the CSN box set.

It already seems a long way from the kind of innocence and sharing exemplified a year or so earlier by Ritchie Yorke. "One late summer's night, Joni had been playing a gig in the east and Nash had driven out to the Los Angeles airport to meet her. He had clearly been pining for her all day; their close relationship was obvious. They drove back to the house, where Joni was received joyously. An hour or so later, she was seated at the piano playing one of her new songs. Everyone was mesmerised." Such contradictions would underlie *Blue*, which moved Joni's music onto a whole other level.

chapter 3:

On A Lonely Road...
Travelling

"By the time of my fourth album, *Blue*, I came to another turning point – the terrible opportunity that people are given in their lives. The day that they discover to the tips of their toes that they're assholes. [Solemn moment, then a gale of laughter.] And you have to work on from there. And decide what your values are. Which parts of you are no longer really necessary. They belong to childhood's end. *Blue* was a turning point in a lot of ways." The album was released in July 1971. It reached Number Fifteen in the US and Number Three in Britain, a million-seller at a time when such feats were exceptional. It was again recorded at A&M studios, with Stephen Stills on bass, James Taylor on vocals and guitar, and Russ Kunkel on drums. 'Sneaky' Pete Kleinow from the Flying Burrito Brothers guested on pedal steel guitar. 'Carey', a single drawn from the LP, spent one week on the US Hot 100 at ninety-three. Those are the bare facts. What is the truth? Something else completely. Joni again, talking to Cameron Crowe: "Honesty? Genius? The *Blue* album, there's hardly a dishonest note in the vocals. At that period of my life, I had no personal defences. I felt like a cellophane wrapper on a pack of cigarettes. I felt like I had absolutely no secrets from the world, and I couldn't pretend in my life to be strong. Or to be happy. But the advantage of it in the music was that there were no defences there either."

The photograph by Tim Considine which dominates the cover of *Blue* is of a pensive Joni, half caught in shadow, eyes closed, mouth turned down in sadness. Her face emerges from a deep shade of royal blue, with all that colour suggests: the blues, nobility, melancholy – 'Blue Train', 'Almost Blue', 'Tangled Up in Blue' – or unresponsiveness:

"You're so cold, I'm turning blue." Corpses, the sky, Joni's eyes on the front cover of *Clouds*, the sea (both off Crete and the Caribbean), infinity, and the divine: in medieval art, blue suggests the presence of God. The album traces a time of disillusion and terror, where they "won't give peace a chance." It is closest in tone to John Lennon's post-Beatles work – and perhaps this album is a counterpart to their 'white' album – plunging back into private emotions.

Rather like Fleetwood Mac's *Rumours* – also the work of emigres to the Golden State – the record derives some of its curiosity from the glimpses it offers into true life romance, Joni swinging between James Taylor and Graham Nash like a pendulum. Contemporary reviews were largely ambivalent. Alun Lewis in *Melody Maker* describes sourly "another volume of vicarious heartache." Joni is now a Rock Star, able to fly at a whim from Laurel Canyon to Amsterdam, or Spain, or the Aegean Islands. Her very success has divorced her from her fans. He then admits that the LP hasn't been off his turntable in five days: "each song seems to have been born whole and perfect and complete with shining guitar and velvety piano." He goes alliteration-mad about her singing, "scaring and swooping in the space of a single syllable." For *Sounds*, Billy Walker considers Joni to be approaching perfection, like "a champion prize-fighter, a great race horse or a Dutch master."

A brilliant observation, as the album draws from just that school of painting, domestic settings exactly captured. It has the stillness and mystery of a Vermeer. The more one looks, the odder *Blue* becomes, seen from a perspective somehow lost to the viewer. Mitchell, too, has the ability to freeze time, so that these portraits of herself, the various men in her life, and her abandoned child, become immortal. In some ways, *Blue* corresponds to Dylan's most mysterious album, *Blood on the Tracks*, also written at a time of domestic upheaval, also endlessly playable because the whole thing is a maze, a game of hide and seek, a puzzle without a solution.

'All I Want' is a song about looking for love, and finding a cocktail of pain, excitement, need, desire and mutual hurt. The language fractures or peters out into nonsense: humming, no less. The music is edgy, with dulcimer, guitar and percussion, while Joni's voice swoops and dives like a drunken seagull. Journalists have always supposed *Blue* to be Joni's nickname for Graham Nash, but the record would actually make

Joni backstage with her band at the Palladium
October 1970.

Joni seated at her piano, onstage at the
August 1970 Isle of Wight Festival.

Joni in concert with the LA Express, London April 1974.

Joni onstage with Tom Scott at Wembley Stadium, London, September 1974, supporting Crosby, Stills & Nash.

Joni in New York 1979 with (l to r) Klaus
Voorman, John Mayall and Commander Cody.

Joni from her 'blue' period.

Joni onstage with Larry Klein, late eighties.

The entrance to Joni's home in Los Angeles. Callers strictly by appointment.

An early nineties shot of Joni with Bruce Springsteen and Sting.

Joni at the New Orleans Jazz & Heritage Festival, 1995.

Joni at her home studio in Bel Air, 1989.

Joni with Peter Gabriel at the NY Coliseum, holding her Billboard Award, 1995.

Joni outside the LA Hard Rock Cafe, 1996, attending the Gibson Guitar Awards.

Joni with her two awards at the 38th Grammy Ceremony in Los Angeles 1996.

Joni with Coolio at the Grammy Awards ceremony, 1996.

more sense if it referred to James Taylor. The word is quietly dropped in at the climax of the song, but the effect is ironic, and the song vibrates with the excitement of a new (possibly illicit) love affair. The lyrics have the same love-hate ambivalence as 'Carey', with its "mean old daddy." Whichever man is meant, the effect of meeting him was devastating. The song is Joni's sexiest yet, the ecstatic repetition of "travelling," the way her voice almost breaks on "want," or lingers on "feel," the way it almost purrs on "sweet romance." Anyone newly in love will identify with the wish to share a bath – to "shampoo you" – as well as a bed. Odd, but touchingly true.

'My Old Man' – directed to Graham Nash – is about a different kind of love, less desperate, more comfortable: even the emblems of loss are domestic. Who else could make a frying pan romantic? Stately piano, and a lovely, meandering melody like a hymn: the musician-lover himself becomes the "warmest chord." There is surely a pun in how this kind of love, marriage in every sense apart from the lack of that piece of paper, keeps away "my blues." 'Little Green', copyrighted in 1967, is almost impenetrable, although obviously about Joni's lost daughter. The unnamed man who "went to California" is perhaps the child's father. The papers are real enough here, with which Joni signs away her child, as is her reaction, "you're sad and you're sorry, but you're not ashamed." The little girl grows up back in Canada, under the Northern lights. Both the guitar accompaniment and Joni's un-ironic, intimate vocal seem a throwback to earlier LPs. But then 'Willy' was also Joni's child, in the song of that name.

'Carey' is James Taylor, both smart and sinister with his "cane," a "mean old Daddy" with whatever Freudian connotations that suggests. Drums drive along this return to nature, dirty fingernails and all, and back to rock 'n' roll and a hot wind straight from Africa. Sexual, or what? And yet, for all this abandon, there is the nagging impression that she wants to be safe at home.

'Blue' is a song about being lost, out at sea, in thick fog. It is a love letter from Crete, sent in a seashell (back to the first album!) so that the song imitates that breathless hush you hear when you place a shell to your ear. If 'Blue' is Taylor, not Nash – and it certainly fits in better with his career profile – this is a song of leave-taking ("let me sail away"), though Joni offers to follow him as he sinks down into hell. When

Hollywood makes a movie about Kurt Cobain, as it must, this would be an ideal song for Courtney Love to sing after the funeral, naked on the beach. Here is an odd mixture of the symbolic and the gross – tattoos, needles, guns, ass. In an abstract song, the way in which the pen with which Joni writes transforms into a syringe – "a pin/underneath the skin" – is truly shocking. The song is a lullaby, as stated, but one to a damaged adult, and one full of pain. As she sings "sail away," Joni's voice does just that. Never can the word "laughs" have been sung with such sadness and disdain. "Blue", "love", "you", "me", are all stretched out almost endlessly, like an aria but one sung by someone herself strung out on love's drug. Even the final piano chord seems oddly unresolved.

'California' sees Mitchell running back home to the safety of home and Graham Nash. Such highly public references – Nash, after all, plays in a rock 'n' roll band, while Taylor joined Joni in Crete – invite few other interpretations. The fact that Taylor himself plays guitar on this song, in which he seems to feature as a ditched lover, makes the whole thing even more bizarrely personal. Of course, the redneck might not be Taylor at all – someone from his wealthy background would hardly need to steal a camera – and yet it was for Taylor that Joni undoubtedly finally left Nash. And the song does have a deeper, or at least parallel, meaning, with news of the deepening conflict in Vietnam destroying dreams of peace and love, the butterflies now turned back to bombers with a vengeance. Still, California is home, and even the police on Sunset Avenue generate homesickness, which is further evoked by Sneaky Pete's pedal steel.

'This Flight Tonight' is a more mysterious song than it first appears. Reading the LP as a story – and that is how it is presented, with cunning repetitions and contrasts – she has again left Nash, and heads for Las Vegas, den of all iniquity, still missing him. There seems to have been a row – "I can't talk to you baby." The stars featured in the song take us back to her lost daughter, and the vocal is startlingly intimate, at times reducing to speech, or a near whisper, or parodied as a harmony band in her own headphones.

From that, the LP moves into the plangent piano introduction to 'River', the saddest Christmas song ever written, a song of escape from someone who has already escaped, in songs on this album, from

Canada, from Crete, from Paris, from Spain, from California. "The best baby I ever had" is presumably Nash, and it seems to have been her who forced the relationship to its end. The way Joni's quiet voice seems to linger endlessly on "fly" and "away" is heart-breaking, as is the end of the song, when the piano almost plays 'Jingle Bells', but the result is a kind of melancholy, wasted echo of that jolliest of songs.

'A Case of You' returns to that lonely northern star, shining through the night. It could be both Nash and (more secretly) her lost daughter being bid goodbye to; the lyrics imply that love is never lost, but can be recreated in the memory, as if new born. Taylor plays second guitar here, which, with the re-evocation of the devil in the second verse, suggests that he too could be the subject of the song. My own uninformed guess is that 'A Case of You' is about Leonard Cohen – though the couple had parted some years before. If so, this would explain its religious imagery, the map of Canada, the lines about northern stars, and particularly the phrase "love is touching souls," which sounds like neither Nash nor Taylor, but straight out of the mouth of 'Laughing Len.' It's a deeply heretic song, in which the changing of Jesus's blood into holy wine transmutes into sexual love. Mind you, what exactly is the point of a wine you can drink twelve bottles of, and still remain standing?

'The Last Time I Saw Richard' harks back to Chuck Mitchell, who does not appear here as a backing musician. She saves a particular and highly specific spleen for that poor man. He gets his own verbal punch in first, but she floors him in the second verse. The song starts out sad, as if his prediction of "pretty lies" has come true, but it ends with a final image of escape (hers, not his). The grub has become a butterfly, and flies away. The way Joni lingers on "gorgeous" is indeed gorgeous.

Timothy White observes that a "Rolodex of songwriters" has borrowed from these tunes. For Mitchell herself, the album took a stunning toll. "We all suffer for our loneliness, but at the time of *Blue* our pop stars never admitted these things." For White, the album has stretched the tape measure for unfathomed personal inquiry "until it snapped free of the spool." Her singing has become correspondingly wilder, flying to heaven, swooping in trills and ululations like a Canadian variation on qawwali (the Sufi music of devotion, as exemplified by Nusrat Fateh Ali Khan). Just as ambitious were Joni's

131

elaborate guitar and dulcimer tunings: "There are certain simple fingerings that were difficult in standard tunings. My left hand is not very facile; my right hand is extremely articulate. At the time that I began to write my own music, Eric Andersen showed me open G and D modal, dropping the bass string. I had always heard beautiful melodies and music in my head, so I just tuned the guitar to those chords, or slipped into a tuning so that the shapes made by the left hand were simplified."

It was anything but simple music. David Sinclair has since described the album as "a ravaging emotional critique of the post-Aquarian age" while Steve Clarke recognised that a generation once told that it could have anything it pleased, now "responded to her mood of disillusionment." For Dave Marsh, her lyrical outlook "becomes more entwined with her own emotions." Barney Hoskyns finds a bridge between the "girlish ingenuousness of her early albums and the artful sagacity" of later work. Here is the essence of nostalgia. Joni's voice can take grains of loss and desire, and turn them into pearls. The most memorable quote comes from Jacques Vassal, perhaps only half translated from the original French: "It shows her kicking back against the corruption of the rich superstar world that she has penetrated, the corrupted values and the smell of too much wine and the fishnet stockings." Follow that! Conversely, Neville Wiggins recently described Joni as one of the few singer-songwriters of the era whose work has not dated horrendously. "Whilst I defy anyone at all sensible to listen to, say, Melanie's scratch 'n' sniff album (let alone smell it) without feeling queasy, Joni causes no such embarrassment!"

A simpler but truer gauge of her importance to the lives of real people, rather than to the ethereal world of rock critics, is the letter posted by R Barry to the *Melody Maker* just after the album's release. Like *Blue* itself, this is straight from the heart, unsolicited apart from the need of its saying. "Each time I play my Joni Mitchell LPs, I find the truth and the love in which her songs are immersed give me the answer to the problems of how life should be lived. Why don't people see the maturity in her words of love, and try to bring a bit of tolerance and kindness into the world?"

That letter describes exactly what makes Mitchell's work so special: her full-tilt search for meaning, using details so commonplace that out of context they would seem ridiculous. Unlike her earlier albums – and those of contemporaries like James Taylor or Cat Stevens – she strips away all covering imagery to portray herself emotionally naked. As she later told Cameron Crowe: "*Blue* really was a turning point in a lot of ways. I perceived a lot of hate in my heart. I perceived my inability to love at that point." Primal therapy, indeed. In 1987, *Rolling Stone* voted *Blue* forty-sixth in their list of the 100 best albums of the past twenty years. "She's restless and insecure, but also earthy and real." It also describes the album as the perfect incarnation of "the-album-as-autobiography," an assertion that Joni was later to vigorously deny.

The final word must go to Nick Kent, ever a man for a killing phrase. The album repeated the "tweeter wreckage and dippy emotions" of earlier LPs, but songs like 'All I Want' also spotlighted "femininity in full flight, giddily thrusting aside native intellect in the throes of a mad passion." With *Blue*, her songwriting reached "territory previously untouched in such determined detail by any other performer, either male and female, before or since. A commitment to dissecting one's own psyche with particular reference to the emotional fibres to barter with one's vulnerability, to reach right in and draw out the innermost perceptions and sculpt those perceptions with a tempered irony. That's where Joni Mitchell absolutely demands to be set apart." High praise indeed, from a man who has also written brilliantly on such psych(ot)ic surfers as Syd Barrett, Lou Reed, and Iggy Stooge.

Talking to Timothy White, Joni denies that she is a 'confessional' songwriter as such: "I feel that the melodies, if they're 'born' first, require words with the same melodic inflections that English has in its 'spoken' forms. People assume that everything I write is autobiographical. If I sing in the first person, they think it's all about me, but many of the characters I write about – even if their tone is entirely first person – have nothing to do with my own life in the intimate sense. It's more like dramatic recitation or theatrical soliloquy." In *Blue*, she did see herself as an "eyewitness reporter," but even there, art needs to tidy up life. "Then I find it won't rhyme, or it lacks a certain dramatic quality, and there's a necessity for exaggeration." This is not lying, it is artifice, "a creative truth. I have, on occasion, sacrificed myself and my own emotional makeup, singing 'I'm selfish and I'm sad,' for instance. These are not attractive things in the context of rock 'n' roll. It's the antithesis of rock 'n' roll – which is 'Honey I'm a lover and I'm bad.' You don't go saying these other things in pop circles, because you're liable to bring terrible results: unpopularity. Which is what you don't want."

Joni started this kind of 'confessional reporting' to sabotage the cult of worship that was beginning to engulf her. *Blue* was an attempt to say "Well, okay, I'm just like you. I'm a lonely person.

"Loneliness is the main thing we have in common with animals. Unfortunately we have this ability to perceive more strongly – unlike, say, the coyote who's born and sits in the bushes until one day his mother bites his nose to the bone and says 'I'm not feeding you anymore!' And then sends him cruelly out into the world, to be on his own." Where he will later inspire one of her finest songs.

To describe the kind of soul-stripping that produced *Blue*, Joni quotes Nietzsche's image of penitents of the spirit, writing in their own blood. Heavy stuff. This is not the Jack Nitzsche who played with the Rolling Stones! "In order to make that album we had to lock the doors in the studio. When the guy from the union came to the studio to take his dues, I couldn't look at him, I'd burst into tears. I was just so thin-skinned. Just all the nerve endings." Even being onstage is another form of loneliness, of non-communication: "Let me be on a pedestal that is not *separating* so much."

Like a reformed alcoholic endlessly revisiting the grounds of her addiction, Joni further purged herself to Bill Flanagan. The album obviously still represents some kind of catharsis to her, precise notes on a nervous breakdown, death and rebirth. "*Blue* was like, 'nothing left to lose, let's spit it out,' and when it was finished I went over to a friend's house and Kris Kristofferson was there. I played it. He said 'Joni, save something for yourself.' It was hard for him to look at it. There was an odd sense of respect, like it was a Diane Arbus photo book or something. I've heard some of the writing called that, and yet I find it hard to relate to those images. These are not strange people in the basement of apartment buildings. These are all of us." Flanagan prompts her onward, like a therapist urging on his patient. The album is just about unequalled. "I'll tell you what you have to go through to get an album like that. That album is probably the purest emotional record that I will ever make in my life. You wouldn't want to go around like that. To survive in the world you've got to have defences. And defences are in themselves a kind of pretension. And at that time in my life, mine just went. They went and you could call it all kind of technical things. Actually it was a great spiritual opportunity but nobody around me knew it was happening."

This is the language of nervous breakdown, of an almost schizophrenic withdrawal and re-ordering of outer reality: life with all the safety devices turned off. "All I knew was that everything became kind of transparent. I could see through myself so clearly. And I saw others so clearly that I couldn't be around people. I heard every bit of artifice in a voice. Maybe it was brought on by nervous exhaustion. Whatever brought it, it was a different, un-drug-induced consciousness. The things that people love now – attitude and artifice and posturing – there was no ability to do those things. I'll never be that way again and I'll never make an album like that again."

James Taylor remembers how such music was created. "It was a wonderful year, performing and recording together. I was pretty unconscious around then, but she was writing the *Blue* album in a single-storey, rough-cut wooden house up on rock piers in Laurel Canyon." The relationship crumbled, and the release of *Blue* coincided with a major change in Joni's life. The Laurel Canyon days were over forever. "It was just an address," Joni bitterly observed. She sold up, and moved into a house facing the ocean, back in her native Canada. It was the same kind of process that had taken Dylan off the road for three years, and into the rural retreat of Woodstock.

Joni, too, needed to regroup her forces. Here, deep in the forests of northern British Columbia, she worked on the songs that were to bloom into *For the Roses*, living simply and largely alone, and continuing her embargo on interviews and live appearances. It was not until 1972 that she returned to the stage, touring with Jackson Browne, and finally unburdened the story of these 'lost years' to Penny Valentine, a sympathetic listener, guaranteed not to ask too many prying questions. Emotionally spent, Joni left Warner Brothers, irked by their promotional policies. Here she was, re-defining the language of rock music, to be greeted by adverts like 'Joni Mitchell is 90% virgin' or 'Joni Mitchell takes forever', whose crassness defies description. *For the Roses* would appear on the new Asylum label, set up by David Geffen, one of her own management team.

This, too, was a signpost to the future. Geffen had been Laura Nyro's manager in New York when Elliot Roberts summoned him west. "Everything was happening so fast in Los Angeles, and the only person I thought could help me was David. He was making a lot of side deals for everyone. See, you could hire David to make deals without having the involvement of David." In *Waiting for the Sun* – the definitive guide to LA rock – Barney Hoskyns traces the growth of Asylum, so named because it offered a refuge to the Laurel Canyon elite. It also boasted a corporate philosophy of 'benevolent protectionism.' Jackson Browne, for one, was deeply grateful. "David may have wanted to have a successful business, but also wanted to be part of a community of friends. He became your champion and years later – after a lot of therapy – he finally got over his need to care-take people, to the detriment of his own life." The repayment for this loyalty was the support – which he reciprocated – of the likes of Crosby, Mitchell, and Young. They "drew great people to them like a magnet," and the new label was to promote Jackson Browne, Linda Rondstadt, and four obscure country-rock sidemen who banded together as The Eagles. It was the exclusiveness of this new order that fuelled attacks on Mitchell and her colleagues from the likes of *Rolling Stone*. Geffen treated his artists like royalty.

He persuaded Atlantic to finance his new label, after its veteran boss Ahmet Ertegun declared that his new colleague might have no ear for music, but sure "has a nose for it." Jerry Wexler had put it more crudely, describing Geffen as a man who would "dive into a pool of pus to come up with a nickel between his teeth." Ron Stone, Elliot Roberts' assistant, assigned Geffen's success, more simply, to sheer hard work. Business was his "entire life." Few people at the time could have predicted how formidable a power base Asylum would become, building a multi-million-dollar industry out of bar bands playing at LA's Troubadour. Geffen sold Asylum to Warner Brothers in 1973 for $7 million, merging with Elektra to create, in the words of Art Fein "a latterday folk-rock axis that took hold of America." He went on to form

136

his own Geffen Records label, on which four of Joni's later albums were to appear, and sued another of his long-term acts, Neil Young, for producing deliberately uncommercial records.

Ron Stone makes a telling comment when he says that while he and Elliot Roberts were in the music business, Geffen was in the "finance business." The story of our times.

Joni Mitchell's desire to escape the fishbowl of publicity – difficult enough, in view of the confessional nature of her songwriting, and her own highly public lifestyle – was blown wide apart by *Rolling Stone* magazine in 1972. The article, dubbed 'Old Lady of the Year', (contemporary slang for a girlfriend, not a senior citizen) named names, some of whom Joni barely knew. As she told Barney Hoskyns, "it was a low blow, and it was unfair. I was not abnormally promiscuous, especially within the context of the free love experiment, so to be turned on by my peer group and made an example made me aware that the Whore/Madonna thing had not been abolished by that experiment. People who were legitimately on that list, like Graham Nash, were gonna call and complain, but then they figured it would fan the flame." Indeed, there were people listed who had got no closer to Joni than interviewing her on LA radio. "Assumptions were made in interpreting the lyrics that this was about so-and-so. All that nonsense that destroys the ability of the listener to identify with a song. Plus, they were misinterpretations. So that was painful and unnecessary, and *Rolling Stone* had a policy for years after that to get me."

Rolling Stone was beginning its long swing rightwards, from creating prophets to making profits, and was pushing investigative journalism into cracks and crevices where it really had no right to go. In another 1972 article, 'Hollywood's Hot 100', the magazine quoted a Hollywood publicist: "It's all so very incestuous: musically, socially, romantically. Graham used to be Joni Mitchell's ole man, after David Crosby, and before James Taylor." So what? The article itself is in the form of one of Pete Frame's family trees, but looser, with lines snaking everywhere. Joni is represented by a pair of lips, and is connected to David Crosby (broken heart), Graham Nash (broken heart), and David Geffen (kiss kiss). She is also connected with Russ Kunkel and Stephen Stills (musical alliances). Cameron Crowe asked for a reaction, and got one.

"I never saw it. The people that were involved in it called up to console me. My victims called first (laughs). It was ludicrous. I mean, even when they were drawing all these brokenhearted lines out of my life and my ability to love well, I wasn't so unique. There was a lot of affection in those relationships. The fact that I couldn't stay in them, for one reason or another, was painful to me. The men involved are good people. I'm fond of them to this day. We have a mutual affection, even though we've gone on to new relationships. Certainly there are pockets of hurt that come. You come a little battered out of a relationship that doesn't go on forever. I don't live in bitterness."

It is fascinating to listen to the sharp insights on her LPs: it would not be so comfortable to have to deal with such acute perceptions on a daily basis. "By confronting these things and linking them through, there's a certain richness that comes in time. Even psychiatrists, mind whores for the most part, don't have a healthy attitude towards depression. They get bored with it." Nevertheless, gently prompted by Crowe, she looks back on her relationship with Graham Nash as tender and enduring. "We lived together for some time – we were married, you might say." It was a time that released her both as a woman and as an artist – the bulk of her best drawings were done in that period from 1969 to 1970. Doubtless as a defence mechanism, "to contend with this hyperactive woman," Nash developed his own skills as a photographer. "Even though the romance ended, the creative aspect of our relationship has continued to branch out."

This is the key to Joni's relationships – a search for creative as well as sexual conjoining. In Leonore Fleischer's book, affairs are hinted at – never confirmed – with Steve Stills, Leonard Cohen, Neil Young, and Warren Beatty, who is rumoured to be the inspiration for Mitchell's 'Coyote', as he was for Carly Simon's 'You're So Vain.' The latter song could also be about James Taylor, whom Simon later married. As Joni acidly commented, when she herself met Taylor, he was almost a complete unknown. "Maybe I helped his career." One thinks immediately of Joan Baez featuring a young Dylan on record and at her live shows, and of the way he publicly dumps her in the film *Don't Look Back*. One thinks also of how Baez has continued to snipe back, in song and in her autobiography, in a way which Mitchell has confined to her wretched first husband.

Rather than trying to compile my own list, I feel it's more germane to note how all of Joni's acknowledged lovers have been musicians, and creative forces in their own right. As she herself said, "we have all interacted, and we have all been the source of many songs for one another." Barney Hoskyns dared to comment that she clearly stayed friends with all these guys. "Wherever possible. See, my mother says things to me like 'Ducks mate for life,' but I guess I'm a serial monogamist."

In the Spring of 1972, Joni embarked on a European tour: her two-year retreat from live performance was over. She played the Manchester Odeon on May 3rd, and London's Festival Hall three days later (a nationwide tour, by her standards). On her return from dates in Frankfurt, Amsterdam, and Paris, she also taped a *Sounds for Saturday* TV show, broadcast in June and notable for her "natural relaxed mood." Jackson Browne opened proceedings each night. His previous visit to Britain had been when supporting Laura Nyro, and he had come to fame accompanying Nico, so for someone of such tender years, he already knew how to placate women of extreme musical temperament. Just to keep things in the family, his first album featured David Crosby and Graham Nash.

The Festival Hall gig started badly, then got worse. Half an hour after its scheduled start, the audience were still barricaded outside the hall, and when finally let in, were greeted with the sight of minions still fiddling with their equipment. Michael Watts of *Melody Maker* had a ringside seat. "There was Jackson Browne, Joni Mitchell and this third, malignant presence on stage, which manifested itself by a series of whistles, screeches and hoots in the PA system, whose volume level was skittish to the point of perversity." As soon as Browne got stuck into a song, the sound died, and he was left mouthing into the mike like a character from a silent movie. In a forty-minute set, he only managed to complete three songs. Still, his time would come.

Joni Mitchell wrested triumph from disaster. Using the house PA, which muffled her bell-like higher notes, she still soared like a bird and stung like a bee. Watts was in awe, seeing her as a kind of "high priestess, virginal and vulnerable, not to be vilified." Alliteration worthy of Joni herself, and surely an unconscious echo – careful of this pop music: it can enter your soul, your mind, your heart... Watts now had the cheek to complain that her one fault was that "the mood of her performances tends to be excessively devotional. When she sits down at the piano, one knows the song is going to be melancholic, and when she takes up the guitar, only slightly less downbeat. She becomes not just a performer but some kind of icon." Worship is in the eye of the beholder.

Penny Valentine uses her more practised eye to note Joni's beige silk trousers, her long blonde hair hanging round her shoulders, with all the appearance of "a creamy snow princess", but also how this fragile look belied "the true tougher performer underneath." This was the same goddess who had been watching Browne from the wings, nervously puffing at a cigarette. Now she was transformed into a Hans Christian Andersen fairy queen, her vocals "pitched to hang like icicles on the night air." The set itself was an interesting blend of new material with the old and known – 'Big Yellow Taxi', 'Clouds', 'For Free' – which she now described as being about a New York street musician – 'Blue', 'Woodstock', 'My Old Man', but no 'Willie'. She interspersed songs with stories of her voyage to Greece with her friend Penelope (appropriately enough). New material included 'You Turn Me On (I'm A Radio)', 'For the Roses', and 'Song for Ludwig', which Valentine described as "the most beautiful song she's ever written, which caught the audience mid-breath." Watts loved its "lovely rolling piano lines." She came back for an encore of 'The Circle Game', with Browne joining in, as Nash and Taylor had done elsewhere, and with the sell-out audience on its feet.

On the home straight of the same tour, Bob Sarlin caught her at Carnegie Hall. From the start, it was clear who was in command, as Joni came out unaccompanied, a "thin, lanky figure in velvet." With little preamble, she launched into 'Blue', something old and something new. It was a virtuoso performance. "Here she was faced with an audience that was surprisingly rowdy – oddly similar to the audiences that usually show up for concerts of much 'heavier' music, the Ripple-and-reds-crowds. But she quieted them with grace and charm. It is her secret weapon, this grace with which she surrounds some of the most concrete and strong-minded lyrics around. She catches her audience by surprise: once captured, it is enraptured." Poetry again: it is as if Joni's verbal dexterity rubs off even onto her professional listeners.

140

Penny Valentine sat listening in Joni's hotel suite overlooking St James' Park. Back in London to record her TV special, and disguised in a beret, she had prowled midnight Piccadilly alone, sketching people in bars. The next morning, she sat dressed simply in jeans and a plain sweater. "There is a tidy casualness about her, a cleanliness and un-rumpled freshness." But this is a complex innocence: Valentine smiles at the bright-red painted toenails Joni wiggles, having kicked off her clogs. She also finds the star surprisingly warm and open, especially for someone Richie Havens once described as "the lady that walks on eggs." In which case, this interview makes a fine omelette.

Have not all her songs been directly autobiographical? "Well, some of them are directly personal, and others seem to be because they're conglomerate feelings. Like that song for Beethoven is written from the point of view of his Muse talking to him." For the muse, read music. Robert Graves wrote *The White Goddess* about his own search for a feminine divinity (given flesh in the figure of Laura Riding): a book which has served since as holy text for poets as diverse as Ted Hughes and Bob Dylan. A muse can both inspire and tear to shreds – look at Richard Thompson's song 'The Calvary Cross', the terrifying portrait of a man in thrall to his own inspiration. Feminist criticism has agonised over what form the Muse can take for a woman artist, and this is directly pertinent to songs by Joni like 'Willy' or 'Blue'. The men here are somehow more than just flesh and blood.

Valentine centres on the song 'Cactus Tree', which seems directly autobiographical in its wish for personal freedom, however painful that may be. "I feel that's a song of modern woman. Yes, it has to do with my experiences, but I know a lot of girls like that, who find that the world is full of lovely men, but they're driven by something else other than settling down to frau-duties." A strange choice of word, suggesting the Third Reich's positioning of woman as the inviolable keeper of hearth and home, while the men went off to conquer Europe, commit genocide, and engage in other masculine pursuits. Joni desires a domestic stability she has never herself known. "Drifting through lives and cities, you never really get to understand a person or place very deeply. You can stay with a person until you may feel very bored. You feel you've explored it all. Then all of a sudden, if you're there long enough, it'll just open up and flash you all over again. But so many people who are searching and travelling come to that point where it's stealing out on them, and they just can't handle that and have to move on."

Valentine ties this back to Joni's own restlessness over the past two years. An innate disappointment haunted the spoken introductions to songs at the Festival Hall gig. Was Joni's decision to return to Canada and settle there a reaction to all this restlessness? "Not really – moving back is like burning your bridges behind you. For one thing, I don't want to lose my alien registration card, because that enables me to work in the States. So I have a house in California – not the one in Laurel Canyon I used to have – for an address. The house in Canada is just a solitary station. It is by the sea and it has enough physical beauty and change of mood so that I can spend two or three weeks there alone."

Over dinner the previous night, Joni had spoken about her dream of this new life, of leading "a kind of Heidi-like existence, with goats and an orchard." Reality had not proved so simple. "The land has a rich melancholy about it. Not in summer, because it's usually very clear, but in the spring and winter it's very brooding, and it's conducive to a certain kind of thinking. But I can't spend a lot of time up there. Socially I have old schoolfriends around Vancouver, Victoria and some of the islands but I need the stimulation of the scene in Los Angeles. The house in Canada is home, but so is the Holiday Inn, in its weird way."

How had this change of scene affected her music? Joni had written lots of new songs, but until they were shared with other people, it didn't seem "a completed art." "I kept calling people in the bar of this lodge, saying "Listen, do you want to hear a song?" and they'd say "That's really nice – know any Gordon Lightfoot?" I really did want to play in front of people, which was a strange feeling, because I had a bad attitude about performing, you know. I felt like what I was writing was too personal to be applauded for. I even thought that maybe the thing to do was to present the songs some different way – like a play or a classical performance where you play everything and then run off stage and let them do whatever they want, applaud or walk out. I was too close to my own work. Now I've gained a distance on most of my songs."

The last rays of the evening sun were filtering across the trees in the park. Joni moved over to the piano, played a little (presumably as a breathing space after all these personal revelations) and picked at some butterscotch – an unintended reference to 'Chelsea Morning', perhaps. She gave a foretaste of her forthcoming album: "Well, I've started on it. I've been into the studio to cut a publishers' dub, when the songs were very new." The kind of thing bootleggers would now kill for.

One can see her in the process of moving into rock music, full speed ahead. "For 'Cold Blue Steel' I got in James Burton, who's really a great guitarist. Like that song is a real paranoid city song – stalking the streets looking for a dealer. I originally thought it needed a sliding steel but we tried that and it didn't work. Finally I ended up with James playing great wah wah – a furtive kind of sound. It's a nice track but in the meantime the bass line and drums didn't work solidly, so I have to re-cut that. I have a take of 'Lesson in Survival' which is really magical, the feeling is there and I don't think I'll do it again – so I have that cut and finished." The creative process, unleashed in a modern recording studio.

Joni shows a true seventies awareness of marketing, of repositioning herself onto the Top Forty playlist. "Then I tried to do 'You Turn Me On (I'm A Radio)'. I've never had a hit record in America, so I got together with some friends and we decided we were going to make this hit – conjure up this bit of magic for AM radio, destined to appeal to DJs. Graham and David came, and Neil lent me his band and he came and played some guitar, and somehow it just didn't work. There were too many chefs, you know. We had a terrific evening, a lot of fun, and the track is nice, but it's like when you do a movie with a cast of thousands. Somehow I prefer movies with unknowns. So I'm going to start looking for people who are untried, who have a different kind of enthusiasm that comes from wanting to support the artist." Perhaps this is – in retrospect – the key change in her musical life.

Joni was outgrowing even the finest rock musicians, and looking for something new. It is significant that she quotes a figure from jazz – rather than rock – to get her point across: "Miles Davis always has a band that are really great, but are cushions for him. It sounds very egotistical, but I really want to go in all directions right now, like a mad thing, right! I'd think 'this is really rock and roll, this song, isn't it?' and I see it with french horns and everything, and I really have to hold myself back or I'll just have a monstrosity on my hands." She assures Valentine (and maybe herself) that she has musical talents as yet untapped. "I could sing much stronger than I do you know, especially on the low register. I've got a voice I haven't used yet and haven't developed, which is very deep and strong and could carry over a loud band. And I'm very tempted to go in that direction experimentally."

As indeed she would, but not fully until *The Hissing of Summer Lawns*. Remember, this was someone who had just released one of the most perfect and profound albums in the history of rock – but she's only concerned with future change. Joni is also aware of not pushing the envelope too hurriedly. "Rushing ahead of ideas is bad. An idea must grow at its own pace. If you push it and it's not ready, it'll just fall apart."

Joni told Cameron Crowe more about her retreat – in both senses – deep into the Canadian wilderness, a wooded estate outside Vancouver. "My idea was to get back to nature. I built a house that I thought would function with or without electricity. I was going to grow gardens and everything. But I found that I was too spoiled already. I had too much choice. I could take the more difficult, old-fashioned way for a short period of time, but the idea of doing it forever would not work." On the gatefold cover, Joni – a symphony of green suede and velvet – sits on the edge of a river on her new Canadian estate. The back cover extends the shot into the wild wood, no other human in sight. The shock comes inside, where a semi-abstract painting of roses folds over to reveal Joni butt-naked, standing on a rock and looking out to sea. She would often walk unclothed from her new house to her own private beach. How she got to the rock is unexplained! A wave slaps at her feet.

"I remember my mother putting on glasses to scrutinise it more closely. Then my father said, 'Myrtle, people do things like this these days.' That was a great attitude. It was the most innocent of nudes, like a Botticelli pose. It was meant to express the lines about looking at the ocean, in 'Lesson in Survival'. Joel Bernstein is the only photographer I would feel comfortable enough to take off my clothes for. We were going to call the album *Judgement of the Moon and Stars*. We were originally going to set that photograph in a circle and replace the daylight sky with starry night so it would be like a Magritte. At that time no-one was paying homage to Magritte. Then Elliot said 'Joni, how would you like to see $5.98 plastered across your ass?' [laughs]. So it became the inside." Crowe adds, gallantly, "not that it was sensational. Like everything Joni does, it was very tasteful."

Talking more recently to Timothy White, Joni elaborates further. "I was building a house in the northern British Columbia forestry with the rustle of the arbutus trees at night finding its way into the music. There was moonlight coming down on black water; it was a very solitary period. It was melancholy exile, there was a sense of failure to it." The figure on the album cover is serene, faintly smiling, yet with a wariness in her eyes. Her body language is slightly tense, carefully posed. With her long hair and green clothes, Joni is almost a creature of the woodland that surrounds her, or like some native spirit of the trees, given human shape. Apart from the invisible photographer, she is totally alone.

Like cuckoos announcing Spring, the English rock press printed two items heralding *For the Roses*. Asylum label boss David Geffen flew into London preparing his first product launch, and talked to Roy Carr of the *NME*. He does not come across as a charming chap: "It's not my job to be popular, except to those people I work for. We are supposed to be tough, and we are. Music makes stars. Managers are like baby doctors in that they help the artist to deliver." How unlike the previous – and next – generation of men in suits, socially and musically distanced from their charges, like butchers from the beasts they market. "It's as hard to 'break' Jackson Browne as it was to do with Joni Mitchell five years ago. We've got to like our artists, because a manager-artist relationship should be a very personal thing, and if we don't get on together at this level then there's going to be no fun in doing it."

It was at about this time that it was rumoured that Joni was living with Geffen – who later came out as one of America's most high-profile gay men, and whose wealth has mushroomed over the years. Asylum eventually bought out Elektra, the finest American label of the late sixties, and one of the worst of the early seventies! Asylum's logo is oddly like a Magritte pastiche, consisting of what looks like a prairie door, rough-hewn out of wood, crossed with Dr Who's TARDIS, and set against a blue sky. Maybe Mitchell had some creative input here too.

From record label boss to fan, an almost unimaginable leap. MJ Higgins wrote to *Melody Maker*'s 'Mail Bag' in June 1972, asking why the wait for the new LP was so long. "I bought *Blue* last summer, nearly a year ago. How can they torture us like this? What do Asylum want? Blood? A pound of flesh?" This kind of deep affection and need for an artist's work underlines Mitchell's comments to Cameron Crowe, about her part of this compact between musician and audience. "I have reclusive fits, though, all the time. Not that it isn't rewarding, you know. It is. I mean, I do it for myself first, but I don't want to do it for myself only. I feel that I can still share my work with people, and they appreciate it. I guess it is my calling." While there are only a handful of multi-millionaires like Geffen, there were – and still are – hundreds of thousands of MJ Higginses out there. Hell, I'm one myself.

Looking back with Timothy White, Joni now accepts that she doesn't handle adrenalin very well – a harbinger of later illness, adrenal problems, and hypoglycaemia, On a lighter note, the title of *For the Roses* was far more facetious than it now reads, as a rather po-faced, post-hippie curlicue. Without beating about the bush, what we are talking about here is, literally, horse-shit. A press advert – and billboard – of the time gives the game away (subtly). A grinning toy horse head surmounts a glass bubble in which pretty ladies of the canyon reside. In Joni's surrealistic drawing, they are surrounded by an eye, lips, a chauffeur-driven limousine, a whale, and a tree whose blossoms could just be faces. In fact the whole thing, from a certain perspective – and under the right combination of drugs, presumably – turns into Joni's own face. "I wanted to use a drawing of a horse's ass for the album cover. I did use it for a billboard ad. It was my joke on the Sunset Strip, the huge drawing of a horse with cars and glamour girls, and it had a balloon coming out of the horse's mouth which said 'For the Roses'. But nobody got the message."

For the Roses was the first of her records to feature a full rhythm section – the session team of Wilton Felder on bass, and drummer Russ Kunkel. The CSN contingent this time around was Steve Stills, imitating a whole rock 'n' roll band on 'Blonde in the Bleachers', and

Graham Nash on harmonica, an instrument he learnt during the long-gone days when the Hollies had been an r&b band. Legendary guitarist James Burton took time off from his duties with Elvis Presley and Emmylou Harris to play on 'Cold Blue Steel'. His solos on Ricky Nelson b-sides had inspired a generation of English guitarists, Richard Thompson prominent among them. (The mind boggles at what would have been achieved if Mitchell, like Linda Rondstadt and Bonnie Raitt, had jammed with early members of Fairport at the LA Troubadour.) Bobbye Hall provided percussion, and Bobby Notkoff "strings." His violin had provided a spectral ghostliness to Neil Young's song 'Running Dry', with Crazy Horse. The most significant addition, however, was one Tommy Scott on woodwinds and reeds: his work ran through the album like a silk thread.

Henry Levy again provided "sound and guidance," while "direction" came from the Geffen Roberts Co: corporate rock, waiting in the wings. The LP was recorded in the tried and tested A&M studios in deepest Hollywood. The English version of the LP – distributed by monolith EMI – censors the lyric sheet. A four-letter expletive, as the broadsheets used to say, is present and correct on the recording of 'Woman of Heart and Mind', but replaced by four dots – appropriately – on the inside sleeve. The CD re-release replaces "fuck" full-square and proud. Richard Williams – now an award-winning sports journalist, then the guru of avant-garde rock in the *Melody Maker* – reviewed the album with the kind of informed enthusiasm he was master of.

What differentiates Joni from her competitors – the name James Taylor remains unspoken – is her lack of self-pity, her "total command of poetic device," her lack of blandness. The album deals with loss, caressing "precious yesterdays like the cover of an old well-thumbed, leather-bound book." Williams once wrote memorably about how underrated Cliff Richard is simply as a singer, an article which forever changed the views of anyone who read it, and this gift of informed praise is here turned on Joni's crowning talent. "Lastly I should mention her voice. There will always be that mildly uncomfortable break between the contralto and soprano registers, but sometimes she can enunciate a word or phrase in a way that comes straight from heaven. Just listen to the way she sings "Movie Queen" in 'Let the Wind Carry Me' – like most of this album, it's the perfect mating of a rigorous intelligence and an earthy sensuality. The product of these two qualities is a third: grace, which suffuses the album."

Another rock heavyweight, Charles Shaar Murray – an Oz schoolkid and the critic who first brought Patti Smith's *Horses* LP to public attention as a masterpiece – opens the batting for the *NME*. Joni retains "that quality of desperate freshness which is occasionally a trifle underwhelming for those accustomed to getting their kicks in less rarefied atmospheres." Like Mr Murray, presumably. He predicts, correctly, that future releases should tide her audience through the "rougher cosmic storms" of the seventies, then spoils it all – in those days before political correctness – with "she is also, as the inside photograph reveals, the possessor of a startlingly fine ass, the like of which I have rarely seen. Who could ask for anything more?"

For the Roses is, musically, a much smoother and more thematically unified album than her previous releases. Lyrically a more public, if less emotionally harrowing album than *Blue*, it extends the range of that record. The songs seem to merge into each other, like movements in a classical suite. The way in which Joni's voice blends with the backing musicians has left the last vestiges of folk behind: this is a luxuriant outgrowth of rock music, edging already towards jazz in its phrasings, like the finest work of Nick Drake.

The album opens with 'Banquet', about a picnic on the sea shore. This is no longer the idealised image of escape from the first album, but a polluted area. Even the seagulls no longer glide poetically, but instead come down to squawk their greed. The chorus is an early condemnation of the pursuit of self-interest which (ironically) grew out of the hippie movement, and fuelled the age of Reagan and Thatcher. Joni's voice cuts deepest during the list of American dreams – religion, hard drugs, ecology – with "some watch their kids grow up," which takes on an extra edge. A shopping list of desires.

'Woodstock' is certainly a long way away from 'Cold Blue Steel and Sweet Fire', a song about addiction more lyrically graphic than anything Lou Reed ever penned. But the smoothness of voice and backing almost disguises – and perhaps under-plays – words that he could barely croak: blood and brown scum, the bashing-in of veins. Indeed, there is even the suggestion that Joni herself is the siren here, lulling James Taylor (one presumes, in both senses) down to an early, romantic rock-star death. Ladies of the Canyon have become the 'Lady Release' of smack.

If the message in the opening track was found in a fortune cookie, the next song finds holy vision in a cheap diner. Shangri-La becomes 'Barangrill'. With her rented Rolls Royce waiting outside, Joni envies a waitress her simplicity, then realises that both of them are as helplessly trapped as one another (this all to a jaunty tune). The revelation comes with the petrol pump attendant, who improvises his own song. Deeply ridiculous, if you listen too close.

'Lesson in Survival' is a return to what Joni does best, a song of hopeless romance, and an impossible man. Her voice breaks free for the first time on the album on "I need more quiet times." Back to the ocean once more, but heavily symbolic this time. One wonders idly whether the friend to whom she goes to unburden all this is the long-suffering Graham Nash: the impossible man is undoubtedly Taylor, and the relationship – for all the talk of magnets and souls at the end – deeply unstable, as it forces her spirit into timidity. We've all been there, and the confusion and pain of this song is its crowning glory.

'Let the Wind Carry Me' takes us back to Joni's rebellious adolescence, as the dancing queen of Saskatoon. A chorus of Jonis is echoed by a chorus of brass, like a musical equivalent of a multi-layered ice-cream. Sickly, but sweet. The desire to settle down and have children, to start the whole process again, flashes before her eyes, but soon passes. Ironically, it is Joni's father who seems to bless this restlessness, and her mother – "always cleaning" – who acts as a brake, and needs to be escaped from. An oddly unresolved song.

'For the Roses' observes – from a distance – how James Taylor is, in turn, escaping her. She traces her own stardom, and its aftermath, the unexpected crucifixion, a chilly evening, and the moon an "empty spotlight." The implication is that the same will happen to him, as indeed it did. It's a very bare rendition – just Joni and her guitar – as if she is singing by and for herself. 'See You Sometime' is a more bitter take on the same theme, the faithless lover now "so jive" and hanging up the phone on her (how different to 'I Don't Know Where I Stand'), even implying that she's only interested in his fame. A very nice person, who, she implies with equal malice, is some kind of cross-dresser: a chorus of wronged Jonis cheerily snap out the injunction to "pack up your suspenders." Note how her voice dips as she sings "undermined": a neat touch. The whole song is a masterful example of Joni's use of a chorus line which changes subtly with the song: Joni would "still," "just" and "sure" like to see him again, despite everything.

'Electricity' is virtually impenetrable, but could be Taylor's reply, or a union man warning of her interfering with his job – or anything, really. It is a private story which doesn't translate. The whole thing is an over-obvious metaphor for Joni's broken heart. 'You Turn Me On (I'm A Radio) is the exact opposite, a simple metaphor of radio as sex: the "country" station has all kinds of connotations. The theme is the same as 'See You Sometime', but so much better expressed, and with a sensuous backing choir and Joni abandoning words at the end for feral yowls. In 'Blonde in the Bleachers', Joni is spurned by Taylor for a groupie, and decides to avoid the "rock 'n' roll" man in future – ironic, as her next two male partners form a rock rhythm section, bass and drums, and as the song ends with a coda that is almost avant-garde jazz. The "unknown child" here becomes the sole subject of 'Woman of Heart and Mind', whose lines, "no child to raise," take on a darker significance for Joni.

Jacoba Atlas regards this song as "an obvious reference to her relationship with Jackson Browne." Still a young man, Browne had been a resident of LA since the age of three, and musically (at least) accompanied Nico – another icy blonde – after she left the Velvet Underground. The first 'unknown' to sign to Asylum, he had briefly been part of the Nitty Gritty Dirt Band, and his song 'Take it Easy' became a major hit single for another Asylum/LA act, the Eagles. He also filled the support slot for Joni's concert appearances, like James Taylor before him. Browne was devastatingly pretty as a young man. The subject here, whoever it is, is like Graham Nash in the earlier song 'Willy', craving a mother, not a partner. The song lopes along, with Joni's weary vocals only perking up on an expletive. The prettiness of the song partially disguises its venom, a trick that Dylan also pulled off with 'Positively 4th Street'. Browne, who, like Mitchell, spent the eighties producing political albums which railed against Reaganism, came back to artistic majesty in the early nineties with I'm *Alive*, an LP to rank among his best work (Joni Mitchell's name does not appear in a long list of friends and musical acquaintances to whom he gives thanks). His most profound album, *The Pretender*, was recorded after the suicide of his wife Phyllis, and deals with regret, self-doubt and grieving, an album far from the sunny LA dream.

The final track on *For the Roses* is something else entirely. *Judgement of the Moon and Stars* is subtitled 'Ludwig's Tune', and it's fairly obvious that this denotes Beethoven, not some second-division German footballer. The singer identifies with the misunderstood genius – also tied to his keyboard – and the way his failure in love (and deafness) is counteracted by his genius. Joni's voice cracks with emotion on the passage about stockings. The song is interrupted – rather than complemented – by an arrangement which bursts out of the speakers like a bomb. Ludwig channels his sexuality into a search for the lost chord. Weird.

Timothy White later saw *For the Roses* as a possible farewell to the music business, "fleshed out under the rustle of arbutus trees in her remote British Columbia hideaway." Gloominess in the lyrics is countermanded by the joy of their delivery: "Mitchell's delightful vocal animation was a leavening factor, her trills, ululations and sandpapery skips along the scale revealing a personality increasingly willing to laugh at its wilfulness." Penny Valentine also picked out the power of her voice, as it "perches and falls like a butterfly on the wind." It was the song to Beethoven, however, that "takes me finally to bed." Quite how or why is not explained.

Nick Kent wrote of a new inner strength: "Mitchell was in no way going to swan back to embrace all that prim Laurel Canyon filigree." With his keen eye for rock 'n' roll sleaze, he hones in on 'The Blonde in the Bleachers' as the finest song yet to deal with groupies, "not to mention being probably the first to spotlight their plight without degenerating into callow obscenities in the 'whip-some-skull-on-me-bitch' tradition." Conversely, the main charge against the album was that of solipsism. *Record Collector* saw the world here as "the narrow one of the pop star, seen through an analytical, slightly jaded eye." Bill Flanagan perceived an obsession with stardom, which possessed and redeemed her, and yet still "tempted her through the airwaves all the way up in Canada." Ironically, then, the album helped establish Mitchell yet more widely as a star. 'You Turn Me On' was a hit single in the States, and 'Cold Blue Steel' received a fair amount of airplay in the UK, without breaking into the charts.

'You Turn Me On (I'm A Radio)' was put out as a single, as a taster for the album. Chris Welch reviewed it in *Melody Maker* on November 25th, 1972, two weeks before the album, and jokily commended it in his usual, inimitable style: "A nice song from Joni, full of charm and fragile humour. When 'ere Miss Mitchell takes to the microphone, my knees tend to sag and the jaw muscles give way. In a word, she turns me on. And I'm a tape recorder." It was a slow burner, but early the following year, made Number Twenty-Five in the US single charts, while in February, the album reached Number Eleven. In November 1973, Nazareth's version of 'This Flight Tonight', taken from *Blue*, reached Number Eleven in the UK, while Joni used it to begin her set for a second BBC radio concert. James Taylor again guested on second guitar. 'You Turn Me On (I'm A Radio)', 'Electricity', 'See You Sometime', and the title track of *For the Roses* – supposedly about her former lover – were all featured.

Taylor's involvement was particularly surprising, in the light of a January 1973 interview with *Rolling Stone*. Taylor's comments are a masterpiece in understatement. "I think I heard a track of it on the radio. I'd be interested to hear it, because I really love Joni's music." Interviewer Stuart Werbin perseveres, as if with a particularly clam-like politician. He casually mentions that there are references to a man in suspenders, and supposes that Taylor would have to hear it. No direct allegations, of course, or even the demand for Taylor to drop his trousers to see what lies underneath! The answer is blandness itself: "Joni's music is much more specifically autobiographical than a lot of other people. Her songs are sometimes really disarmingly specific." To which Werbin replies, with matching irony, that this is "her most disarmingly specific album" yet.

In December 1972, Joni played a sell-out residency at the LA Troubadour for four nights – Thursday through to Sunday. The intimacy of the venue gave her a chance to play new material, and take risks onstage. Steve Ferguson opened the show, a local black singer, songwriter, and pianist also associated with Asylum – he and Joni both contributed to Rod Taylor's debut LP. Ferguson even dedicated a piano instrumental to slide guitarist Ry Cooder, but fame never came knocking at that particular door.

Greeted with a huge bouquet of red roses, Joni played for almost two-and-a-half hours, solo. Most fascinating were her long intros to some of the newer material, a cross between stream-of-consciousness and a shaggy dog story. This, for example, prefaced 'Barangrill': "Sometimes it takes a personal crisis to turn you on the spiritual path. During your childhood and your teens you go through many crises. Everybody should go through it, it's a good experience. You go through a re-evaluation of yourself. Anybody with a smile on their face is enlightened. Everybody knows more than you. I walked into a restaurant a while back, and I saw three waitresses and thought they were the Trinity. I moved closer and I saw they were all wearing black diamond earrings. While going through some guru books, it said that some people look to Mecca, some to the Cross, and some to the City National Bank. But I decided they were all wrong. It was happening right here in the restaurant."

The story was continued over to 'Judgement of the Moon and Stars': "While looking for the guru, I found a book on the spiritual development of Beethoven. I wrote him a song, and was gonna call it 'Roll Over Beethoven Revisited', but I decided it to call it 'Ludwig's tune'. No disrespect intended." Tom Scott delivered a fine clarinet solo to 'For Free', while still sitting, incognito, among the audience. He joined her on stage for 'Let the Wind Carry Me' and 'Cold Blue Steel', both from the new record. Joni's tinkling piano rang and echoed through the club, like a mountain stream. Less apt was Mike Rosen's description for *Sounds*. Joni was dressed in a floor length dress, sunshine hair spilling past her shoulders and "snowy white teeth reflecting from the stage lights." Not so much Garbo as Dracula!

Unaware of such compliments, Joni went into another rap: "I always wanted to have a hit, I never had a hit you know, so I made one up. I decided there were some ways to make a hit, increase the chances. You put a long part at the beginning and over the end so the DJs can talk over it. Take a tender situation and translate it into commonly-appealing songs for the DJs. It'd have to be a little bit corny, so I wrote this song called 'Oh Honey you turn me on, I'm a radio'." Her rendition is followed by "unabandoned applause." Joni encores with 'The Circle Game', getting this coolest of audiences to sing along as if at a children's birthday party.

In August of that year, Joni appeared with Neil Young and the Eagles at the tiny Topanga Canyon Corral, on the outskirts of LA, playing twice nightly. Admission was a princely $4, and all proceeds went to an anti-condominium movement, opposing the building of high-rise flats in Topanga. Ecology in action. Joni was already moving on, musically. The *Spring Songs* bootleg, taped at Duke University in February, includes performances of 'Free Man in Paris', 'People's Parties', 'Same Situation' and 'Just Like This Train', from her forthcoming LP. As she told Cameron Crowe, *Court and Spark* contains a lot of songs written up in Canada. "The title song was written up on my land there. It deals with a story based on Vancouver and the Sunshine Coast."

The album was about as popular as she got, although Asylum seemed to spend more time promoting their new signing Bob Dylan – who soon skidaddled back to CBS. On March 16th, it topped the US album charts. Joni's first-all electric album, *Court and Spark* boasted an all-star cast drawn from CSN and the Crusaders, as well as members of Tom Scott's LA Express – whose drummer, John Guerin, was also soon to guest in Joni's personal life. Robbie Robertson, Jose Feliciano, and Wayne Perkins filled in on electric guitar, and comedy duo Cheech and Chong – dopes in any language – added a stoned rap to 'Twisted'. When Joni returned to LA, she had seemingly resolved her ambivalent feelings about wealth and fame. As Bill Flanagan observed: "She made a slick, jazzy album that made her a superstar." The musical catalyst was Tom Scott. Having been introduced to his version of 'Woodstock' by Henry Lewy, Joni checked out an early form of the LA Express – seasoned session men all – at an LA club. Scott's most difficult challenge was that Joni was neither interested nor schooled in the technical side of things, not even knowing the names for notes on the piano. "As gifted and talented and fantastic as she was, she has no technical knowledge whatsoever. She's a perfectionist, and that's something I can respond to immediately."

Michael Watts made much the same point in his review of the new album for *Melody Maker*. "Of all the female writers and singers postdating Joan Baez in pop music, Joni Mitchell seems to have arrived at the most complete definition of herself as an artist. True, she's not witty, like Dory Previn, as sophisticated as Bette Midler or La Streisand, not as stylistically far-ranging as Carole King, but few other rock musicians, male or female, have so refined personal expression that it succeeds as genuine art." She should be sitting at Dylan's right hand. "The cards are face up, the King and Queen, they say."

The album was previewed by the 'taster' of a single, 'Raised on Robbery', reviewed for *Sounds* by John Peel, the rock oracle of Britain. An early champion of her work, Peel felt she had since "fallen back on making money by making the noises that people expected of her." This, however, was something new, "with Andrews Sisters-like harmonies over a crisp backing stuffed with wah wah guitar." Sounds good enough to eat. Peel concludes with the injunction to "place an order for your copy now," and when has that man ever been wrong?

Previewing the American import of the LP for home listeners, Steve Clarke, in *NME*, praised the record's humour and depth of feeling: "Buy this record, it's pure enjoyment." *Disc* was equally snappy, reckoning the English release was "worth every penny of anyone's money," and certainly the £2.45 in new decimal coinage which it actually cost.

The real heavyweight response to *Court and Spark* came in *Rolling Stone*. Jon Landau's review was modestly titled 'An individual struggling with notions of freedom and paradox: Joni Mitchell, a delicate balance', which sounds more like a PhD thesis than a rock album review. As did the review itself: "The lyrics lead us through concentric circles that define an almost Zen-like dilemma. The freer the writer becomes, the more unhappy she finds herself; the more she surrenders her freedom, the less willing she is to accept the resulting compromise. Joni Mitchell seems destined to remain in a state of permanent dissatisfaction – always knowing what she would like to do, always more depressed when it is done." His conclusion, at least, makes sense: *Court and Spark* forces its listener both to laugh and to cry, and does so with "infinite grace."

Writing in the short-lived, but magisterial *Let It Rock*, Graham Taylor sees the album as completing a major change in Joni's work. She has shed early romanticism to reach the "serious intent and everyday language" of *Court and Spark*. And he is so right.

The album opens with a fullness of sound new for a Joni Mitchell record. If there is a narrative here, it is one private to the singer, but the songs do seem to flow together as a suite: even the gaps between tracks are virtually non-existent. A song-by-song analysis is less fruitful here: Mitchell was moving towards the flow and artistic unity of *The Hissing of Summer Lawns*, the album as movie rather than a collection of snapshots. 'Court and Spark' itself means 'to woo and to have', and the would-be lover described in the title track combines the musician in 'For Free' and the "child of god" from 'Woodstock', with a dash of Charles Manson (and perhaps Jackson Browne!). Love as religious sacrifice. The conflict in the song is between San Francisco – Peoples Park – and Los Angeles, sense and sensibility, maya and mammon. LA wins, at least for the moment.

'Help Me' hits a delicious folk-jazz groove, much like the best of Tim Buckley. Joni's vocals are suitably exuberant, hitting the same wonderful uncertainty at the start of a love affair as 'I Don't Know Where I Stand'. A new romance, to her, is like another wedding for Elizabeth Taylor: endlessly repeated. It's ironic, after 'Cactus Tree', that here she meets a man who equally likes and demands his own freedom. Notice the mention of stockings again in this song, a constant motif for Joni. The bouncy 'Free Man in Paris', which features Jose Feliciano on guitar, is a surprise present for Asylum boss David Geffen, Joni's travelling companion, in whose persona the song is sung. Freedom is, again, the subject. For a successful businessman – and Geffen is America's closest equivalent to Richard Branson – it is kept at bay by telephone calls and people endlessly wanting favours. Joni's vocal is exuberant, set to a bouncy r&b rhythm, with Steve Cropper licks on the guitar. There is a slight ambivalence, for Joni too – especially in cross-dressing mode – wants to be a "free man," and helps in her own way to stoke the "star-making machinery behind the popular song," by referring teasingly to rock star lovers.

Paris is Joni's own favourite place of escape. It is a staging post between Crete and Laurel Canyon in 'California' and a place of untroubled sensuality: "In France They Kiss On Main Street." She's back to California with a vengeance, though, in 'People's Parties', an LA party from hell. The ladies of the canyon have become seventies people, all passport smiles and photo beauties. 'Same Situation' is plangent, a study in decadence which is oddly reminiscent of Procol Harum, clunky piano and clever wordplay. Perhaps the golden youth is Jackson Browne, whose list of partners rivals Joni's, from Nico onwards.

Side two of the vinyl edition opens with 'Car on the Hill', and a full chorus of Joni Mitchells. The boy has grown away, and the spark is gone. It's a beautiful arrangement, smooth as cream – driving music, in both senses. 'Down to You' leads back into the soundscape of *Blue*, piano-led, melodically ravishing, and lovingly evoking the kind of man who blows hot and cold. There is an ominous quality here, like Bernard Herrmann's *Hitchcock* soundtracks, luxuriant decay. It also partakes of something of Lou Reed's spoilt masterpiece, *Berlin*, sharing the bleak chill of 'Sad Song'. As in 'People's Parties', friendship seems one of the first casualties in this brave new world. 'Just Like This Train' is rockier, about a love that she hopes will endure, watching her boyfriend's hair recede. If this is a leftover song to James Taylor, her wish has certainly come true! The guitar sounds like a train whistle, and the rhythm section like train wheels picking up speed. The arrangement rolls along, until it dies away at the end as the train moves out of view.

'Raised on Robbery' goes back to Joni's early love of fifties rock 'n' roll, and is very Canadian, in her vocals, and in the reference to her favourite ice-hockey team. This sounds like the Band on 'Rock of Ages', when they stretch out with Allan Toussaint's horns, here largely due to the presence of Robbie Robertson's wiry guitar. Joni is back scuffling again, trying to make the rent, and the whole thing is a siren song to sex and money. Her so-called 'virginal' image is shot to pieces here. In 'Trouble Child', Joni visits a friend in hospital, who has obviously overdosed on the good life: if this is the boy of the first song, he's certainly learnt some bad habits along the way. The band breaks just like those Malibu waves. Solo trumpet leads into 'Twisted', the first non-Joni Mitchell composition to feature on her LPs – snazzy and comic and bubbly, with a nasty aftertaste. The craziness bubbling under throughout the LP surfaces here: Joni puts on her jazz voice, skipping over the words like a high jumper, giggling, harmonising with herself – now there's a trick – and taking risks, improvising like a horn player.

Court and Spark is a strange combination, Mitchell's most commercial and musically accessible offering, the narrative of which, behind the lyrics, remains oblique. The title itself is a private code, the front-cover drawing impenetrable – a figure twisted like a Francis Bacon face rising in front of mountains, the whole thing framed by the singer's own handwriting, and in a still-sicklier tinge of yellow. It must be a unique album cover which boasts two signatures by the artist within. The inside cover shot has replaced the semi-religious trance of the *Blue* sleeve with a sexual grin, her eyes closed and lipsticked mouth half open in ecstasy. Joni's hair is swept back to reveal a black ear-stud. A necklace snakes around her throat. Most importantly, the songs here are based on life in the modern city – even the countryside is seen from a train, and the opening track sees her seemingly confined to her home, an impression strongly reinforced by 'Car on a Hill', in which Joni waits at home for a unnamed "sugar to show", gazing out of the window for signs of his car. 'Raised on Robbery' is set in a hotel lobby, 'Trouble Child' in a hospital, 'Twisted' in a psychiatrist's chair. Even at a party, the singer feels alone and trapped. Not just court, but caught, like a fish.

The musical union with Tom Scott drew much favourable comment. Dave Marsh praised "the emotional rushes that such a union creates," as Joni pares her lyrics down to the bone, and Scott's music accentuates them as never before. It is a perfect pairing: we not only feel the romance of her voice in songs like 'Help Me', "but the well-paced music of Tom Scott and crew sends a shiver of recognition up our spines." *Record Collector*'s Debbie Pead (surely an alias) responded both to the fact that you could dance to this LP – as Joni doubtless did herself – and also listen hard. "Even the quieter numbers have the power of organised emotional chaos behind them." In 'Just Like This Train', for example, the music's rhythm and atmosphere dramatises the lyrics, their meter echoed by the band, while Larry Carlton conjures up a train whistle on his guitar. For Mike Allen, her band was faultlessly tasteful. Like her first LP, a half-way concept, *Court and Spark* ends "on a comic and deceptive note; the misfit winds up in the home for certifieds, her 'right to be human' is threatened, and the final track is a song of schizophrenia, a witty and detached version of Joni herself."

Nick Kent, with his well-trained nose for madness, does not discern anything of the sort. The album comes as a mild disappointment. LA Express add textural richness, but sometimes sound a touch too "menthol-muzak-orientated," and are dangerously close to what has recently been canonised as 'Easy' – i.e. musical crap. Lyrically, Mitchell is "simply seeing it through, coming to terms with herself and trying to store away fear and uncertainty with a positivism which... stands as the crock of gold at the rainbow's end of all self-consciously great art, performed as a kind of exquisite personal exorcism." I think that means he likes it.

Years later, Timothy White described the record as "an immaculate jazz-rock exploration, the wide-open aural landscapes in which the singer loses, re-discovers and surrenders herself." It was a direction envied and imitated by everyone from David Bowie to Jimmy Page. The "lustrous gleam" of this music even reached a young Madonna, then a teenager in Pontiac, Michigan. She told *Billboard* that "in high school I worshipped Joni Mitchell and sang everything from *Court and Spark*, my coming-of-age record." White himself sees the album as a specifically LA album, in which that city's open, "freeway-entwined" landscape became an aural panorama. 'Car on the Hill', for example, used a 'doppler' effect, for which the wavelength and frequency of the horn passages were carefully altered and panned. "I wanted to make them move like traffic, so their pitch would change as they came nearer and then rode past." Twenty years on, Barney Hoskyns asked Joni if she was still living on nerves and feelings. "No. I still swing by them, but I don't live there."

Joni opened 1974 with a burst of performing energy, and the year saw two major concerts in London which could not have been more different in setting and intensity. The year culminated in the release of her first (legal) live album, recorded on this seemingly never-ending tour with the LA Express. For this year, at least, Joni played at being a conventional rock star. It didn't last, of course. In February, Al Rudis reported back to England for *Melody Maker* about a concert held at the Chicago Auditorium. He was, perhaps, a biased witness: "She has a beautiful voice... there is nothing else like its warmth, strength and fragility all tied up in one. She has a beautiful presence, rough hewn and sophisticated. But most of all, she has a beautiful mind." Can anyone imagine anything so positive appearing in the rock press now, bending over backwards, as it is, to be ironic, and post-modern, and uncommitted?

As to the concert, Tom Scott's LA Express started with six solid instrumentals – hors d'oeuvres for the main course, no doubt. Then

Joni came on, opening with 'This Flight Tonight'. Scott himself supplied neat musical fills on melodica – beloved of dub reggae – on 'Turn me on, I'm a Radio', while the rest of the band "cooked like chefs." Each song followed the last, "like crystal-clear rain drops," until Joni chose to break up the flow by telling a story. Suddenly, all 3,892 of the audience – even the lighting booths were overflowing – were at home in her living room. This is an old Roy Harper trick, to suddenly interrupt his own set and engage in verbal free-fall, with much the same result. "The story wandered hither and yon, with many digressions about a Japanese-Canadian artist who was fixing up his island home so that planes flying over would be able to enjoy his environmental art from the air. We heard about the ravages of Cabin Fever, the dread City Longing freaks, and we got a short lecture on how a Canadian relative of the manzanita tree grows in solid granite and has young and old branches co-existing side by side with no generation gap."

At least one member of the audience had enough by this point, so began yelling for some music. Not being Harper, who usually engages in a pointless verbal battle at this point, Joni wrapped things up with the soothing "So then this song came to me." A couple of songs later, somebody shouted out for 'White Rabbit'. Quick as the proverbial flash, Joni replied "I'm getting slick, but I'm not that Slick." After the intermission, Joni came out solo, and performed nine numbers, joined for the last two on soprano sax by Tom Scott. Highlights were 'People's Parties', a "chilling little voyage into some private hells," and the eerie 'Car on a Hill'. The last song before the inevitable encores was her hit single 'Raised on Robbery', and she ended proceedings with 'Twisted'.

Chuck Pulin reported another Stateside gig for *Sounds*, and gave us precious insights into the audience Joni attracted. In retrospect, her archetypal fan sounds close to the teenage Madonna. "The Radio City Music Hall audience, made up largely of teenage girls, sat with idolatry expressions, almost cooing with joy. The male section of the audience seemed to comprise dates or boyfriends or elder brothers, but in any event the New York gals jumped or danced with joy, running up to the front of the stage with flowers for Joni. Her piano was so bedecked with flowers it seemed it would collapse under the weight, and during her two-hour set many wept, while others cried out 'We Love You Joni'."

The interval came immediately after the six LA Express numbers – luckily, no-one died of over excitement during this portion of the show – and Joni opened up the second half with 'This Flight Tonight', playing a set largely drawn from *Court and Spark*. Encores of – again – 'Raised on Robbery' and 'Twisted' had the audience dancing, and Joni exiting with a grin that spread into a large smile. "The crisp, clear sound and the subtle lighting were flawless, whilst Joni's poise and manner of chatting to the audience were a delight. The experience of seeing her was unforgettable." Not much critical detachment there, thank God.

In early April, *NME* announced "London dates by Joni," two concerts at the barn-like New Victoria Theatre on Saturday and Sunday April 20th and 21st. Ticket prices had risen to £1, £1.50, £2 and £2.50. A single, 'Help Me' – which reached Number Seven in the States – was rush-released to coincide with the concerts, for those too poor or mean to buy the album. Joni strode onstage in a loose-fitting top, jeans, her hair now curly and with a centre parting, cheeks glowing with makeup. For the second half, she changed into a powder-blue evening gown. As Rob Mackie observed, "she looks a little harder and tougher, from folk waif to rock 'n' roll lady." LA Express again opened up with a half-hour of jazz-funk doodlings, of which only a John Coltrane tune stood out. Their line-up was Scott on woodwinds, reeds and triangle, Robben Ford on fluid lead guitar, Max Bennett on fender bass, and John Guerin on drums. A new addition was Roger Kellaway, who had played keyboards with Melanie, and acted as her musical arranger. The entrance of Joni, on amplified acoustic guitar, brought things into focus, though she was obviously nervous, standing awkwardly as if she had never been onstage before, her voice slightly flat. She opened with 'This Flight Tonight', Scott adding soprano at the end; in fact, most numbers started with Joni solo, the band gradually joining in. Then straight into 'You Turn Me On (I'm A Radio)', ending the song wordlessly harmonising with Ford's guitar. Robben Ford had recently appeared at the Marquee, backing bluesman Jimmy Witherspoon, and like the best of the blues – BB King, Jimmy Page, and Robert Plant – voice echoed guitar, as Joni lilted and whooped without any sense of strain.

Though himself not a very good singer (at least by comparison), Tom Scott provided backing vocals for 'Free Man in Paris'. Still without addressing the audience, Joni moved to the piano for 'The Same Situation', and oddly, it was a mistake that helped break the ice. Joni suddenly started to play something different, much to the confusion of the band. (Bob Dylan does this all the time nowadays, on purpose!) She explained "I've been working on this other thing, I know it wasn't what we were doing, but I'd like to throw it in." She then told the audience that she and the band had just had a two week lay-off, so that things were a little rusty. They tried the song again, with Joni's injunction to her band, "OK, on your spots." They followed up with 'Just Like This Train' – in which Scott's soprano sax almost drowned Joni out – and over-twiddly arrangements of 'Rainy Night House' and 'Woodstock'.

The second set was far more assured. 'Cactus Tree' came unadorned, while 'Big Yellow Taxi' had some lyrics changed, so that it became a big yellow tractor. Joni then rambled on about being at a party where all the food was white, and the furnishings transparent, and everyone had Richard Nixon's face – sounds a long way from life in, say, Barnsley. "Speedfreak," a member of the audience shouted, prompting Joni's baffled response: "No, I'm just a naturally compulsive talker." For 'People's Parties', her phrasing was near perfect. NME's Steve Clarke hallucinated that "she seemed to have butterflies in her voice, holding down notes long and low until they disappeared." Picking up a dulcimer, she sang 'All I Want', 'A Case of You' and 'Blue', followed by another long preamble, then 'For the Roses' and 'Cold Blue Steel', made eerie by Scott's offstage sax solo, like an unseen ghost. Rob McKie described how, live, "singing with the deep siren voices of addiction, and wiggling gracefully behind her guitar at the same time, she made the song even more unsettling than it was on For the Roses. There are times when the lady's lyrics seem like they've been dragged, protesting, right out of your subconscious."

Lots more material from the new LP followed, as well as a band-accompanied version of 'Both Sides Now', in which Joni added "yes I have" after the line "they say I've changed," and "sometimes still" after "I look at love that way." She encored with 'The Last Time I Saw Richard', mimicking the sharp tones of a New York barmaid. Throughout, she was reappraising older material, with a slightly ironic twist where once all was sung straight. The concert ended with

'Twisted', before which Joni spoke of LA Express, explaining to the audience that "I finally understood what jazz was all about playing with these guys." Then Joni went on to a party – no interviews, no photos – where she chatted self-consciously with Rod Stewart, then stepped into a black limousine, surrounded by bodyguards. As she sang in the updated 'For Free', she now had "about sixteen" men to escort her to the halls. For *NME*, legendary rock photographer Joe Stevens captured her haunted face, "gaunt without being wasted," staring out of a limousine, like a mythological being.

The LA Express reminded some reviewers of The Section, a soft rock combo who backed the likes of Carole King and James Taylor. The biggest shock to her English audience was seeing Joni with a backing band: Rob McKie's analysis is sensible, yet wacky enough to deserve repeating: "Joni's voice is so much stronger for the backdrop. It's like a puppy can have a lot of fun playing with you, and chasing the ball or the stick, but when you see him frisking with another puppy, it's another ball-game." As to the atmosphere Joni can create onstage, Michael Watts captures it in an over-the-top piece of writing for *Melody Maker*, also reverting to the canine world for his opening metaphor: "You'd be a pretty boneheaded mutt not to feel challenged by her presence and the splendid mystery of her music. There's nothing equivocal about shivers bristling on the spine as she hovers into view. Joni Mitchell is disturbing in a very real way, because after watching and listening to her for a while you start thinking she's not just a woman, she's woman, embodying all male desires and expectations."

When you get this kind of journalistic overkill, the next step is inevitably media martyrdom – and that was soon to follow.

Crosby, Stills, Nash & Young were also back with a vengeance, on speaking terms again, if not exactly friends. Like Joni's, their live concerts showed energy, if nothing else. The first gig of their world tour, in Seattle, had seen them on stage for four hours. This was stadium rock at its most overweening, playing what Crosby boasted were "enormous halls" – did he mispronounce a letter there? – as befitted the biggest band in the world at that point. "Stephen Stills liked that. It was enormously satisfying for him to have the Beach Boys, Santana, the Band, Joni Mitchell open for us. That was quite something." Graham Nash was always the most likeable of the four, and speaking to Steve Lake of *Melody Maker*, discussed the difference in mood between the band's two studio LPs: "When we started the first album, we were all in love, and everything was sunny. And then just before the second album, Joni and me split up, Neil got divorced from his wife, Stephen hadn't seen Judy in months, and the week before we were due to start, David's lady Christine was killed in a crash. That's the difference between CSN and CSNY. It started out real weird."

The presence of Neil Young – once a buddy of Charles Manson – often seems to have that effect. Similarly weird to Steve Lake was the incestuous nature of the Laurel Canyon mafia. How did it feel to have songs like 'Lady of the Island' and 'Our House' – written specifically for Joni Mitchell – still floating around four and five years later? Graham thinks hard about this, brow furrowed in concentration. He is diplomacy itself: "I think that this isn't really so different from you reading an interview you did a couple of years ago. You'd probably think, 'yeah, I believed that then, but that's not where I am now.' But I've never felt hesitant about opening myself up in that way. It's painful sometimes. I don't think I could sing 'Our House' now." Joni joined the European leg of the CSNY tour, as did Jesse Colin Young, her old friend from the New York folk circuit. He too had relocated to the West Coast, with his band the Youngbloods, the ultimate in good-time, laid-back vibes. They even had a keyboard player called Banana. On September 11th, 1974, Joni and Jesse appeared at Wembley stadium, along with the Band, at an event unlikely to be forgotten by anyone lucky enough to attend. For all that, it certainly wasn't Woodstock revisited.

Barbara Charone attempted to interview CSNY, holding court in their West End hideaway like decadent princes. Despite Elliot Roberts' best attempts, none of them would speak to her. Neil Young was lost somewhere behind his mirror shades, too exhausted to communicate, while Nash was surly, and Stills aggressive, spitting on the floor – punk rock, anyone? Crosby was his usual amiable self, but whacked. "Suddenly the bathroom door opened and Joni Mitchell walked out carrying a small replica of a wooden ship she'd only just finished. Crosby looked embarrassed and pointed to the door." Onstage the next morning, Jesse Colin Young – a singer of the utmost delicacy – was put on stage half an hour before the concert is even advertised to start, but played well anyway. The Band gave an adequate but disappointing account of themselves. Joni Mitchell's onstage mixture of intimacy and moodiness is almost impossible to pull off in daylight and in such a huge and impersonal arena, but as at the Isle of Wight, she gave her all.

She was, however, already preaching to the converted. Nick Kent's keen eyes scanned the audience, and found a fairly tame cross-section of "the suburban denim long-hair" out to enjoy itself. "There are also a lot of girls in long skirts, sporting that lank, benign look of confused femininity which is synonymous with the younger Joni Mitchell bedsitter aficionado." First, the LA Express swung smoothly through a half-hour of jazzy instrumentals – "knife-edged flares were dutifully creased" – then Joni appeared, in cream-coloured Bill Blass summer wear, trousers and a blazer, oddly reminiscent of Brian Eno (though Mitchell has far more hair!). She opened nervously with 'Free Man in Paris', but soon settled down. 'Woman of Heart and Mind' was particularly outstanding, and the whole band rocked gently on 'Big Yellow Taxi'.

The first half of the set ended with 'Woodstock', which Charone praised in its new incarnation as "a sophisticated supper-club swing." Nick Kent was more cynical: despite a "rather ill-judged back-up job" from Scott and partners, she is owed a debut of gratitude, simply because performing 'Woodstock' precludes CSNY from singing it themselves! There was a fifteen-minute break, to rearrange some microphones, then Joni came back solo, and communicated more directly. Her dulcimer-accompanied version of 'All I Want' miraculously grabbed the attention of the 72,000 strong crowd, as did fine versions of 'Rainy Night House', 'The Last Time I Saw Richard' and 'This Flight Tonight.' The LA Express returned, and rocked out on 'Help Me', closing on a sleazy version of 'Twisted', with Annie Ross herself appearing on stage. Backstage, Jimmy Page was proclaiming his undying love for Mitchell at high volume, though he preferred her indoor gig: "it was more – uh – intimate." Joni had triumphed against all the odds, though acting as a mere warm-up act for CSNY she was, as Barbara Charone commented, "in the wrong place at the wrong time."

The CSNY tour rumbled around the world and Joni returned to LA exhausted, after fifty-four live dates in less than a year, and having confronted her own loneliness. It was time for a major change in her personal life: she was no longer a young girl seemingly with the whole world at her feet. David Devoss of *Time* magazine came round to interview her, and she made him dinner, three meticulously cooked courses, with roast beef and yorkshire pudding like her mother used to make, and spiced apple dumplings. The kitchen was her favourite room in the house: "Maybe I'm growing old, but I enjoy taking care of this place."

Time regarded her as an icon, an "organic earth mother with a growing throng of dedicated, denim worshippers." Meanwhile, on with the show. The double live album *Miles of Aisles* was a souvenir of her world tour with the LA Express, though the three concerts sampled were all near to home. Most tracks were taken from a four-day residency at Hollywood's Universal Amphitheatre in August, spliced with two earlier performances, at the LA Music Centre and Berkeley Community Centre. The cover shot – which literally interprets the album's title – is not identified, but is an interesting mixture of reality and art. A photo of an auditorium taken by Joni – her painted toenails peep out at the bottom of the shot – extends left and right into paint and apparent infinity, woods and waves. Onstage, a band is setting up, playing to an empty auditorium. Inside the complex packaging are two photos of a happy Joni, one alone, dressed in black with microphone and guitar, one offstage with her band, in beret and dressed in green.

The album hit Number Two in the USA, with advance orders of $1,000,000: in February 1975, *Miles of Aisles* came straight in at Number Ten in the British album charts. It had already gone gold in the States, having passed the million sales mark, exceptional for a live album. Advance orders in Britain topped 20,000, while the live single 'Big Yellow Taxi' was issued here in late January as a taster. The LA Express line-up was Tom Scott himself on woodwinds and reeds, with Robben Ford on guitar, Larry Nash on keyboards, Max Bennett on bass, and John Guerin on drums. Guerin also helped Henry Lewy to engineer the album. Joni played piano, guitar and dulcimer: at least half the album is her 'unplugged'. "Joni, you have more flash than Mick Jagger, Richard Nixon or Gomer Pyle – combined!" an enthusiastic fan shouts between numbers, and both performer and the exuberant audience join in healing laughter. Side One of the original vinyl release is upbeat and happy. 'You Turn Me On (I'm A Radio)' boasts tinkly piano and funky rhythm: Joni's voice is slinky and seductive. At the end, she seems to release her vocals like a skyward-drifting balloon, scatting wordlessly in a duet with the guitar like Van Morrison (though without his gruff growls and grimaces). 'Big Yellow Taxi' is taken at a quicker lick, with witty bass – listen if you don't believe me – and Joni's voice taking on the timbre of an electric piano. The words have been updated: as in Joni's New Victoria Theatre performance in London, the taxi is a big yellow tractor, and there's also an extra, ironic "again" when she sings about the disappearance of her old man. 'Rainy Night House' drifts and her voice surfs the backing, rather like Tim Buckley's on his *Blue Afternoon* LP, bottomless pools of melancholy. Drums kick the song into a settled rhythm, and this time Joni duets high with Tom Scott's flute, until the song ends funkily. Fascinating. The controversial respray job on 'Woodstock' updates it for a new decade, and sounds surprisingly optimistic, though her voice twists nastily on "smog," and stretches out on the "children/garden" half-rhyme. There is an exuberant addition, in that everyone is singing and dancing and having fun at the festival. On the LP, the end of Side One neatly coincides with an interval.

Joni opens Side Two – a sombre suite of songs indeed – with an acoustic 'Cactus Tree' and a particularly bare 'Cold Blue Steel', her plaintive vocals matched by Scott's soprano sax. As her voice plunges low on "down," the saxophone soars, like a soul fleeing a dead junkie. 'Woman of Heart and Mind' is particularly intense on the lines "no child to raise": it starts with the kind of sad majesty on which Mitchell has a copyright. She moves from guitar to dulcimer on 'A Case of You', sung with devastating nostalgia, and to piano for 'Blue'. The way she emotes "lots of laughs" is enough to make you cry – as, indeed, she seems to when she half-sobs on the word "Blue" itself. Her cough at the end speaks volumes.

Side Three lightens up immeasurably with her chorus song 'Circle Game.' As she retunes her guitar, the audience – largely female – shout out requests, while Joni raps to fill in the time, along the lines of "a major difference between the performing arts and being a painter is a painter does a painting and that's it. Nobody ever said to Van Gogh 'paint a starry night again, man'! Let's sing this song together, it doesn't sound good with one lonely voice. The more out of tune voices on it, the better." Joni gets her "best out of tune voice" out specially, and gives an extraordinarily intimate performance, as if the audience is listening to her most secret thoughts. They sing pretty well, too. The version is optimistic rather than sad, "there'll be plenty of new days" she adds. 'People's Parties' is much barer than the album version – just Joni and her guitar – and she kind of shakes her voice out at the end of each verse, like washing flapping on a clothes-line. Someone prophetically shouts out for 'All I Want' and gets it. 'For Free' is little different from the BBC radio performance, with bell-like piano, and Tom Scott coming in on saxophone right at the end, almost subliminally. 'Both Sides Now' sees the band back – at long last – and Joni seemingly singing to herself. LA Express swing gently, and she seems to be thinking about the words for the first time, adding "once upon a time" like a footnote. She deliberately sings against the tune at times, to make the familiar strange again. Triumphal.

Side Four is all band-enhanced. 'Carey' takes on a calypso tinge, like the lighter works of Kevin Ayers, and is robbed of any bitterness. She likes mean old daddies, at least sometimes. The cool swing of later-period Steely Dan is here in embryo. Good time music. 'The Last Time I Saw Richard' immortalises her Bronx waitress impression, and is accepting rather than confrontational. She closes with two new songs: "They're love songs of course, one of them is very hopeful and the other is the portrait of a disappointment. My favourite theme. A little yin-yang here for you, folks." 'Jericho' has a swooning quality, with the texture of Joni's voice perfectly attuned to her band, not least the drummer, which is probably not accidental. A song of trust, of opening yourself to love, like a flower. 'Love for Money' paints the downside of LA, its endless parade of casualties and "40 watt successes." Her vocals are like a saxophone, so that lyrics elide with one another and lack the crystal clarity of earlier work, replaced by a soothing flow, which half-disguises the sting of the lyrics. A song of bruises and battles, prefiguring *The Hissing of Summer Lawns* in both meaning and musical texture.

If the new rearrangements remind me of anything, it is of Dylan's

1978 tour, his Las Vegas pastiche, which classily reworks his greatest hits, though Mitchell lacks both his bitter self-irony, and his protean need to constantly reinvent himself. Reviewing the album for *Circus* magazine, Viola James talks of Joni's warm relationship with her audience. "John Guerin is Joni's current room-mate, but even more important, he's the heartbeat behind her cooking rhythm section... the LA Express serves as a kind of musical sauce that helps to make even the most poignant and personal realisations more palatable." Barbara Charone in *Sounds* thought the album "wisely put together," concentrating on re-interpretations rather than greatest hits.

The album has faded in retrospect, "a secondary if entertaining package" according to Dave Marsh, while Timothy White praises its "graceful facility." Contemporaries like David Bowie and Jimmy Page were dumbfounded at the time by its sheer musicality. "She brings tears to my eyes," Page commented. "What can I say?" After the tour, she granted a rare interview to Malka. Her thoughts on inspiration predicted the move she would now make, away from the conventional song into a new conceptual and jazz-based music. It would baffle as many as it inspired. "I feel often that I have just run dry, and all of a sudden things just come pouring out. I have a fear that I might become a tunesmith, that I would be able to write songs, not poetry. It's a mystery, the creative process. You throw a question at the muses and maybe they drop something back on you."

Domestically too, things were settling into place. Mitchell returned to settle with John Guerin in her new home in exclusive Bel Air – a sixteen-room hacienda, where she lives to this day. As Leonore Fleischer reported, it was an Eden of tranquillity: "Joni and John live quietly, seeing a few friends, making a little music, playing a little cribbage. The Bel Air house contains a skylight studio at the top of the curving staircase. The room is furnished minimally – a couple of stools, an easel, and a large table that holds Joni's sketches and sketching paraphernalia. There is no mirror in the room; she finds them distracting when she works." An interview at the time related further scenes of domestic contentment, and an unexpected passion for indoor games. There was a goldfish pond, a swimming pool, Chinese paper dragons by the door, and Joni and John playing backgammon on a table in the sun.

On Christmas Eve, she joined Linda Rondstadt, Carly Simon and James Taylor singing Christmas songs on the streets of Los Angeles. The next year, 1975, began quietly. With an all-star audience of George Harrison, Ringo Starr, Grateful Dead, the Band, and Cat Stevens, she attended LA's Roxy Theatre to see a cataclysmic concert by the (then) barely known Bob Marley and the Wailers. In March, she and Tom Scott won a Grammy for 'Best Arrangement Accompanying Vocalist' for 'Down to You', off *Court and Spark*. A long way from scuffling around Yorktown, earning the odd dollar! The single version of 'Big Yellow Taxi' reached twenty-four in the US singles chart. Endless adoration and a succession of smooth and successful albums and concerts seemed to stretch into the future, forever. It was not to be. In fact, Joni was just about to take the greatest artistic risk of her whole life.

chapter 4:

Jazz In The Ruins

The more perceptive among rock critics recognised that, for all its surface smoothness, Mitchell's work was reaching some kind of crisis point, as was rock music in general. Punk and new wave were as yet seeds in the wind, but Joni could already feel the breeze. In *NME*, feared scribe Nick Kent – whose immersion in narcotics and consequent skeletal looks gave even Keith Richards a run for his money – examined the 'feminine factor' in rock. The match which lit his fuse was a recent lead story in *Time* magazine, hardly a rock oracle. Linda Rondstadt, Maria Muldaur, Wendy Waldman, and Bonnie Raitt had all been singled out as having what it takes. "Yup, the girls are taking over." The cover shot alone, of Joni, brought out Kent's fangs. "It portrays her as some gossamer-thread apparition from a Mormon Tabernacle 'Bride of Jesus' hootenany – a bonafide Pete Seeger wet dream." Thus primed, Kent ripped through the *Time* parade of female singer-songwriters like a serial killer. "I think that perhaps the facet that I find the most offensive is that they're all so damn good-natured. Only 'rock poetess' Patti Smith looks capable of really stepping out, and even then it's at the cost of a whole passel of emasculation. Looks like it's just down to Joni after all – so one might as well begin by separating her from present company."

Which he does, brutally. Wiping the ink, or blood, from his fingers, he starts in on our Joni. Even Jann Weiner and *Rolling Stone* had been permanently ensconced in sack-cloth and ashes for their "unfortunate" bestowal of Groupie of the Year award on Joni. Not quite accurate, but when has truth ever got in the way of entertainment? This was followed by "a graphic survey of who-was-screwing-who in the Los Angeles circuit (our Joan scored pretty high here, as one could imagine)." Kent reports that Mitchell froze in horror, refused all interviews, and "her house bully-boys, CSNY" immediately rallied to her defence. What annoys Kent most is not Joni herself, but the way the media appear to fawn over her. He skewers the *Time* article – a kind of prequel to *Hello* magazine, whose writer dines with Mitchell and John Guerin, who was now firmly established as man about the house.

"Guerin thumbs a tattered copy of *Arizona Highway*. They are going to a little town to buy turquoise next week, but only from a certain Italian craftsman. 'We should call to see if he'll be there.' 'John, no!' Joni yells from across the room. 'We're taking the train. Let's just go and wander around. It's more romantic that way'." This charming conversation, which shows the singer's innate romanticism – and good business sense – becomes, for Kent, a fault line which he pursues through her records, a kind of devastating tweeness. He also rips into her belief in "a male muse called Art," in which she is in soulful communication in the cover shot to *Blue*. What would Kent make of *Pour Down Like Silver* – the Thompsons lost in Allah – or Van Morrison up among the clouds on *Astral Weeks*, or Nick Drake's *Bryter Layter*, or John Coltrane's hawk-like stare on *A Love Supreme* – in fact, any album which contains some mighty act of spiritual transformation? He quotes, ironically, what I hope this present book will show to be the bottom line of Mitchell's whole being.

"I feel like I'm married to this guy called Art. I'm responsible to my Art above all else. My family consists of pieces of work that go out in the world. Instead of hanging around for 19 years they leave the nest early." This is something she gave up her own daughter to pursue – not that Kent is aware of that. It's also interesting, in retrospect, that Mitchell's longest period of domesticity, with her second husband, was also, artistically, her most barren period. Kent ends by admitting that, in musical terms, Joni is out there on "her very own highway," having outstripped all the competition in sight, male as well as female, "in the-art-of-penning-the-intelligent-love-paean sweepstakes." His mention of the androgynous Patti Smith is interesting, for she is a harbinger of punk and new wave, a tide which will sweep the whole singer-songwriter, mellow, Laurel Canyon, 'whispering Bob Harris' scene down the plughole, leaving Mitchell coldly alone, respected but largely ignored.

Jacoba Atlas concurs in her article *First Lady of the Canyon*, which also appeared early in 1975. Mitchell has gone from "from being a soft, genteel writer to being a biting, insightful, chronicler of the human heart and condition." As an artist, she lives "very close to the bone."

In January 1976, *The Hissing of Summer Lawns*, again using members of LA Express – but not Tom Scott – hit Number Four in the States and fourteen in the UK. The single 'In France They Kiss on Main Street' peaked at Number Sixty-Six in the USA. Those are the facts. Everything else is conjecture. The album remains one of the most compelling yet produced in the whole rock canon. It circles in a select orbit with the likes of *Astral Weeks*, the third Velvet Underground LP, Tim Buckley's *Starsailor*, Nico's *The Marble Index*, and the Beach Boys' unreleased *Smile*. Albums in touch with strange worlds.

As Joni writes in her sleeve notes, laid out like a poem around her body as it floats in a swimming pool, "This record is a total work conceived graphically, musically, lyrically and accidentally – as a whole. The performances were guided by the given compositional structures and the audibly inspired beauty of every player. The whole unfolds like a mystery." It's a mystery she is not prepared to unravel, merely throwing in more unrelated clues. The album seems to be an analogue for the singer's own life. If folk singer Bobby Neuwirth (Dylan's minder in *Don't Look Back*) was the midwife for the most personal song here, then "the child filtered thru Genesis at Jackfish Lake, Saskatchewan is rebellious and mystical and insists that its conception was immaculate."

The first people to be thanked are Myrt and Bill Anderson, Joni's parents. The places mirror her own progress – North Battleford, New York, Saskatoon, Bel Air – and career. Burbank was the home of her first record company, Burundi supplied the percussion and natives on the cover, as did the *National Geographic* magazine. As to Orange County, and the deep, deep heart of Dixie, who knows? The founts of country music and American jazz, perhaps. Joni also thanks long-term engineer Henry Lewy, and Blue – James Taylor – but not Graham Nash, though both sing on the opening track, with another old lover, Dave

Crosby. The musical driving force is the drumming of her (then) husband, John Guerin, who seems to be the principal dedicatee here, "for showing me the root of the chord and where I was."

Thanks also go to "Helpful Henry the Housewife's Delight," which I take to be cocaine, though it may well be a brand of oven gloves. Like all the albums named earlier, whose inner core remains publicly inaccessible, this record is moulded by some kind of drug experience. Like them, it places the artist in his or own secret orbit, looking at the world from a distance. In some cases, like Skip Spence's *Oar* or the later ravings of Syd Barrett, such music can be interesting merely as case notes; in others – as in the work of Nick Drake – it unlocks the contemporary world, and sees it anew.

To return to the facts, for *The Hissing of Summer Lawns* Joni adds Moog and arp-Farfisa keyboards to piano and guitar, and Jeff 'Skunk' Baxter from Steely Dan comes in on guitar, but otherwise the musicians used are much as on *Court and Spark*. The album's title refers to water sprinklers on the lush lawns of Los Angeles – a city resting perilously on what was once desert – and how they sound like a huge snake rustling ominously through the undergrowth, like the insects at the start of David Lynch's movie *Blue Velvet*. There, too, a suburban world peels back to reveal layers of depravity and decadence. The city on the front cover of the album is New York, crossed with Saskatoon, while the mansion on the back cover, viewed from the air, is the singer's own Bel Air home. The blue of the swimming pool matches the blue of a trailer on the front, the only other colours in Joni's drawing being grey for the sky, and a kind of olive green for the grass – maybe Central Park, maybe the suburbs – across which black and white natives drag a giant snake, apparently towards a church. On the original LP sleeve, the central figures are embossed, to make them stand out as if by magic from the ground.

The rhythm track on 'Jungle Line' is taken from a recording made by the French Government in 1967, and released as a single, 'Burundi Black'. Later, Adam and the Ants picked it up, and it underlay the overblown drum sound of the early eighties. What Mitchell is doing here is an early example of sampling, a technique largely developed by Can's enigmatic bassman Holger Czukay. The 1974 Nonesuch release of *Music from the Heart of Burundi* reveals that "drumming of this kind was once reserved for kings and powerful aristocrats." Rock stars are the latest equivalent. "The drummers were traditionally Hutu of Karuzi, in northern Burundi. The lead drummer calls upon his fellow 'warriors of the drum', inviting them to attack their instruments. The drums are tubular, made from the scooped-out trunk of a large tree – drummers play in standing position (the drums are as high as their waists), striking the skin with two sticks. The Hutu are the majority population, and tend to be short in stature and less martial. The Tutsi are renowned for their graceful dancing, and as a race are tall and slender. As the drummers created a rhythm, Watusi youths re-enacted famous battle and victory scenes in dance form, gracefully leaping and shaking their heads, a short spear balanced delicately between three fingers in each hand."

This ritual tension turned serious in 1972, when ethnic fighting broke out between Tutsis and Hutu. This resulted in the death of more than 200,000 Burundians and more than 80,000 Hutu subsequently fled the country. The fighting broke out again in 1995, and the culture celebrated here is already a matter largely of ethnography and history, rather than a living tradition.

All part of the puzzle. This is an album that has constantly been reassessed. Artists like Annie Lennox and Prince – as was – have named it as her best LP, and a profound influence on their own work. This provided a vindication for Joni, talking much later to Bill Flanagan, as some critical responses of the time were as savage as the natives on the sleeve. "I was so pleased when Prince said it was his favourite. It was called all sorts of awful names. Of all my children, that was the one that really got beat up on the playground. So for him to say that in the same rag (*Rolling Stone*) that kind of started the war against it was a treat for me." Much of this hostility was from the change of narrator in her songs. "I had been writing 'I' this and 'I' that. And it was easier to stomach or something, because when I started writing 'you', people said 'Who does she think she is?' And 'Why is she taking potshots at us?' This simple dramatic device became a large point of contention. That constituted an enormous change for some of my fans. If a person you met when they were vulnerable suddenly got strong it would threaten you, because you have to readjust your role. Sometimes somebody's strength makes another person weak.

175

Some people have a hard time making those transitions."

Early albums deal mainly in narrative, about characters like Marcie, but in *Blue* she wrote some extremely personal songs, "a series of self-portraits, scrapings of the soul." Her return to narrative here did not go down well with those who expected her work always to be confessional. They "saw themselves more than they wanted to. Then they would get mad at me." Mike Allen compares the opening track with 'Night in the City': both differentiate the "'them' of the crowd" from the wild, rushing "us." Joni is still singing to her own constituency. She has simply turned a close focus onto it, which – as Lemuel Gulliver also found – can be distinctly uncomfortable.

Rolling Stone's staff voted it the worst LP of the year, failing to recognise an album which anticipated the later craze for world music, the LA riots, and much more. Talking to Timothy White, the scars had obviously not yet healed for Joni, twenty years on: "There was a big stink about that. It was taboo, you see. I don't think I realised how culturally isolated we were. In white culture it was problematic, but it got good reviews in the black magazines where it was accidentally reviewed because there was an illustration of a black person on the cover. I thought it was adventuresome, but it was shocking how frightened people were of it. I think the record was inadvertently holding up a mirror to a change that people were on the brink of in this hemisphere, and people were disturbed by the teetering they were experiencing. The Third World was becoming more important and they were disorientated."

She told Alan Jackson that "I got a telegram from Paul and Linda McCartney that year saying "We really liked it." It was the only good review that it got, and then it was almost a sympathy telegram. It was destroyed on so many levels, and that really hurt. There's no way, just on a level of craftsmanship, that you could say it was the worst record made that year. If they'd just said they hated it you could take it, because it would be a personal opinion. But to say 'it's the worst. Stay as you are and bore us, or change and betray us.' That's your choice." Mitchell shrugged, pausing to light another cigarette.

She has slightly rewritten pop history here. *The Hissing of Summer Lawns* received all kind of critical responses, from the damning to the ecstatic. The main initial reaction was a pleasurable sense of puzzlement.

S tephen Holden, in *Rolling Stone*, finds the album "a great collection
of pop poems with a distracting soundtrack." The characters Joni
creates are all stereotypes – and this before the Specials were even
thought of – acting out social rituals of power and submission. That's
the good news. Unfortunately, these lyrics are set to "insubstantial
music," and there are no tunes to speak of. The music is both
pretentiously chic and boring, prey to "pseudo-avant-gardeism." Joni
Mitchell ought to work with someone of her own stature, like pianist
Keith Jarrett, whose work is "spiritually and romantically related."
Related, but probably incompatible. If I were one of the musicians
responsible for the miraculous musical shadings of this album, I would
have sought Holden out, and punched him on the nose.

British critics were awestruck. In *Sounds*, Alan Lewis recognises that
her music has moved on with the times, from the sunny sixties to "that
thin line between hope and despair down which we all walk in the
1970s, the jungle which lurks without (and within) the city, the
gathering darkness which people seek to banish with love and sex and
music and drugs." Each line here hits a nerve. Lewis hears ravishing
melodies and "new, subtle nuances of sound and tone." Similarly,
Michael Watts in *Melody Maker* finds this mysterious album "a
delightful torture," and compares the way it juxtaposes "primitive and
sophisticated" with the work of Harold Pinter. As Pinter once described
his plays as summoning up the weasel in the cocktail cabinet, this
seems pretty apt. He also name-checks David Hockney's paintings of LA
swimming pools. Both artists make the everyday unreal and intriguing.
The album possesses a "cool and damaged beauty that lingers long after
the last playing."

A ngus MacKinnon was the first reviewer to notice that *Apocalypse
Now* was more than just another Vietnam movie. Writing for
Streetlife, he similarly takes *The Hissing of Summer Lawns* as a work of
the utmost importance: "A socio-cultural overview, a many-layered and
fascinating behavioural model. Rather like a prism, refracting different
streams of light and colour as it is angled differently towards the sun."
The result is a musical labyrinth. Here MacKinnon really lets himself go.
"The cover's pictorial metaphor of lush, tropical vegetation represents
the terminal effects of collective social atrophy. What was initially a

cautious strand of weed pushing up between the neatly-laid patio tiles will end up a dense, choking carpet of creeper tendrils."

This dream – of Woodstock, perhaps – acts like an opiate, drugging a whole generation. Here are "small-town agonies, every level of society is equally myopic, dream-orientated." Archetypes interlock, unravelling further each time you listen to the record. On the inside photo, Mitchell allows herself to remain passive, an observer. The swimming pool is a restful womb. The other alternative is to cleave a way through the undergrowth, like a snake, to become 'La Carmeuse de Serpents', the snake enchantress from Henri Rousseau's painting of that name, rustling through his exotic jungle canvases.

"Maybe that's only the start of it. The album is a shimmering, evanescent windscreen. Guitarists provide crystalflow accompaniment, with a rich mix of electric pianos, rippled over bass and drums (John Guerin himself). Careful solos, deft arrangements, all re-emphasising the cover motif in their depth and luxuriance." Crucially, MacKinnon hints at the underlying sexual politics of the album, in which men are seen as redundant, and women unsatisfied.

From the vantage point of the late nineties, Simon Reynolds and Joy Press see the album as a key work in female liberation. "While men seek 'street' credibility, women more often explore the 'great indoors', sharing fantasies together or writing diaries alone." Mitchell was never really at home on the streets, and 'The Boho Dance' is her response to a slumming male bohemian who has dared to sneer at her for no longer being street credible.

This is why the album proved to be so disturbing. Male fans had secretly relished her portrayal of emotional frailty, fantasising about being the knight in shining armour who would come to her rescue, and found it hard to accept her new sense of detachment. Like much feminist criticism – especially that written by men – this analysis overstates an already good case, while hectoring the reader. Some of the most fervent critics – and fans – of Mitchell's confessional style have been women, or gay men like Paul Gambaccini.

Equally interesting is Reynolds' and Press' critique of Mitchell's vocals on this album, high in the mix so that it glides over the music rather than intersecting with it: "For all its somersaults and swerves, her voice is self-possessed. It glides and swoons, pirouettes and weaves. For rock fans, Mitchell's fluttery, quavering folky-jazzy voice can seem too feminine for (dis)comfort." For "rock fans" here, read males, that blighted half of the human race. Fortunately, Joni Mitchell herself has more charity in her own soul, investing pathos rather than triumph into these songs of men rightfully deserted by their partners.

If "rock" fans found it so disturbing, strange then that the album sold well, and was judged rock LP of the year, both in *Sounds* and in the heavily rockist *New Musical Express*, which sees her as exploding all such categories: "She now stands apart from both rock and folk, inhabiting a sophisticated world where those musics meet with jazz. She has no imitators because she is beyond imitation." The record was "not quite a rock album" but did reflect the progress and refinement of sixties popular music. Debbie Pead described it as a "song cycle," blazing the way for rock-jazz albums of the sophistication of Steely Dan's *Aja* and Weather Report's *Heavy Weather*. Paul Gambaccini saw her setting a new direction: "more musically ambitious, less emphasis on melody, less intricacy in lyric."

Talking to Cameron Crowe in 1979, Joni recognised a reaction that was bound to come. "I had stopped being confessional. I think they were ready to nail me, anyway. It was my second year in office. The cartoonists had their fun. There weren't enough good jokes left, so it was time to get a new president. It's politics." It's a misreading of the actual critical response, but why ruin a good anecdote with facts? Mitchell describes The *Hissing of Summer Lawns* as a "suburban album," based firmly in uptown LA. This was a key to the backlash which followed. "People thought suddenly that I was secure in my success, that I was being a snot and was attacking them. The basic theme of the album was just any summer day in any neighbourhood when people turn their sprinklers on all up and down the block. It's just that hiss of suburbia. People thought it was very narcissistic of me to be swimming around in a pool. It was an act of activity. As opposed to sexual posturing, which runs through the business – nobody ever pointed a finger at narcissism *there*."

In retrospect, though, she feels that the times have caught up with her. "Perhaps there was a weary tone in my voice that irritated people, but there was so much of it that was accessible." The unkindest cut of all was the appearance on Neil Young's 1975 LP *Zuma* of the song 'Stupid Girl', supposedly about Mitchell. It is sung in sorrow rather than anger. *Zuma* was released the same year as *The Hissing of Summer Lawns*, and verse two of *Stupid Girl* seems inspired by the inside shot of the Mitchell LP, with Joni as a beautiful fish, "flopping on the summer sand," waiting for a wave. The song shares the sense of exasperation – "you've really got a lot to learn" – which many felt at the time, not least because of her attacks on fellow rock musicians as not technically capable of interpreting her new music. "I had no choice but to go with jazz musicians." This, of course, was also true in her private life.

Nick Kent told Barney Hoskyns about her behaviour in those days in *Waiting for the Sun*, a kind of rock music alternative to Kenneth Anger's *Hollywood Babylon*. Dish the dirt, Nick: "She was unbelievably snobbish. She'd walk into a room and if she needed something she'd get some other rock star to ask a mere mortal to get her a drink. She was like Bianca Jagger – she wouldn't talk to anyone who wasn't famous because it would fuck with her aura so badly she wouldn't be able to have these superior thoughts." Hence Young's picture of her in a Mercedes-Benz, hiding from him so that he couldn't see her eyes. The unkindest cut of all is the *Zuma* artwork which, whether by accident or design, reads like a parody of Joni's artwork at its worst: faux naive, a naked woman carried by a seagull – crossed with a vulture – over cactus trees and mountains.

Joni herself was content to leave others to interpret her latest work: "I can't speak for how you're perceived. Life is short and you have an opportunity to explore as much of it as time and fortune allow." The opening track, 'In France They Kiss on Main Street', harks back to 'Free Man in Paris', to a half-invented Eden which sounds more like an idealised memory of her Canadian adolescence. The time is the fifties, with Brando still (semi) coherent, formal dances, pinball and rock 'n' roll. A "war of independence" is being waged for sexual freedom – in particular for women – despite attempts to break it "in churches and schools." Musically, the chorus and clipped guitar break are reminiscent of Steely Dan – though her laughter as she delivers the line on raising Jesus is a world away from their overbred cynicism. 'The Jungle Line' is Joni's *homage* to jazz – she imitates horns on her synthesiser – though the first sound is Burundi drumming, and chants. Much later, Peter

Gabriel reinvigorated his career by sampling native percussion, then adding technology on top: Joni got there first. Drug taking, the "poppy poison" of opiates, is not a vicarious walk on the wild side, but a metaphor for enslavement. The scene seems to be a downtown cellar, a five-piece band playing jazz, from which Mitchell hallucinates the song. The snake is an extemporisation of spit on a trumpet. Punk rock, anyone?

'Edith and the Kingpin' deals with the same demi-monde – a development of James Joyce's Nighttown from *Ulysses*, or TS Eliot's *The Waste Land*. A cocaine dealer – "snow" bending to the spoon – seeks out another victim. Absence of spirit, and a seduction not of the flesh but the soul. All this is set to a lolloping, gorgeous tune, like the sinister encrustations of later period Elvis Costello, the crooner from hell. The lyrics are doubly ironic, considering the cocaine glamour of California at that time, and Mitchell's own admitted partaking, which glows out, anyway, from the glazed sheen of photographs of her at the time, and her over-bright eyes.

'Don't Interrupt the Sorrow' is a poem of almost impenetrable mystery, written to her muse (female now), and set not so much to a tune, as to a divine slither of notes. Again, a man enslaves a woman, though Mitchell repeats the message of 'Cactus Tree', that since the age of 17 no-one has controlled her, least of all any man. Alcohol is the drug of choice – the way she sings "Rhine wine" would sell buckets of the stuff, if advertised. Joni's early virginal image is turned around, so that she becomes the Virgin herself, strong at the crucifixion. The feeling expressed in the line "when your man gets weak" seems endemic to the whole album.

'Shades of Scarlet Conquering' is straight out of *Gone with the Wind*, which the young Joni must have seen in all its technicolour glory, and likewise chronicles the death of a decadent civilisation, one that enslaved its black workers, literally. Its very tune is cinematic, and Joni's singing divine. The song features a big production, as on David Accles' 'Montana Song', another search for roots. There's something in the totality of celebration of womanhood here which evokes Dylan's awed 'Sad Eyed Lady of the Lowlands', but this is also partly a self-portrait. The last line, sung, then half-spoken, is a call to revolution: "A woman must have everything."

The title track has an (unconscious) steal from Bowie, "a diamond dog," and reminds us of 'Richard' and the ice-skater he married, and ensconced in his kingdom, literally behind barbed wire. The woman seems to be half a prisoner, but carries within her the seeds of wildness and escape. She stays, for the moment at least. Ironically, the song is a collaboration with her then boyfriend John Guerin, who Mitchell is shortly herself to leave. Joni's voice is matter-of-fact, counteracted by a second voice of wildness and seduction. The song lopes, like a wolf. 'The Boho Dance' looks back to Joni's scuffling days, its title drawn from social commentator and style guru Tom Wolfe. The band from the opening songs is now washed up. There's fancy piano, and a vocal that drifts towards the easy-listening style of Carole King, singing bitter lyrics, then in the line "don't you get sensitive on me" predicts the sassy spite of Chrissie Hynde. Even in the denim democracy, Mitchell pressed her jeans, and sewed lace along the seams. She tells off the proud male for his slumming, just as she herself was criticised in 'The Last Time I Saw Richard' for undue romanticism. The image of laddered nylons is pure Joni, somewhere between "the streets" and fake glamour.

A short instrumental segue leads into 'Harry's House' which re-runs the title track, though here the woman does have the courage to leave. Harry is an archetypal businessman, taking a big yellow taxi ride to a sales conference, past images of female perfection – shop dummies in fishnet tights, models shopping, memories of his own wife, oiled and perfect in a swimming pool, like Joni on the inside cover. The song dances along on a sea of brass, then changes speed to quote from the Harry 'Sweets' Edison/Jon Hendricks tune 'Centerpiece'. Joni's voice slurs into big town jazz, with piano flourishes courtesy of Joe Sample. The picture of domestic contentment given here is ironic, for after some overdubbed nagging, Harry's wife first traps him like a fish, then chucks him away: female emancipation, though the song's sympathy is with Harry, as the song is told from his perspective.

'Sweet Bird' returns to the imagery of the first album, with Joni out "on this horizon line" admiring a seabird's poise and powers of escape. A meditation by Harry's ex-wife, perhaps, and also reminiscent of Neil Young's early song 'Expecting to Fly'. The vocal floats above percussive backing, and fades away on sweet repetition, like a mantra.

'Shadows and Light' sets Joni's unaccompanied voice against a multi-tracked chorus, backed by synthesiser, with a hymn-like, sacerdotal feel. The lyrics are stream of consciousness, abstract, weird. They seem to evoke a balance between evil and goodness, freedom and entrapment. Stephen Holden interprets this song as the key to the whole album: "While acknowledging the power of devils and gods, Mitchell perceives them as male myths, necessary for the creation of inevitably patriarchal systems." That is to over-interpret, but it is certainly a "man" who here governs wrong and right, and throughout the album men are frauds or victims, women strong and triumphant. Which still doesn't explain 'Shadows and Light'. Mike Allen sees the song as a quest for solace rather than solitude, thus revealing "her as a restless perfectionist. The eagle eye always finds a disturbing and distracting shadow in the midst of every apparently glowing situation. And just that shadow is enough to make her flinch."

You pays your money. My own view is that the song sees Joni working through her own contradictions, and failing to resolve them. Its division into cruelty and delight is pure William Blake, from his Prophetic Books, which – like this song – no-one really understands. The fun is to invent your own interpretation. Mitchell's next album, *Hejira*, resolves this quandary in travel. Life as a road movie. The answer lies in flight, literally so in 'Sweet Bird'.

Joni Mitchell went back on the road with a vengeance in late 1975, joining Bob Dylan's Rolling Thunder Revue, largely as a spectator. An extraordinary phenomenon, it was a throwback to the days of the package tour. Dylan had gathered all kinds of old friends from Greenwich Village days, and they criss-crossed north America playing small theatres, and community halls. Dylan was giving some of the greatest performances of his career, in white clown make up – through which his eyes glittered like a coked-up snake – and huge feathered hats, singing the highly personal narratives from *Blood on the Tracks* as if he was in mortal danger. His band were playing a new kind of free-form rock, and the likes of Joan Baez, Roger McGuinn, David Blue, and Allen Ginsburg gave him a safety net for his nightly musical high-wire act. The presence of his partner Sara on the tour – and the particularly charged versions of 'Idiot Wind' and 'Isis' which resulted – added an extra layer of tension, and the couple were soon to separate for good.

The Rolling Thunder Revue was a long goodbye to Dylan's musical past, and the marriage in which he had found sanctuary after the apocalyptic 1966 world tour.

Mitchell performed at several concerts with the Revue, though she asked not to be included in *Renaldo and Clara* a highly confusing four-hour movie directed by Dylan himself, and using footage drawn from the tour, in which everyone appears as a character other than themselves. Joni does appear in the background of a couple of scenes, defiantly herself. Playwright Sam Shepard later published his logbook of this extraordinary tour, whose edgy photos and disjointed narrative tell their own story of ego-death and frazzled nerves. "Joni Mitchell is cross-legged on the floor, barefoot, writing something in a notebook. She bites her lip and looks over to Rick Danko, who's smashing the shit out of a pinball machine. The high spirit of competition has seized us all. Headlines in the paper seem like messages delivered from outside the walls. This feeling of separateness weasels its way into everything. You find yourself expanding to the smell of arrogant power or deflating to total depression. Then everything filters away to the elevators. To music. To another marathon night to the break of day."

It all sounds like a middle-aged adolescence, or the scene Joni had already turned into a song in 'People's Parties'. On November 16th, 1975, the troupe received a phone call inviting them to drop by the Tuscarora Indian Reservation. Robert Shelton takes up the story. Without speakers or amplifiers, troupe musicians including Joni Mitchell and Eric Andersen showed up at the Indian's community house. "Song swapping between this troupe and the Indians reached some intense moments: Tuscaroras did traditional songs and dances to drumbeating. While Dylan sang, a few of the younger Indian children played tag around the community house." Joni also appears on the double bootleg *Flagging Down the Double Es*, recorded at the Maple Leaf Gardens, Toronto. Revisiting ancient haunts.

Talking to Cameron Crowe, she recalls her involvement: "I joined Rolling Thunder as a spectator. I would have been content to follow it for three cities just as an observer, but since I was there I was asked to participate. Then, for mystical reasons of my own, I made a pact that I would stay on the thing until it was over. It was a trial of sorts for me. I went out in a foot-soldier position. I made up songs onstage. I sang in

French, badly. I did a lot of things to prevent myself from getting in the way. What was in it for me hadn't anything to do with applause or the performing aspect. It was simply to be allowed to remain an observer and a witness to an incredible spectacle. I preferred to be invisible. [Laughs nervously] I've got my own reasons why." Especially after an impromptu gig at a Correctional Institution one December afternoon. This turned out to be a pocket-sized gymnasium, to an audience made up almost entirely of black inmates, none of whom had the slightest inkling who Bob Dylan or Joni Mitchell were, or particularly cared. It was visiting day, and those who were not receiving conjugal visits had the alternative of watching the show, as second best.

Indeed, as Bob Spitz reports in his biography of Dylan – panned by the critics but grudgingly admired by Dylan himself – if it had not been for the presence onstage of Roberta Flack that day, there could well have been a riot, with Joni herself as the cause. It must have been like *The Hissing of Summer Lawns* coming to brutal life: forget *Rolling Stone*, this was a genuinely bad review. "The inmates couldn't relate at all to Joni Mitchell's creamy white pastorales. Two minutes into her set, hoots and catcalls sailed up over the makeshift stage, thawing Joni's icy composure. That tomcat face of hers puckered into a wicked sneer. 'We came here to give you love,' she lectured them. 'If you can't handle it, that's your problem'." Rob Stoner remembers: "Talk about wrong moves – that warmed-over sixties shit was the worst thing she could have said to them. it was like the neat chick on *Romper Room* – 'Do-Bee says Respect your Visitors.' I mean, you could see guys giving each other looks that said 'Throw that bitch out here and we'll teach her a thing or two about clouds'."

She appeared, in front of a somewhat larger audience, at the Revue's Madison Square Garden concert on 20th December, a five-hour benefit for Hurricane Carter. "Well, it looks like I'm here to fight someone tonight" declared the compere for the night. "I never knew that Bob Dylan was this big." Joni, her chic appearance contrasting markedly with the worn jeans of the Thunder hillbillies, sang four new songs in the first half, and appeared for the encores. The Rolling Thunder tour took its toll on her health, and she acquired a reputation for cancelling dates. One she certainly managed was a January 1976 concert in Austin, Texas, where Dylan appeared unexpectedly, duetted with her on 'Both Sides

Now' – one hopes it was better than his murdering of 'Big Yellow Taxi' on *Dylan* – and performed 'Girl from the North Country' solo. The reconvened Rolling Thunder Revue failed to rekindle the spark of the previous year. After a particularly disappointing second 'Night of the Hurricane' at Houston, Dylan returned to Malibu to rethink his career, having spent a few days in Texas, hanging out with Joni and Doug Sahm.

Joni has her own sharp views of the whole experience. Talking to Phil Sutcliffe of *Q*, she reveals her own variety of road madness: "For my own amusement on that tour, I had taken to ripping off cops. I would use my wits and try and get a piece of cop paraphernalia off 'em – I got hats and jackets and tie-clips and badges. One time I chased a cop and he wouldn't give me anything so I said 'what if I get a gang and we pin you up against a wall and you tell your superior you were outnumbered.' The smile came over just one corner of his mouth and he said 'Go get your gang.' It was really a charming game. I would introduce myself as Mademoiselle Oink, the liaison officer between rock 'n' roll and the cops." One dreads to imagine the police reaction if fellow Los Angeles resident Ice T, author of 'Cop Killer' had tried the same game: collecting bullet holes, perhaps. Joni's own desire to disguise herself as a black man was in direct contrast to the Rolling Thunder tour.

"Bobby and Joan Baez were in whiteface and they were going to rescue Hurricane Carter. I had talked to Hurricane on the phone several times, and I was alone in perceiving that he was a violent person and an opportunist. I thought, Oh my God, we're a bunch of white patsy liberals. This is a bad person. He's fakin' it. So when we got to the last show, at Madison Square Garden, Joan Baez asked me to introduce Mohammed Ali. I was in a cynical mood. I said, what I'll say is – and I never would've – 'We're here tonight on behalf of one jive-ass nigger who could have been champion of the world, and I'd like to introduce you to another one who is.' She stared at me, and immediately removed me from this introductory role. Anyway, Hurricane was released and the next day he brutally beat up this woman..."

In January 1976, Joni began a major tour of the States, headlining 5,000-seat auditoria, and backed by a reformed LA Express. Dates were announced for late May for concerts in London and Glasgow, but

I can find no record of them actually taking place. Asylum released 'In France They Kiss On Main Street' as a single. Caroline Coon, a fellow painter, and one time head of the Release organisation for helping drug casualties at rock festivals, was ecstatic. Writing for *Melody Maker*, she felt mad to realise that "I've monitored the radio, all stations, and I've not heard Joni's voice once in months." *The Hissing of Summer Lawns* had labelled her as eccentric in programmer's minds, so her music disappeared into the avant-garde ghetto of late-night radio and the *Old Grey Whistle Test*. Coon – soon to be involved in the British punk revolution, when she helped manage the Clash – is justifiably angry. "Don't UK deejays understand that she is everything we dream a rock 'n' roll artist should be: original, committed, a poet, a fine musician, funny and wry, deep and sad – pleasure incorporated."

Readers of *Melody Maker* obviously agreed. In the poll results for 1976, she headed the international section of female singers, over – in order of diminishing votes – Kiki Dee, Diana Ross, Grace Slick, Curved Air's Sonja Kristina, Emmylou Harris, Patti Smith – first swallow of a new wave summer – Maggie Bell, Linda Rondstadt, and Karen Carpenter (already well on the way to starving herself to death). A mixed bunch, which Joni topped with ease. A list of the previous winners of this trophy is instructive: Joni Mitchell in 1970, 1971, and 1972, Carly Simon in 1973, Joni Mitchell again in 1974 and 1975. What went wrong in 1973?

Whether Mitchell did or did not appear on a British stage in 1976, journalists kept fans informed, via their front-row dispatches. Dick Richmond reported from St Louis: the LA Express now lacked its former leader Tom Scott, who was replaced by David Lewell, while Victor Feldman had taken the place of keyboard player Roger Kelloway. Guitarist Robben Ford remained, as did rhythm section Max Bennett and John Guerin. Richmond reveals more of the musical history of these men, which was encyclopaedic: Bennett had played with Peggy Lee and Frank Zappa, Lewell with Cold Blood, Woody Hermann and the Pointer Sisters. Most bizarre was Feldman, who had played drums with the Glenn Miller orchestra in London while still in short pants: subsequent gigs included Benny Goodman, Henry Mancini, Quincy Jones, Elvis Presley and Neil Diamond. Very

Woodstock. This was his first live tour for 15 years.

As on the previous tour, the band opened with 40 minutes of polite jazz rock, crossing over into funk. Their final number, a Guerin tune called 'Down the Middle', was a throwback to the swing of the war years, doubtless reviving old memories for Feldman. Joni's set stretched through a massive 21 songs, starting with 'Help Me' and encoring with 'Jericho'. 'Talk to Me', 'Coyote' and 'Don Juan's Reckless Daughter' were brand new, while 'Both Sides Now' and 'You Turn Me On (I'm a Radio)' were both notable by their absence. Pop fodder, no longer required. Richmond is clearly unimpressed with Joni, talking of instrumental rather than vocal peaks, though he concedes that her rendition of 'Cold Blue Steel' was striking, especially when Lewell appeared from the darkness to play "little accent notes" on clarinet. As the words ended, Lewell picked out the melody, and again faded into the dark. Spooky. Joni's presence on stage was "stoic," and at times her voice slurred, or flattened, or grew indistinct. She was dressed in a woven top, with an Inca-style charm around her neck. One triumph was 'Rainy Night House', in which she sang in a folk idiom against a jazz-rock backing, her voice rising like a cowboy yodel. 'Jungle Line' matched her vocals with a mass of feverish drumming, not heard "since Johnny Weissmuller made his first Tarzan movie"!

Peter Crescenti updated the readers of *Sounds* on the tour when it reached Nassau Coliseum. The audience was an interesting cross-section of sixties veterans – some with their children, some burned out – new-wave trendies, and teenyboppers. Joni slid around stage, dressed in a gangster's black suit, with wide-brim hat. Very androgynous. She looked like a cross between the *Young Americans* and *Pin-ups* era Bowie, "super-slender, with her padded shoulders and blonde hair tucked neatly and completely away under her sinister black hat." Her voice sounded "tour weary," though it grew spirited on 'Raised on Robbery', and the exotic frenzy of 'Jungle Line'.

Joni's perfectionism – or should that read 'irritability'? – showed through on 'Free Man in Paris', when she stopped the band after a few seconds, to get her guitar tone right. You want stage effects, lights, action? Joni donned a Yellow Taxi cap – from Memphis, as was a new song about 'Furry Lewis' – to sing her big hit single, and the crowd sang along without any prompting from the stage. The title subbed onto Crescenti's piece says it all: 'Who's frail and blonde and rocks like a bitch?'

The breakup of her relationship with John Guerin sent Mitchell travelling across the States by car, and writing the songs which became the album *Hejira*. The principal musical change for the album is the slithery electric bass of Jaco Pastorius – like the snake which once hissed on summer lawns. Pastorius's life was a paradigm of the American dream, turning into nightmare. He was the Sid Vicious of jazz, with considerably more musical ability! From 'white trash' origins, he grew into a hippy beach bum, playing covers in a bar band, until discovered by jazz pianist Paul Bley. After recording with Pat Metheny and Herbie Hancock, he joined state-of-the-art pioneers Weather Report. Drug abuse brought on a form of schizophrenia. Pastorius even raided a record store to steal his own albums. Turfed offstage at the 1983 Playboy Jazz Festival by Bill Cosby for playing heavy feedback – shades of Dylan at Forest Hills – he transformed his chosen artform, then died penniless and a drug addict. Romantic in hindsight, but hell to live with.

Pastorius completely overhauled the way Joni heard music, his jazz tones and upfront melodies spilling all over her subsequent work. As she told Sean O'Hagan, "He had a big bushy ego that ruffled a lot of people but even his arrogance was appealing to me. Life got him in the end, but he just didn't know when to stop, and a lot of people were waiting for him on the way down. It was a real tragedy." Her basic band was otherwise much as before: the departing John Guerin continued to play drums, and Tom Scott returned from the wilderness. 'Stupid Girl' forgiven or forgotten, Neil Young provides harmonica on one track. On *Hejira*'s front cover, Mitchell comes out as a secret cigarette smoker. For those in the know, visual references to snow, the general air of whiteness, and Joni's distant eyes, also hint at a stronger stimulant still, the white powder of cocaine.

Joni is dressed in black on a winter lake – back to Canada – with an endless and empty highway superimposed on her cloak, which has the unfortunate result of plumping her out to Mama Cass dimensions. On the back cover, two Torvill and Dean lookalikes pose on ice skates, unconvincingly. The girl is wearing a wedding dress. On the inside gatefold, Joni is herself on skates, dressed as a black bird – crow or vulture. The seagull fixations have finally got her, and the result is oddly reminiscent of Richard Thompson's posing as a giant fly on his first album, though he at least was joking. Mind you, the songs are all credited to 'Crazy Crow Music' and the cover refers to a conjunction of two songs herein, 'Song for Sharon' and 'Black Crow'. A tacky sleeve for a wintry and deadly serious record.

Hejira was released in November 1976, and by December it had reached 13 in the USA album charts. Years' later, Barney Hoskyns asked Mitchell what she considered the most underrated music of her career. "I would say Hejira. It was not understood at all, but that was a really well written album. Basically it was kinda kissed off. It's a travelling album, it was written driving from New York to Los Angeles over a period of time, and people who take it with them, especially if they're driving across America, really find it gets to them." It works on the M25 just as well. Timothy White also finds the album misunderstood, praising its "other-worldly eroticism," which "treads on a metaphysical plain in terms of inner experience, dream states, psychic journeys and flights of imagination." Joni's reply is more matter of fact.

"Hejira came out of another of my sabbaticals, another time when I flipped out and quit show business for a time. This instance was in '76. I'd been out with Dylan's Rolling Thunder Revue, which was an amazing experience, studying mysticism and ego malformation like you wouldn't believe. Everybody took all their vices to the nth degree and came out of it born again or into AA. Afterward, I drove back across the country by myself, and I used to stay in places like the light-housekeeping units along the Gulf Coast. I gave up everything but smoking, and I'd run on the beach and hit health food stores. In New Orleans, I wore wigs and pawned myself off as someone else. Meanwhile, nobody knew where I was. I'd do these disappearing acts. I'd pass through some seedy town with a pinball arcade, fall in with people who worked on the machines, people staying alive, shoplifting, whatever. They don't know who you are: 'Why are you driving that white Mercedes? Oh, you're driving it across country for somebody else.' You know, make up some name, and hang out. Great experiences, almost like the prince and the pauper. So whenever possible during these breakdowns in my career I would pawn myself off as someone else, or go to some distant clime and intentionally seek out a strata of society I was sure I would have never have gotten near otherwise."

Joni had been cooling her heels on the beach at Neil Young's house one day - he also owns a lake and some mountains. Some friends had come by, and said they fancied driving across the country.

So they all did.

Reviewers had to come to terms with an album that was a radical departure, not just for Joni, but for rock music in general. Writing in *Rolling Stone*, Ariel Swartley thought that Mitchell had all but abandoned "melodies anyone can whistle" for long meditative verses which end in a single-line refrain. She has developed a "sexual roughness which she uses with precision," employing her voice to create continuities and climaxes. "The album is held together by the motion of her music, as unceasing and hypnotic as the freeways she describes in her songs." A road movie set to music.

The endless highway is an umbilical cord which relates people to events, like Shakespeare's Forest of Arden, a place where obligations of wealth and power can be momentarily forgotten. 'For Free', for real. The singer moves "between the long taught myth that a woman should make a total commitment to love, and the hard-won discovery that a career may require the same all-consuming passion." It is Joni's own uncertainty, "the alternating warmth and chill," which fascinates, and makes the album ultimately an optimistic one. Other critics concurred. Malcom Heyhoe found it her most musically adventurous outing to date, anchored by the interaction between her guitar, Pastorius's bass and Carlton's lead, which "twists and trembles like a snake wriggling furtively through dense undergrowth." As to Joni, she is "complex, mysterious, vulnerable and enigmatic, and much more too. She is human." You don't say!

In *Melody Maker*, Michael Watts explains the Arabic word 'hejira' as describing the flight of Mohammed from Mecca in 622 AD. Joni's flight is one into herself, a return to her confessional style, a coming to terms with her past. "She has never sounded more isolated, more enclosed within herself, than in these songs of perpetual, melancholic journeys across landscapes of almost supernatural detachment." This begs the

191

question of what the effect on Joni was of watching a clown-faced Dylan burning his way through 'Isis' – that endlessly strange song, which deals with just such a quest – every night with Rolling Thunder. Watts senses that something is dying in Mitchell's inner world. "It's a work of autumnal hues. The summer lawns fade from green to gold to brown." In *Sounds*, Tim Lott notices the sparseness of the arrangements – never more than four instruments on any track – and the way they punctuate rather than overwhelm the words. There are no solos. In turn, Joni's lyrics have been refocused back onto their author, while her voice is "utterly relaxed, completely intense." Lott himself resorts to poetry. Or at least very. Short. Paragraphs.

"Timeless and majestic, this is the music for the spirit.
Intellectual and inspired, this is music for the mind.
Rhythmic and subtle, this is music for the body.
The music of tomorrow, this is the tip of the iceberg."

Follow that!

The original title of *Hejira* was to have been *Travelling*. The album has an open-ended feel; songs loom at the listener from and back into silence, as if endless narratives, briefly overheard. There are two reference points in the whole of rock. Dylan's *Blood on the Tracks* also records the aftermath of a relationship breaking down, because of his own essential rootlessness, "to keep on keeping on," and the melancholy self-analysis which results. Unjustly obscure, Mighty Baby's second LP *A Jug of Love* – Sufi fuelled – has the same kind of resigned acceptance about life on the road, as a metaphor for life itself, and the same chugging backdrop: chord driven, on electric piano or guitar. Largely acoustic, but kind of propelled.

The album starts mid-stream. Joni hitches both roads and men. 'Coyote' is half trickster myth, half Reynardine, a predatory male, half animal in his sheer lust. He is also a country farmer, impure and simple. The song is, literally, a kiss-off, and the "white lines" Joni is addicted to have other meanings. The song is half spoken, half crooned, with the occasional deep, throaty laugh. The music sounds like traffic: take that, Kraftwerk. Images of flight begin here, with the hawk and the Eagles, also white line pioneers.

The lost flyer Amelia Earhart was the subject of (at least half of) the first LP from Plainsong, whose lead singer was Iain Matthews of *Woodstock* fame. The song on *Hejira* named after her opens with an echo of 'Woodstock', and ends referring to 'Both Sides Now'. Joni has spent her life looking at clouds, "from icy altitudes," but the haughty superstar described by Nick Kent has crashed to earth – like Amelia, like Icarus. The 'Eskimo' of the previous song. A swooning performance, with a particularly nice touch when the line "strings of my guitar" is followed by a solid strum. The music summons up both flight and frost, vibes tinkling like ice.

Joni's voice in 'Furry Sings the Blues' is full of quiet, sad respect, with Neil Young bringing his own mournfulness even to harmonica (a considerable feat), which makes Furry's bitterness all the more startling, a punch in the guts. A kind of distant cousin of 'For Free', and a reproof to all those – like Led Zeppelin – who have ripped off black culture. Next stop, *Mingus*. The Memphis blues, again. After all those images of flight, this one is about stasis: with only one leg and no teeth, Furry ain't going nowhere. Talking to Phil Sutcliffe, Joni described the genesis of the song. She had gone to see old Beal Street, which now looked like a Western ghost town, three blocks long. Cranes with wrecking balls stood, as if in mourning, and there was a modern movie theatre showing "black machine gun movies" right next to the statue of trumpet player WC Handy. As she drove along, a tumbleweed drifted across in front of the car.

"Standing in front of one of the many pawn shops was a guy in a purplish-blue shirt, bald, smoking a stogie. He looks at me and says "Oh Joni Mitchell?" I think, culturally this is impossible. I mentioned Furry Lewis and he says "Oh sure, he's a friend of mine. Meet me tonight and we'll go over and see him. Bring a bottle of Jack Daniels and a carton of Pall Mall cigarettes." Furry was in his eighties or nineties, and senile at this point. Lived in a little shanty in the ghetto. It was quite a nice visit until I said to him – meaning to be close to him – 'I play in open tunings too.' People must have ridiculed him, because he leaned upon the bed and said (hoarse old voice) 'Ah kin play in Spanish tonnin'.' Real defensive. Somehow or other I must have insulted him. He just said 'I don't like her' as I wrote in the song."

A Strange Boy is some kind of transubstantiation of her feelings for her lost daughter. Poet Thom Gunn writes the same kind of tributes to the brain-damaged on the streets of San Francisco, and the subject here sounds like a slightly more grown up version of Grace Slick's 'Lather'. He certainly isn't Jackson Browne. It's sung like a hymn, almost choking on the line about love, "the greatest poison and medicine of all." Joni is both flight and stasis, surf and the sand it thunders on. The final image is straight out of a late sixties horror film, or the acid-damaged bands of the time (the Virgin Sleep's 'Halliford House' a particular touchstone), the glass pupils of a thousand dolls. We're back with the young Joni watching Powell and Pressburger's *The Tales of Hoffmann*. Eyes everywhere.

Hejira namechecks Benny Goodman, of all people, and traces an icy path between birth and death, "the forceps and the stone," visiting a graveyard, the song finishing where it began. Even the music swings like a pendulum. The lack of any chorus adds to the unresolved quality of the whole piece. A song of endless winter. 'Song for Sharon' is a letter in verse, effortlessly anecdotal, music as flow – matching the song which moves from Staten Island to Manhattan to North Dakota to Maidstone – with a ghost of the theme tune to *M.A.S.H.*, of all things. Back to nylons, here worn under cowboy jeans, and after those songs of independence, this begins with a craving for bridal lace. Sorry to sound pretentious, but this has something of the sad harmonies of Wordsworth's 'Prelude'. Winter skaters appear in both, as a symbol of harmony and grace. The same theme appears in 'Anchorage' by Michelle Shocked. The single singer compares her life to a friend's domestic harmony, the kind Mitchell also sees in her own parents, or in her joky sleeve-note to engineer Henry Lewy, who "appears courtesy of Nado Lewy." Here Joni is a new Eve, a diamond snake around her arm, and the final image of "green pastures" could mean her own (forthcoming) marriage, or endless independence. 'Black Crow' comes back to the flying motif, mirroring Joni on her endless highway, with edgy backing, a hint of John Martyn's echoplexed guitar and white funk rhythms. Martyn has also made the journey from pure folk to dirty jazz, and her voice slurps like his, especially on the way it plunges downward on the repeated word "diving." Ted Hughes created a whole mythology in his poetry collection *Crow*, the beady-eyed scavenger as an endless, unconquerable force: here it doubles Joni's troubled soul.

Depending on the listener's mood, 'Blue Motel Room' can sound alluring or deeply fake. Joni's torch-song stylings here are overdone, as if she's singing in a false accent. It's a question of getting the register right – "Boom boom" is OK here; "pachyderm" is like a princess slumming. A song about going home, and about abandoning travel if the lover stops his midnight creep. The use of "blue" is self-referential. 'Refuge of the Roads' replaces the cliched acoustic bass of the previous track with Pastorius driving this road song onwards, playing lead lines on electric bass, so that the music is interestingly full of holes. Joni provides an abstract narrative over the top, drifting here and there, making wonderful use of the song's chorus line. The lyrics evoke not Wordsworth but Keats, a superfluity of sensuality. They move through spring into summer, ending with an image of the earth as a bright star in the sky. There is a Sufi-like sense of the singer's own insignificance, whereas on earlier LPs she was at the centre of the universe. Here, travel has not so much broadened the mind, as diminished self-esteem.

The old, arrogant Joni melts down on this record. Though she remains a free spirit, she is now strong – and modest – enough to allow men to take the initiative, or prove ungovernable, or offer sanctuary. In *The Hissing of Summer Lawns* they were a lost race, barely needed.

It is an album, also, that has grown with time. Steve Clarke considered that it "echoed the stark beauty of *Blue*, only this time around, Mitchell's rhythms derived from jazz and not rock." *Record Collector* thought it was perhaps Mitchell's finest achievement, intense but stoic. After all, the album begins with the words "no regrets." For Timothy White, it is a work "whereby she entered an entirely new realm of creativity, producing a ghostly, ethereal record of stalking, abandon and flight." Joni is exploring a dark eroticism. White compares her new style with the kind of direction in which Henry Miller was pushing Anais Nin, advising her to concentrate on the carnal and "leave out the poetry." My own favoured comparison is with the Tim Buckley of *Greetings from LA*, the double-edged ecstasy of "I talk in tongues." Like Joni, he learns how to unlock himself, a "sweet surrender" to everyday lovers, and to the sexual rush of the music.

Cameron Crowe asked Joni how the songs on *Hejira* came to be written. "Mostly while I was travelling in the car. That's why there were no piano songs. *Hejira* was an obscure word, but it said exactly what I wanted. Running away, honourably. It dealt with the leaving of a relationship, without the sense of failure that accompanied the breakup of my previous relationship. I felt that it was not necessarily anybody's fault. It was a new attitude." As to *Hejira*'s sleeve, the front cover combined – in an "incredibly difficult printing job" – shots by Joel Bernstein taken on a frozen lake with a studio portrait by Norman Seef. "Norman used a very difficult and strange psychological process. He'd try to get a shot of everyone he worked with, crying. He could be a cruel overlord, but he took great photographs. At that point, my stock was up. They let me do all sorts of expensive things in terms of art. On *Hissing*, we did this fancy embossing on the cover. Even Madonna couldn't get embossing these days."

On 25th November, 1976, Joni appeared at the Band's farewell concert, held at the Winterland, San Francisco. It was, self-consciously, the end of an era, with the new wave spitting from the wings. In a weird conjunction of marriage and funeral, 5000 celebrants sat down for a turkey dinner, then tables and chairs were removed, chandeliers lowered, and confetti showered the stage, as the Band revved up with a particularly rowdy 'Up on Cripple Creek'. Neil Young appeared, wearing a torn army jacket, and followed a breathtaking reading of 'Helpless' with a version of fellow Canadian Ian Tyson's 'Four Strong Winds'. For both, Joni provided discreet backing vocals, offstage. Indeed, Harvey Kuberlik felt that the Canadian trio of Young, Mitchell, and Robbie Robertson could "easily replace the current Beach Boy blend."

The Band had rehearsed onstage with Joni the previous night. Her own short set opened with 'Coyote', backed by the Band and the genuinely creepy Dr John on conga. It was a strange context in which to hear Garth Hudson's organ arpeggios – more usually associated with Bob Dylan's live apocalypses – and Robertson's wah wah guitar. The Band's relaxed shuffle seems to slow Mitchell down, making her vocals drag. The musical effect was much like an elephant dancing, extraordinary but uncomfortable. Nevertheless, 'Coyote' was a song which Barney Hoskyns thought "with its allusions to drugs and late night studio sessions" summed up the secret history of the Band. Pianist Richard Manuel was already well on the way to an early grave: he was later to hang himself after yet another gig on the revival circuit. Like Gene Clark or Gram Parsons, his was a primal melancholy not conducive to a long life.

Joni was as intolerant as their own guitarist of the Band's innate sloppiness and dislike of rehearsals, and had earlier expressed doubts about their ability to back her. Their arranger John Simon had written out charts for them to follow. Even so, their support on 'Shadows and Light' – an abstract song, seemingly at odds with the 'greatest hits' nature of the evening – was noticeably shaky, and perhaps her third song, 'Furry Sings the Blues' was not quite appropriate either. In its picture of a dying musical scene, it was spot-on, of course. Though her set diminished the pulse and excitement generated by louder acts, Hoskyns thought that at least she looked the part, "like a rock 'n' roll hippie maiden." Her blonde hair centrally parted, she wore a purple top and what looked to be a hand painted dress, with an Indian charm around her neck. With Neil Young, Mitchell joined the Band to supply backing harmonies on 'Acadian Driftwood', a song too delicate to flower in live performance, so omitted from both the triple album drawn from the event, and the resulting movie.

Martin Scorsese had been involved in the filming of *Woodstock*, and here he shot rock performances on 35mm – like they were real music, or something – and from seven camera angles. In the film of *The Last Waltz*, live music was interspersed with interviews, with events redrafted so that they made a coherent narrative. Thus, the Band's salty anecdotes about women on the road cuts directly into Joni – the least groupie-like of female singers – performing 'Coyote', about just such an encounter. The concert as filmed ends with a stage full of rock stars – dinosaurs waiting to turn into fossils – singing 'I Shall Be Released'. Joni shares a mike with Neil Young; stage right are Dylan and Van Morrison, with Ringo Starr on drums set up above the fray, Eric Clapton and Ron Wood on guitars. Also joining in are Neil Diamond, Ronnie Hawkins, Bobby Charles, and Paul Butterfield. Onstage, the music finally petered out at 2am, with a version of 'Don't Do It', then everyone went back to the hotel for an all-night party.

In November 1976, Joni had also taken part in a tribute to another endangered species, the 'California Celebrates the Whales Day' at the Memorial Auditorium, Sacramento, with the likes of John Sebastian,

Country Joe McDonald, and Fred Neil, whose song 'Dolphins' could not have been more appropriate. These two high-profile concerts presaged another retreat from the public spotlight. Mitchell was developing a reputation for unreliability. Talking to Cameron Crowe, she admits that she has probably cancelled more shows than she has actually played. "There was one time that I was onstage for one song. And I left. I felt very bad for the audience, but it was impossible for me to continue. It's not easy to leave an audience sitting there. I was still in bad health from going out on Rolling Thunder, which was mad. Heavy drama, no sleep – a circus. I'd requested before the show went out to get out of it. It was too late, I had bronchitis. A bone in my spine was out of place and was pinching like crazy. So I was in emotional pain. I was going out with someone in the band, and we were in the process of splitting up. We were in a Quonset hut, and the sound was just ricocheting. And I just made the decision."

This from someone who once scuffled for any gig going, and had once had a sharp hunger for any chance to push her career forward. The pressures on her were not only internal. 1977 was the year in which the new wave began to break through, with their virulently expressed antipathy to the Laurel Canyon elite. Elvis Costello's reaction to Linda Rondstadt's weak-kneed cover of his painful masterpiece 'Alison' was particularly intemperate. Joni herself was described as "looking like a Beverly Hills housewife" at the premiere of *The Last Waltz*. She too was now one of the enemy. At home, groups like the Dead Kennedys were even more disturbing to hippie conformity, their name alone inducing apoplexy in the otherwise terminally laid-back, while as to their single, 'California Uber Alles'... Anyone who wished to keep up trimmed trouser width and hair, exchanged cocaine for amphetamine sulphate, and expressed a newly-learnt abhorrence for the likes of Joni Mitchell, even though in musical terms she had helped lead the way. Leonore Fleischer's brief biography, published in the same year, is unsensational and to the point, but reads more like an obituary than a study of an artist in full flow.

The book ends by describing how her new music had taken Joni away from her customary subject matter, "the fragile nature of the heart and the complex byways it takes in its searches for another heart" – and into realms of expression that many of her fans "may be too perplexed to follow." In terms of experimentation, Joni's long-term followers had some even greater shocks in store.

Throughout 1977, Mitchell worked on her forthcoming album, a double, called, with obvious autobiographical intent, *Don Juan's Reckless Daughter*. The general view of this record nowadays was not too delicately put by Debbie Pead: Joni "seemed in imminent danger of disappearing up the proverbial anal passage." The album reached twenty-five in the US album charts in February 1978, earning her an eighth and final gold disc, and made Number Twenty in Britain. One surprise was the involvement of jazz heavyweight Wayne Shorter. Born in Newark, New Jersey in 1933, Shorter had played with everyone from Art Blakey and the Jazz Messengers to Miles Davis – joining his odyssey from *ESP* to *Bitches Brew* – to Weather Report. His early post-bop fierceness mutated into a tenderness that he made his own: Shorter's theoretical views on music were based on many conversations with John Coltrane, the man who turned the art-form upside down by concentrating on chords rather than tunes. A far cry from the polite white jazz of Tom Scott's LA Express, whose 1976 album (without Tom Scott) was the essence of bloodlessness. This was the real thing, and marked the beginning of many years of musical collaboration which took Mitchell far from the musical mainstream.

She recognised her luck in finding such a colleague: "I'm a painter first. I think about music in terms of paintings and shapes. Anyone who I add as a sweetening colour, I want them to play more than notes. I want them to play somewhat illustratively. I read music tediously, so I have no language as a musician, only the language of metaphor. Wayne was the first musician whose native tongue was metaphor." A world away from hide-bound rock players, whose imagination was too prosaic to help fuel the journey for the places she wanted her voice to go.

"The first record I put him on, he said 'What I'm going to play, it's like, you're in Hyde Park and there's a nanny and a baby and a boat and you're just nudging it.' And he played all these dotted lines. So that was a thrill because he was the first player who spoke to me in terms of illustration. I can't do a record without him now. I'll say to him 'OK Wayne, you're the bird here. Play me some high-heel shoes.' He knows exactly what I'm talking about. He's free to scribble and from the scribblings, this piece is magnificent, that's experimental. If it's not congealed, it pays four takes later. He knows I'm going to take his bad line out and keep his good line. And it's a wonderful way to work." Anyone who dares edit Shorter must themselves be possessed of an iron will, and a firm belief in their own musical capabilities. The thought of, say, Kate Bush taking such liberties makes the senses reel.

The transitional Afro-Latin rhythms of *Don Juan's Reckless Daughter* were inspired by a visit Joni made to the Rio de Janeiro Carnival. The album gained her a new audience among black writers and musicians. Charles Mingus loved its "nerviness," even its sleeve, with a blackfaced Joni dressed as a man. Strange currents swirled around and through the record, which has never had its proper critical due. John Guerin may have quit Joni's personal life, but his drums remain her musical bedrock.

Her new amour, Don Alias, is part of a four-man percussion unit, employing bongos, congas, claves, snare drums, sandpiper, shakers, ankle bells, bass drum and coffee cups. Goodbye Burundi, hello Brazil! Alias has a long musical pedigree, playing percussion on albums by Blood, Sweat and Tears, Ian Hunter, Tony Williams' Lifetime, Weather Report, Return to Forever, and the Mahavishnu Orchestra. He also plays on the debut LP by Jaco Pastorius, who again supplies electric bass, plus cowbells. Larry Carlton is back on lead guitar. New faces this time around include pianist Michel Colombier, a vocal line-up of disco queen Chaka Khan, Glenn Frey from the Eagles, and fellow Asylum Records artist John David Souther. A whole orchestra is at her disposal in New York. Joni seems to be leasing out some forms of control. She has brought in English jazz maestro Michael Gibbs as arranger, and uses studios in London and New York, as well as Hollywood. One track, 'The Tenth World', is written by the band, with Mitchell only on backing vocals.

The album itself abounds in mystery. Its title seems to refer to Joni as a female acting out the sexual freedom previously enjoyed by some men. Don Juan is a counterpart to Casanova. It is also the name given to the Yacqui Indian whom Carlos Castaneda – a graduate of UCLA – supposedly meets in his quartet of cult books. In these, psychedelic drugs are used to initiate the author into the spirit world. Central to Castaneda's revelations is that under the influence of peyote he finds that he can take flight, like the birds – an image which permeates Joni's songs. She must have been aware of his work – the first volume of which was published in 1968 – and, like the Eagles, must have taken his ideas on board. The album in question, for example, credits 'El Bwyd' for providing "the split tongued spirit." Joni also gives thanks to Krims for "part of the magic" – presumably he supplied the doves. The cover is set against a painted backdrop of orange desert and green sky. On the front, Joni, her skin dyed black, wearing a moustache, shades, and dressed like a pimp, is performing magic tricks. The teeth alone give the game away.

Joni had been walking down Hollywood Boulevard one day, looking for a costume for a Hollywood party, when, as she told Mick Brown, "all of a sudden this black kid goes by with a New York walk – you know, the diddybop, with one leg shorter than the other, and the hand curled back – and gave me this most radiant grin and said "Looking good sister." It was such a genuine, sweet smile; it woke up the spirit in me. I began walking behind him, imitating his walk. He just took me into this very fun-loving mood. So I thought, I'm going to go to this party not as him but as his spirit." So, dressed in a blue polyester suit, a cocaine spoon in the shape of a cocaine-spoon, an Afro wig and copious amounts of "Lena Horne pancake," Joni would attend parties as a black man. A kind of reverse of Michael Jackson's move in the opposite direction, rebuilding himself as white.

On the album cover, she also appears as herself, arms outstretched, clad in black top hat and a long, diaphanous dress patterned with teddy bears and a bare woman. A child in bow tie and sneakers stares at the ground. On the back cover is a childhood photo of the singer, banging a drum, dressed as a native Indian, and wearing feathers in her hair. Her expression is fierce, and a speech bubble is appended, containing one word: "How." A greeting from Hollywood Indians, everywhere. The album's inside cover contains more white doves in flight, but the real weirdness comes in the liner bags. On the first, Joni is a black disco dancer, in stack heels, with a speech bubble of "Mooslems, Moooslems! Hey Hey Hey." The real Joni replies "Baila Mi Rumba." The second bag has Joni turning her back, saying "In My Dweams We Fwy." A red balloon floats free.

As a possible clue to all this, and the general ambience of the times,

Joni told Sean O'Hagan that "I was never a big druggie, but I had my moments. I wrote some songs on cocaine, 'cause initially it can be a creative catalyst. In the end it'll fry you, kill the heart. I found it sent all the energy up my spine into the top of the brain. It kills the soul and gives you delusions of grandeur as it shuts down your emotional centre. Perfect drug for a hit man but not so good for a musician." The musical influence, at least, rubbed off. O'Hagan's band, the High Llamas, are currently recycling late-sixties California harmonies into a creamy concoction stuffed with melody and string quartets. One presumes that the pun in the band's name is completely intended!

The album was officially released in Britain in the first week of January, 1978. The critical reaction was muted, and, in some cases, downright hostile. In *Rolling Stone*, Janet Maslin's review was subtitled 'Gambling and Losing'. Joni "has never been an interesting chronicler of experience other than her own. There's nothing said here that she hasn't said better before, except those things she should have kept to herself." Joni sounds drowsy and disengaged.

Michael Watts finds the album "if not a failure, then certainly not a conspicuous success." Melodies "are just not there." *Sounds* gave *Don Juan* five stars, which indicated "a very important platter." According to Tony Mitchell, his near namesake had used her travels to create an early kind of world music, "styles encountered during sojourns in exotic places." Writing for the *Sunday Times*, Derek Jewell found her "unique, magical, adventurous, and, since perfection in the pop world would defeat its nature, humanly fallible." He was also forced to admit that she had problems creating a proper balance "between the demands of the lyrics and the structure of the music." Perhaps the most interesting comment – which I would take more positively than perhaps it was intended – is by Janet Maslin. For her, the album is built on the premise that "blacks and Third World people have more rhythm, more fun, and a secret mysterious viewpoint" that Joni presumes to share.

Originally a double album, no one side of which exceeded a measly 17 minutes – the whole thing lasting less than an hour – and now a double CD (available in Britain on import only) *Don Juan's Reckless Daughter* could easily have been cut to just one, to its artistic benefit.

Its running order is also ill-conceived, with tracks apparently placed at random. The album is about a meeting place of cultures, black and white.

The opening track, 'Cotton Avenue', is understated at first – with acoustic guitar and wordless vocals – then Pastorius's electric bass thuds in. The music is full of self-confidence. The "shiny people" who attend this black juke joint are presented unironically, unlike in the later REM track. It all sounds unreal, like something read from a book. Fast strummed guitar leads into 'Talk to Me', which starts with Joni drunk, peeing in a car park, and ends with her smitten by the strong, dark, silent type of man (Don Alias?). Her attempts at jive-talk are deeply embarrassing, though. No-one ever called Shakespeare Willy the Shake, she misquotes his line from Hamlet's soliloquy – it's fortune, not romance – and as to her imitation of a chicken squawk... ! The whole thing is gawkily adolescent.

'Jericho' was slinky and smooth on *Miles of Aisles*, lots of wah wah guitar, electric piano, and a swooning vocal. The studio version here is sharper, more percussive, the singing more desperate. Wayne Shorter's soprano sax drifts in and out of the mix, turning Joni's vocals into a conversation. A song about willing on a new love, while fully aware of how fragile and difficult the whole process can be. If the previous set of lyrics misquoted – and demeaned – Shakespeare, this song emulates him.

Turn over the (vinyl) disc, and it's straight into 'Paprika Plains'. Piano notes fall like raindrops, then the song starts with rain coming down on the kind of dance hall pictured in 'Cotton Avenue'. Joni goes into free-association and back to her Canadian girlhood (and vocally down to a throaty growl), banging a tin drum like the hero of Gunter Grass's novel. The music crests up to two climaxes, like thunder and lightning, then into a long instrumental passage, acoustic jazz-flecked piano and sonorous orchestra, like something out of Gershwin.

The lyric sheet (but not the record) extemporises here into a jumbled vision of native Canadians camped out on empty plains, their enclave viewed from a helicopter, then an atomic blast, then the earth as a beach ball, childhood memories of shuttered blinds, Joni's sharp talons slashing the globe to see a river winding like a snake, and natives with grim faces. All this has to be imagined – perhaps it would have been better recited – and then Joni's voice comes in again, and we're back at the dance hall, with her giving herself to her new man: "I'm floating back to you." A crash of drums, and Wayne Shorter lets rip into a meaty solo, which dies away before he's really had time to unwind, then back comes the orchestra, underpinned by Pastorius's bass, for a brief coda. As a masterwork, it isn't quite grand enough, and the orchestra sounds tinny.

'Otis and Marlena' is set in a Miami from hell, where old people sun themselves like tortoises and have face-lifts. Joni's voice has an unpleasant, snobby sound to it, to match the song. Meanwhile, "Muslems stick up Washington" – featuring military drums – perhaps suggesting the slow death of the American empire, except that the line has no resonance, so is hardly alarming. This song leads straight into 'The Tenth World', not so much an instrumental as a rhythm track. If one is charitable, this is a fascinating polyrhythmic exercise which predicts the later rise of World music. If not, it sounds like Santana warming up over breakfast. Nothing really develops. It all sounds very Hollywood.

The percussion is more reined in, and ominous, on the next song. Joni first performed 'Dreamland' with the Rolling Thunder Revue: Roger McGuinn was so impressed that he recorded it himself. The vibrant "dreamland" of black culture is compared to the dead world of ageing whites in 'Otis and Marlena', and the snow-deadened New York to which she flies back. Chaka Khan throws in another voice, and the two circle, like ritual dancers. On an earlier album, Woodstock was a dream "some of us had" and dreams have driven the last three songs here as, in turn, vision, self delusion, and escape.

The album continues to perk up – too late – on side four. The title track, which should in any logical world have come first, has the depth and resonance of Joni's best work. The setting is again Paprika Plain. Though over wordy – the song tells rather than shows, a common poetic mistake – it identifies the underlying tension in Mitchell's work. Images of flight (the eagle) against the hypnotically primeval (the snake). And it's got nice bass booms from Pastorius, who sounds like he's sinking depth charges. Joni's vocal is eager, sexy, intimate, urgent: I always get a tingle down my spine when I hear the way she delivers "skin to skin." Chrissie Hynde's whole vocal style could have been taken from this track. 'Off Night Backstreet' is a cheerful song of jealousy, set to a swing, and with an almost subliminal orchestra. Lyrically, the song deserts the seaside for the city: Joni becomes – in terms of love – the kind of urban backstreet along which she walks on the back cover of her first LP. She is back in New York, no longer ingenue, but something close to a hooker, just as the man here is virtually a pimp. The rhythms, and Joni's drifting vocal – the way she stretches out "drain" as if through clenched teeth – are 100% sexual. The album is climaxing at last.

The final track, 'The Silky Veils of Ardor', is post-coital, with Joni purring like Eartha Kitt. Its use of folk song motifs is also fateful, and the song reads like an epitaph. Back to just Joni and her guitar, but with a sense of innate rhythm, and jazz inflections a million miles away from her first three LPs. Thematically, it's a return to *Paprika Plains* and *Dreamland*, where – in turn – time and space yield up visions. This song even sounds as if it is sung half-asleep. It gives the same sense of eavesdropping on a private, interior monologue as Van Morrison's *Veedon Fleece* album, or Dylan's song 'Dark Eyes'. The album ends with a "pretty little white dove" – image of peace, and magic tricks, and the species which Noah sent out to seek landfall. On the inside cover art, this single bird becomes a flock, flying towards the viewer. "In my dreams we fly" – but just as all art is a waking dream, the dream here is incomplete and lacks development or any kind of emotional centre. The baby talk on the inner bags – "in my dweems we fwy" – is just that: infantile. The album as a whole reflects the front cover; there are no real mysteries here. What we perceive instead is a series of conjuring tricks. Technique, not witchcraft.

Don Juan's Reckless Daughter is part of a larger magic trick, a disappearing act, but this time for real. We are losing sight of Joni as a central character, and this dissolving of self-identity is to remain true of all her later work. None of her later projects will ever quite have the inner logic of *Blue* or *The Hissing of Summer Lawns*, or their force.

Rock history has not been kind to this album. Debbie Pead in *Record Collector* – whose articles embalm their subjects in the very finest aspic – found that "the poetic and occasionally pretentious profusion of words" confirmed the belief of many that she should have stuck with *Blue*. Dave Marsh thought that it was a double album that should have been a single disc, "choking with overblown ideas and an obsessively loose musical framework." What he did admire was the "spirit of romantic and artistic wanderlust that percolates through her work." Bill Flanagan really hit the nail on the head. This confessional poet was now putting to music "a life of success, travel, mature love affairs and temptations," a world true to her, but with which most of her audience could no longer identify. "When Mitchell went from 'I' to singing about characters with names, listeners thought she was making fun of lights less bright than she – although Mitchell eyed her creations with no more scrutiny or harshness than she'd ever used to describe herself." Here she is, describing a world of Foster Grants and Pagliacci summer frocks, "breathing an air so rarefied that the songs had little to do with the lives of all those listeners stuck on the ground."

The fact that she was doing so satirically, and predicting the rise of the yuppies, who lived by such trademarks as if holy relics, is lost on Flanagan, but his analysis is spot-on. Joni was now a star, shining down from a different firmament.

Charles Mingus first contacted Joni in April 1978, with a view to her taking part in his adaptation of TS Eliot's 'Four Quartets', a poem which itself adopts musical form. Mingus, a legendary bassist and jazz composer, had become a recluse, fighting the effects of Lou Gehrig's disease, a form of sclerosis. As Timothy White recognised, the two musicians were fellow spirits. Both were natural born rebels. "Having built his reputation on left turns, such as 1963's *Hora Decubitus*, on which he deconstructed free-jazz sonorities and 12-bar blues while abandoning conventional beat concerns, Mingus was sympathetic to Mitchell's periodic urge for going AWOL artistically." For all that, Joni found any attempt to condense Eliot's tightly wound verse impossible, declaring "I'd rather condense the Bible."

Mingus called again. He had written what were to prove his final six melodies – he titled them 'Joni I-VI' – and wanted her to write lyrics. Critical reaction to her own work, accusations that she had lost the ability to write good tunes, might have persuaded her to agree. Mitchell spent over a year on the project, the first time she had given up sole musical control, and worked mainly at her new home, an apartment in New York's Regency Hotel. Mingus died in Mexico, aged 56, on January 5th, 1979, putting even more pressure on Joni to come up with a fitting tribute, which was written and recorded by late spring of the same year. "Mingus wanted his stock to go up before he died, here was an element of choosing me to write his epitaph, help ensure he got a bigger funeral." She included tape recordings of his voice, to link tracks, and titled the album after her dead colleague. It was not a venture likely to make anyone's fortune.

Joe Smith, Chairman of the newly amalgamated Elektra/Asylum, was impressed by the result, if puzzled as to how to deal with it. "She has taken a chunk out of her career and accomplished something truly monumental. When we received this album, I got on a conference call and talked with all our promotion men. If any radio station calls itself a trend-setter, it must recognise this album and Charles Mingus. I'm having a contest for my promotion men. First prize is they get to keep their jobs." Joni talked to Cameron Crowe a few months later. He asked her if Mingus could be as difficult as his reputation suggested. "Immediately I felt this kind of sweet giddiness when I met him. Like I was in for some fun. He teased me a lot. He called me hillbilly; it was charming. We went through some of the old songs. 'Goodbye Pork Pie Hat' was the one we decided on immediately. Charlie put on this one record and just before he played it, he said 'Now this song has five melodies going on at once.' I said 'Yeah, I bet you want me to write five different sets of words for each one of the melodies, right?' And he grinned and said 'Right.' He put on the record, and it was one of the fastest, smokingest things you ever heard, with all these melodies going on at once."

Joni was not cast in the role of easing Mingus's fear of dying. "No, that was up to him. It wasn't in that personal role that I was his comforter. It was a professional partnership with a lot of affection. But one day I called him up and I said 'How are you, Charles?' I never really asked him too much about his illness, but that day I did. And he said, 'Oh, I'm dying. I thought I knew how to do it, but now I'm not too sure.' At that point I had three songs to finish, and I thought, Oh boy, I want him to be in the studio when I start to cut them. I want his approval on this. I want him to like my direction. This was a unique position. I've never worked for somebody else before. Although in the treatment of the music, it was more my version of jazz. As far as the music was finally recorded. He's more traditional in a way – anti-electronics and anti-avant-garde. I'm looking to make modern American music. So I just hoped that he would like what I was doing. I was taking someplace where I would be true to myself. It was never meant as a commemorative album while we were making it. I never really believed completely that he was going to die. His spirit was so strong."

Before his death, Mingus had heard everything apart from 'God must be a Boogie Man', based on the first four pages of his autobiography, *Beneath the Underdog*. Joni had to find a new way of writing: "I had to find my own phrasing for the notes. I had a block for three months. It's hard for me to take someone else's story and tell only his story in a song." She solved this by writing what stirred her own pulse. Mingus had showered her with information about the legendary Lester Young. He used to tap dance in his parents' band, and himself married a white woman. Together, they travelled through the deep south, at a time when such things were virtually taboo. All wonderful material, but it didn't intersect with Joni's own life. She needed something out of her own experience with which to anchor this raw information. What she wanted, and got, was a miracle.

"Then something very magical happened. One night, Don Alias and I – he plays congas on the album, and he and I have been very close for the period of the last two years – were on the subway, and I got off, I don't know why, two stops early. We came up into this cloud of steam coming out of a New York manhole. Two blocks ahead of us, under these orangeish New York lights, we see a crowd gathered. So we head towards the crowd. When we get up on it, it's a group of black men, surrounding two small black boys. It's about midnight, and the two boys are dancing this very robot-like mime dance. One of the guys in the crowd slaps his leg and says 'Isn't that something. I thought tap dancing was gone forever.' Immediately I'm thinking about Lester Young. They were dancing under one of those cloth awnings that goes out to the curb of a bar. I look up – and the name of the bar is the Pork Pie Hat. The music they were dancing to was jazz coming off the jukebox inside. There were big blown-up pictures of Lester Young all around the place. It was wild. So that became the last verse of the song. In my mind, that filled in a piece of the puzzle. It had the past and the present, and the two boys represented the future, the next generation. To me, the song then had a life of its own."

*M*ingus was released in July 1979. It made number 17 in the American album charts, and 24 in Britain. Joni later told *Folk Roots*: "I lost my airplay when I made the *Mingus* album. I did some of my best work at a time when I had fallen from grace." Her current partner, Don Alias, again appears on congas, joined from *Don Juan* by Wayne Shorter and Jaco Pastorius. The drummer this time around is Weather Report's Pete Erskine. Herbie Hancock (like Shorter, a long-term Miles Davis collaborator) plays electric piano, and Emil Richards percussion. The final credit is simply to 'Wolves'. No Musicians Union fees, and years before the Hollywood movie, sharing top billing with Kevin Costner.

Recording sessions again spanned the country, between Hollywood and Hendrix's old stamping ground, the Electric Lady Studios in New York. Joni's sleeve notes talk of being immediately captivated by his "joyous mischief." Mingus found her "dog-paddling around in the currents of black classical music" and pushed her fully in. The actual recording process was challenging. Each song was recorded three or four times, and musicians contributing were a virtual roll-call of contemporary jazz: Tony Williams, Stanley Clarke, Gerry Mulligan, John McLaughlin, and Jan Hammer. Mingus's original drummer, Danny Richmond, was originally cast in the role of narrator. If ever Joni gets the box-set treatment, perhaps some of these lost tapes will surface. Joni describes the final versions as "audio paintings," and to these she has added archive tapes supplied by Mingus's widow. The man remained a magician to the end. On the day of the jazz maestro's cremation, 56 sperm whales "beached themselves on the Mexican coastline and were removed by fire." Mingus's ashes were carried to the source of the Ganges, and scattered there at dawn.

Such coincidences fuelled Joni's own imagination, but the resulting album spluttered rather than flamed in the review columns. For *Dark Star* magazine, a quarterly English love letter to West Coast music, Cliff Ash searched for something positive to say. The album might not make much sense now, but it would be "a grower," revealing its treasures over time. Oddly enough, he turned out to be right, but he was a lone voice at the time. The critics had turned nasty. Michael Watts saw Mitchell trying for a new, more personal style, "and finding only idiosyncrasy." For John Gaskell, it was particularly tragic that a songwriter second only to Lennon and McCartney should release such "a dreary product." Angus MacKinnon admires her bravery, reaching high "only to find ironic clouds, vague and tantalising shapes and reflections. She must be disappointed." The main problem is that she can't sing jazz, sounding like the would-be country singer at the end of the movie *Nashville*, trying to front a gospel choir. For Sandy Robertson, the album is "self-consciously precious, a maddeningly white attempt at blackness." Joni's work is "lacking in abandon." The cover paintings are more intense than the music.

That, at least, is undeniable. The front cover is subtitled 'Abundance and Decline' and is pure abstract expressionism, with two figures, who could be Joni and Mingus, half lost in a swirl of colour. There is a strong erotic charge to the image, with lots of surging white paint. The figure on the right is either sucking or blowing some kind of white tube, while the figure on the left seems to be displaying a naked male member – unless that's just my own dirty mind. It could be a carrot! Whatever, the painting captures the explicit hedonism of Mingus's own autobiography, in which he is seduced in a upmarket brothel, in Laurel Canyon, of all places. Less contentious is the back cover image, a poignant take on the musician sitting in his wheelchair, back turned on the viewer, lost underneath a white floppy hat, and hiding in the shade. He gazes towards what just might be a swimming pool. Inside are two more vibrant images of Mingus, full face. In the second, he has the look of Falstaff, in the first he is lost in artistic contemplation, in the middle of his music, just like the photo of Joni on the front cover of *Blue*.

As to the music, it holds up far better than expected, unified in sound and tone. Joni has invented, single-handed, the tribute album format which would prove so popular a decade down the tracks. As an original Joni Mitchell product, it still disappoints: as a side project, it is fascinating, and exudes honesty. If it had been unreleased at the time, like the Beach Boys' *Smile* or Prince's *Black Album*, it would have accrued a cult following, scratchy bootleg tapes passed around between consenting fans in private, like slivers of the holy cross. The closest parallel, bizarre as it might seem, is the work of Gavin Bryars, in particular *The Sinking of the Titanic*, where an intellectually fascinating exercise is also aurally of swooning beauty.

The album starts with a short recording of Mingus's birthday party (his favourite expletive half-blanked out on the lyric sheet). The first song, 'God must be a Boogie Man', is taken virtually verbatim from the opening pages of *Beneath the Underdog*. For obvious reasons, Joni changes the spelling of 'boogie' from Mingus's original 'bogie', which suggests something unpleasant up his nose. The music captures something of the flavour of the book, a rumbunctious saga of childhood racism and under-age sex in a downtown Los Angeles far removed from Mitchell's usual take on that city. The narrative continues through musical precocity, pimping (very politically incorrect these days) and incarceration in Bellevue mental hospital. Musically, Pastorius's bass counterpoints Joni's fruity vocals, and ragged chorus.

A short 'rap' – which then indicated a dialogue, not a rhyming rant – on Mingus's funeral, and planned longevity (which is not to be), then 'A Chair in the Sky' opens, like *Paprika Plains*, with rainfall. Mitchell becomes Mingus, playing bebop in New York. Plangent electric piano, as Joni sing-talks, her voice taking on the tones of Shorter's sax. 'The Wolf That Lives in Lindsey' is about a heavy-duty killer who runs amok through "the hills of Hollywood," clearing human wreckage. Real wolves, and heavily-strummed guitar, evoke nightmare. The rap "It's a Muggin'..." is a (very) short vocal between Joni and Charles, then there's the slow swoon of 'Sweet Sucker Dance'. It's a song which reinvigorates an old cliche, and her vocal isn't quite jazz, flying over the music like a bird. Deeply pleasurable, if largely meaningless. Mingus recalls that he always had spare change, then straight into the gambler's tale of 'The Dry Cleaner from Des Moines' – a song that gives new meaning to being "cleaned out." Big band jazz, a virtuous flourish from Pastorius, and Joni's tongue-twisting singing, full of slang. Exhilarating. Shorter comes into his own, kicked on by the superb rhythm section; Joni is a whole chorus of sirens.

'Goodbye Pork Pie Hat' has been much criticised, and the Billie Holiday imitation at first edges dangerously close to pastiche, or performing in blackface. But that's the point of this song, still chancy, about miscegenation, the marriage of black and white. Joni puts real emotion into the line about embracing her black lover in the streets of contemporary New York, thinking what could have been their fate in earlier times. The whole project becomes a matter of blood and

211

passion, not an exercise. The "we" in the last verse is certainly Joni, not some construct, and the sight of black children tap dancing comes like an epiphany, as she emerges – literally – from the underground. Wayne Shorter plays at being Lester Young, street noise replicates the sounds that once emerged from Birdland, and in the song Mingus lives on, down in Mexico, slowly being healed. With his death, the tune's title takes on an extra resonance. In turn, this LP throws light back onto *Don Juan's Reckless Daughter*.

On that album, too, Joni had dared to cross racial and sexual boundaries. Even its baby language can be re-read as some kind of multi-cultural common language, accessible to all. The photograph of Joni as a child, dressed as a native Indian, suddenly becomes of enormous import (in other photographs of the time she dresses as a cowboy, covering both bases). One thinks, too, of Neil Young, once dubbed a Hollywood Indian because of his love for dressing up in feathers and buckskin, and that mysterious, autobiographical song 'Broken Arrow'. 'Paprika Plains' was obviously intended as some kind of major statement, in which she either imagines or invents her first contact with races other than the white settlers from whom she herself descended. The dream therein, literally unspoken, is of contact with another civilisation. Suddenly the African roots of *The Hissing of Summer Lawns* and the Moorish pilgrimage of *Hejira* also fall into place, earlier journeys into the Third World. Joni was blazing these happy trails years before Paul Simon was to set his poetry to a beat drawn from Africa – on *Graceland* (perhaps itself an unconscious echo of Joni's song 'Dreamland') – and Latin America.

The *Mingus* album was the culmination of this journey, communication on equal terms and with every sense working overtime, with someone of a different race, sex, and musical background. It is a baton that has not yet been picked up, although collaborations like those between Ali Faka Toure and Ry Cooder follow its lonely example. The problem is that, for all its ambition, the actual album did not free either of the two imaginations present. As Angus MacKinnon commented in *New Musical Express*, it would perhaps have been more interesting to see what the two would have made of Eliot's 'Four Quartets', giving each the chance to create anew, and meet midway. The album we have is ennobled, but limited, by the weight of respect that

Joni was obliged to convey, with Mingus so newly dead, his ashes so recently scattered.

Later, Bill Flanagan felt that for all her good intentions, Mitchell's lyrics sometimes obscured Mingus's melodies, rather than opening them up. Roland Kirk had also written words for 'Goodbye Pork Pie Hat', but they "didn't step on Mingus's mood." Debbie Pead watched it reduce Joni's music to "a minority interest", which, perhaps as a result, was her last venture into modern jazz. As she told *Rolling Stone*, "I started working in a genre that was neither this nor that. People didn't know where I fit in anymore, so they didn't play me at all. I was considered an expatriate from pop music, meanwhile the jazz folks thought 'Who is this white chick?'." There is an interesting parallel here with Julie Driscoll, who went from straight pop to a wondrous blend of soul, blues and psychedelia on the *Streetnoise* double – with organist Brian Auger – then plunged deep into the world of improvised jazz. Which is where she remains, working with her husband Keith Tippett, and playing experimental music of wild, wordless extravagance, to small but select audiences.

Meanwhile, Mingus's widow Susan gathered together some of his old alumni as 'Mingus Dynasty', to tour his music worldwide. With jazz revolutionary Charlie Haden depping on bass, the band recorded an album for Elektra, *Chair in the Sky*, which takes back three tunes from Mitchell's vocal versions, and restores them as instrumentals. Is there a small hint of reproof in Susan Mingus's comments in June 1980? "The Joni Mitchell album was a start. And Mingus would have gotten great joy out of all this. But at the same time, it underlines the importance of keeping the music going the way that Mingus would have played it."

Bill Flanagan talked to Joni about the long-term effects of this collaboration, which she regarded as crucial. "Charlie's work was based on blues – with this wide polyphonic harmony that I had gradually gotten into, ironically because of the open tunings. Those tunings originally came from black blues players, but I had modernised them by putting them into the very broad twentieth-century harmony. I don't think up until that point I could really sing rock 'n' roll. Now my *roots* have changed, I can feel that as if it's part of my being. It's not pretentious. It's a spirit." Like a plant, or a multi-national corporation,

Joni was looking for growth. She assumed that she was in sync with her times, a leader of fashion, and that others would follow. First, she tried to play with rock musicians, as she pushed her work from folk to folk-rock. "They couldn't play my music because it's so eccentric. They would try, but the straight-ahead 2/4 rock 'n' roll running through it would steamroller right over a bar of 3/4. People figure out how to play my chords. The way I play them in open tunings you can do it all with one finger. So with a simple left hand I was getting these chords that I liked the sound of, but which look like minor ninth inversions. Write these chords out and they have long names."

Instead, she found herself out in the wilderness, having escaped any easily identifiable category, into which she could be slotted. "I've never been a jazz musician, but I have been called jazz in the rock 'n' roll press. And jazz – they don't want to have anything to do with me. 'Who is this Joni-come-lately?' So I'm a person without a country now." It's particularly ironic, therefore, that when a record executive first heard her later album *Dog Eat Dog*, he exclaimed "I really like this one. It's jazzy!" Suddenly jazz was high fashion! Mitchell: "Sting, being a huge pop star and craving virtuosity, has now made the possibility of playing with virtuosos and still being popular kind of hip. It was always my optimism that eventually we would have an American music – it wouldn't be all divided into these little cliquey camps. It seems to me a crime against the artistic impulse to persecute a person for being broad-minded."

Tom Scott was the first musician whom she could tell, "you're playing the Doppler effect; just give me straight lines," and he would immediately respond. She remembers with a shudder how rock musicians would patronise her. "They'd laugh. 'Aww, isn't that cute? She's trying to tell us how to play.' Never negatively, but appeasingly." It was Russ Kunkel who finally said "Joni, you better get yourself a jazz drummer." But what has happened to all the tunes? "The album with Charles is incredibly melodic. What it is, is more melody."

chapter 5:

Lost In The Eighties

Rock 'n' roll stars used to have a heyday of a few months, before being shunted onto the revival circuit, or back to the car wash. Joni's peers – Dylan, Cohen, Neil Young, Lou Reed, Richard Thompson – had a different kind of problem: how exactly to "keep on keeping on." Icons of the late sixties, they had to work out a way to keep their music relevant, and to survive a climate in which all their ideals were undermined. Exactly what does a spokes(wo)man for a generation do, when that generation is moving into middle age. Unlike, say, Elvis who simply atrophied and grew paunchy, all the above had the priceless gift of writing their own songs. They could remain in the shadows if they so chose, endlessly reinterpreted by younger musicians. The real problem came with live performance, where demands for 'greatest hits' conflicted with their own desire to move on. Dylan squared the circle by continuing to reinterpret his old songs so radically that sometimes it was difficult to recognise them, while the whole 'Unplugged' craze covered both bases. As an artist (as yet) neither the subject of a tribute album or an MTV acoustic retread, and who now rarely performs live or broadcasts, Joni's path has been a particularly lonely one.

For the next fifteen years, her work was to be shunned by radio programmers and fashionable journalists. Only a small coterie of fans followed her years in the media wilderness, while she quietly produced some of the most tuneful and relevant music of her whole career. As Joni quipped in 1988, "the worst curse I ever heard was a Yiddish curse which said 'May you be wise among fools.' What a horrible feeling." She also tangled with the bureaucrats, an enemy as coiled and slithery as any snake that ever hissed on summer lawns. With eleven of her backing musicians, Joni was forced to contest a costly legal battle over tax. The California State Board of Equalisation had alleged, in a test case, that she owed an additional 15 per cent of her income from the years 1972-1976, her commercial peak.

An artistic control clause in her recording contract was interpreted as meaning that her musicians were taxable independents. Literally, the cost of being free. Being in the right, Mitchell won her money back, but only after ten years battling an implacable and tireless foe. Later, the Geffen company – a private bureaucracy – put a stop on Joni's royalties, setting against them 'unrecouped monies', spent on promoting her 'product'. It is difficult to believe that this would have happened had she not been seen to be in commercial decline. Geffen later refunded the cash, but trust cannot be won back so easily. It was a colder, more grasping world out there, and Joni had been wise to retain complete ownership of her own songs, her primary source of income, and her own private pension fund. The dispute with Geffen intensified when Joni learned via complaints from fans that tracks on her earlier albums had been rescheduled on cassette "with no artistic reasoning behind it at all, so that tracks would more easily fit the format." A typical corporate bungle, and one particularly galling to somebody who programmed her albums so carefully.

Anger is the best spur to complacency. With typical self-awareness, Joni addressed such issues direct in a major interview, right at the hinge of her career. She put an end to the civil war with *Rolling Stone* magazine, speaking with Cameron Crowe over three days in 1979. Sitting on a sofa in her manager's LA office, dressed simply in a tan blouse, slacks and no makeup, Joni talked rapidly, while structuring her words and thoughts "like a third draft."

She announced from the start that she would censor some of her replies, for the sake of her parents: "very old-fashioned and moral people." One presumes, therefore, that they had also never listened to her albums, as graphic as any in rock. Joni also attempted to retune her public image. Introspection was only part of it. Away from work, "I love to dance. I'm a rowdy. I'm a good timer." As in her songs, she illustrates this with an anecdote. It is an everyday story about media folk, set in an exclusive club in Hollywood.

"Linda Rondstadt was running through the parking lot being pursued by photographers, Jerry Brown was upstairs, Bob Dylan was full of his new Christian enthusiasm – 'hey Jerry, you ever thought of running this state with Christian government?' Lauren Hutton was there, Rod Stewart. There were a lot of people and this little postage stamp of a dance floor. These are all people who dance, in one way or another, in their acts. I just wanted to dance, so I asked a couple of people to dance with me and nobody would. They were all incredibly shy. It was just like the fifties, when none of the guys would dance." Joni goes to the ladies' room, where a friend confides that her peers thought of Joni as "a very sad person," and so someone to avoid. She is a victim of her own press.

As to the new wave, then sweeping her own career far out to sea, "I understand the punk movement. It reminds me of a very exciting time in my own life. It's nothing new – I was a punk in the fifties." So much of music is politics, the equivalent of kissing babies. Even among the LA scene, Joni feels a kind of outsider. "The Eagles have really stretched out thematically. Jackson Browne writes fine songs. Linda Rondstadt is very special. I'm a great appreciator of all those people. But at a certain point, I was denied any kind of positive feedback from a lot of sources. Like I go to a party and everybody shows up. I figure everybody must have a tape of their album on 'em, I figure 'Let's sit down and play these things.' A lot of times I would be the only one who would end up being that pushy."

Looking to the future, "I don't know where I'm going. I never really do. My songs could come out any shape at this point. I am thinking now of keeping it simpler. I feel myself returning more to basics and to my roots in folk music. But I don't even know what that simplicity might turn out like."

Geographically, Joni is now "spread across this continent in a very disorganised manner," with residences which match her own progress, and her moods. The rural estate she owns in Canada is "wild and natural." Her apartment in New York brings her "directness," the daily challenges of street encounters. As for her home in Bel Air, "California represents old friends and health. I love to swim. If there's anything that I love about this place here it's the luxury of being able to swim, which is like flying to me. I could get in the pool, float around for about two hours and never touch the sides. That's better than any psychiatrist to me. I'm working out my body, working out my lungs – the poor things are blackened with cigarette smoke – and looking at nature. I don't have that in New York."

Crowe challenges her on this, asking whether great art comes from hunger and pain, and if so, how can she justify her wealth and comfort? "Pain has very little to do with environment. You can be sitting at the most beautiful place in the world, and not be able to see it for pain. So no, misery knows no rent bracket (laughs). In my life, I've confronted a lot of my devils. A lot of them were pretty silly, but they were incredibly real at the time. I don't feel guilty for my success or my lifestyle."

More important is the fact of her own mortality, as for us all: "In my lifetime, I've had so many brushes with death myself, not that I'm saying that I'm not afraid to die – of course I still am. Afraid of it. 'Cause it's so final. As far as a ceremony, of how I would like it to be treated, I'm not really sure. I mean, it's an inevitable thing. I'm confident that I'll live to be in my eighties. So I have a more immediate problem than confronting death." This is how to age gracefully, especially difficult when you are embedded in people's memories as forever young. Joni recently met some Hollywood veterans, *en masse*. "They were drinking toasts to Marilyn Monroe, and there were lots of stories flying around about people who they had known. There was a tremendous amount of glamour represented. *Well tended* glamour. The fourth face-lift. Maintaining the youthful silhouette. I looked around and thought, is *this* the way that we must go in this town? Is our hippie philosophy going to surrender to this?"

At the age of 36, she must also confront childlessness, at least as that is publicly perceived. No mention yet of her illegitimate daughter. "That's a constant battle with me. Is my maternity to amount to a lot of black plastic? Am I going to annually bear this litter of songs and send them out into the marketplace and have them crucified for this reason. In a few years I'll be past a safe childbearing age. I wouldn't just frivolously get pregnant and bring a child into this world. The children of celebrities have been notoriously troubled."

Crowe carries on with the zeal of a professional analyst. What does she think of Dave Crosby's quote that she is "about as modest as Mussolini"? Joni smiles, and shakes her head. "I like to work myself up to a state of enthusiasm about anything I do; otherwise, what's the point? I'm not talking about arrogance. That's probably where Crosby's quote comes from." A sidestep as neat as any politician's. Finally, then, what makes her happy? "It might finally be a beautiful face that would make me put the microphone down. I would just be thinking fondly of someone who I love. You can strive and strive and strive to be happy, but happiness will sneak up on you in the most peculiar ways. Some days the way the light strikes things. Or for some beautifully immature reason like finding myself running to the kitchen to make myself some toast. Happiness comes to me even on a bad day. In very, very strange ways. I'm very happy in my life right now."

One recent cause of happiness is her decision to go back on the road, with a band including Pat Metheny and Jaco Pastorius. She is looking for a rich meltdown of all kinds of musical categories. Free music, in the widest sense. "With these players, we're talking about young musicians who have no real musical or categorical preferences. We all love rock 'n' roll. We all love folk music. And we all love jazz. If anything, we want to be considered a musical event. We're going to do some traditional African ceremonial drum pieces. I would like to get loose enough to dance." Part of a wider loosening up, and division of boundaries. "Jaco is also a fantastic keyboard player. In this band, we're trying to switch instruments. It should be very creative."

In 1979, Joni toured America with a crack band, playing the most complex live music of her career. Don Alias had supplanted John Guerin on the drum kit and elsewhere, while Jaco Pastorius remained on bass. New faces included fusion ace and lead guitarist Pat Metheny, with his long-time musical partner Lyle Mays on keyboards. Metheny had just released three highly-regarded jazz albums with the German ECM label, and was on the cusp of adding rock to the mixture, a formula which would bring him world fame. His future collaborators would range from Ornette Coleman to David Bowie, but it was Joni who first brought him to a mass audience. On saxophone was Michael Brecker, also set to break through as a major player in fusion music, and who had already worked with Billy Cobham, James Taylor, and Yoko Ono, as disparate a trio as anyone could name. Ten years on, he played with Paul Simon when he toured *Rhythm of the Saints*, music highly influenced by Joni. Mitchell herself played electric rhythm guitar, while backing vocals were provided by doo-wop group The Persuasions. Founded in 1962 on the back streets of Brooklyn, they are still going strong, mixing r&b and gospel harmonies.

The results were extravagant, and still discussed in awe by those lucky enough to witness the tour. Music before its time, a rich and creamy melange of jazz and rock elements, effortlessly cool, with Joni's vocals sailing over the whole affair, like a bird in flight.

A September gig at Santa Barbara County Bowl was recorded for a forthcoming live album, and mixed back at the trusty old A&M studios in Hollywood. The *California* bootleg, taped at the Greek Theatre, Hollywood that same month, has much the same set list, adding a version of 'Raised on Robbery'. The official LP, a double subsequently converted into a single CD by shedding three tracks, was released a year later. *Shadows and Light* takes songs from *The Hissing of Summer Lawns* and the three albums that followed, though it does culminate with a retread of 'Woodstock'. Only one track – 'Free Man in Paris' – overlaps with *Miles of Aisles.*

The album did something towards restoring Mitchell to public favour, reaching Number Thirty-Eight in the US album charts, and Number Sixty-Three in the UK. In December, a *Shadows and Light* concert special was aired on the Showtime TV channel, splicing live recordings with still photographs similar to the collage on the front cover of *Hejira*. That has long been commercially unavailable, but on CD the music is still miraculous, with never a dropped note, or glitch. Weightless melodies, moving from limpid to savage on the turn of a bar. Joni leaves her band plenty of room to improvise, most notably on 'The Dry Cleaner from Des Moines', which sounds like Frank Zappa on the edge of self control.

Reviewers missed the point. Patrick Humphries later wrote a biography of Richard Thompson which movingly caught the essence of that locked enigma, while lacking any real insight into his music. 'A Sailor's Life', sailing boldly into uncharted waters, is "tepid." Similarly, he admits to the readers of *Melody Maker* that he has never been "that impressed by Joni Mitchell," though anyone involved with "Crosby, Stills and Nash obviously merits attention (and some degree of sympathy)." He admires her switch from "guitar totin' folkie to jazz siren," but spoils even that by describing Joni's lonely and difficult musical journey as "superficial." Here, she is "up to her pectorals" in jazz, and the results sound cold, contrived and uninvolved. In *Sounds*, John Gill sneered too at her musical progress. Folk, rock and cool jazz collide in a "disjointed muddle of personalities and modes." Even the crowd singalong on 'Boogie Man' sounds like "a bunch of Scotsmen in Trafalgar Square on New Year's Eve."

Along with Paul Morley, *NME*'s Ian Penman is perhaps the most destructive critic in rock music. His importation of trendy literary theory was like a virus, sapping the enthusiasm of that wonderful paper, and leading into a morass of self-reverential tripe. He identifies "skid and drift" here and occasional laziness: "no matter how 'tight' a musician is, how necessary is it to solo (for soloing)? God made little green ECM labels for those kind of things." Breathtaking stuff: a gratuitous sideswipe at the most revered jazz record company since Blue Note, after a weasel question. I think someone like Coltrane or Hendrix could tell Mr Penman *exactly* why it was necessary to solo. Like breathing, or something. Penman favourably compares Joni to that "rock 'n' roll conservative" Neil Young – about as wrong as you can get – and then buries her in gibberish: "Ms Mitchell has expanded all her ranges, often to excess. We find contradictions and movements stolen from a number of genres, from Torchy to more archaeological avenues – *recherche du vamps perdu*." The more you read that, the less it makes sense. Note the self-important use of the royal "we"!

One turns in relief to Paul Keers, whose appreciation of the record is not drowned out by the sound of his own cleverness. His review is the only one to correspond to what my own ears hear, now: "Joni's voice twists and turns like silk in the wind, moving gracefully over the aggressive choppy rhythms of her band. It is very much a group performance, with improvisations, solos, and long instrumental passages just as prominent as Joni's vocals. As jazz is meant to be played live, it's on this double album that you can really appreciate the success and sophistication of those recent compositions."

Shadows and Light is itself playing complex games, at least in its packaging. On the front cover, Joni's face merges with a cymbal – bashed by her current lover! – while the inside shots show her using video to make photo-montages with a vaguely *Twin Peaks* menace to them. 'Introduction' also uses juxtaposition, a snatch of the title track, then a key scene from James Dean in *Rebel without a Cause*:

"You can't be idealistic all of your life."
"Except to yourself."

This is followed by Frankie Lymon singing 'I'm not a Juvenile Delinquent'. Dean killed himself in a car crash: Lymon died of a heroin OD, aged 26. Joni herself keeps on keeping on, and the music segues into a particularly joyous 'In France They Kiss on Main Street'. Metheny's guitar tinkles, and the lyrics celebrate teenage rock 'n' roll, out on the street.

In 'Edith and the Kingpin', the band imitates a typewriter, on cue, and Mitchell's voice is even swoonier than on the record. Deeply gorgeous. 'Coyote' is urgent, bass driven, with Joni impersonating her lover's deep voice, and telling the story like a master raconteur. Lovely chording from Metheny. 'Goodbye Pork Pie Hat' opens with Brecker's smoky sax, and Joni's vocal is shadowed by electric piano arpeggios. The rhythm section is spectacular, booming bass and precise drumming, so that every beat counts. Just to make things clear, the lyrics this time round say "Don and I look up." Halfway through, Brecker breaks free, like (a) bird.

'The Dry Cleaner from Des Moines' begins with just voice and Alias's drums, which almost talk, then in come the band, and Joni responds to them, her melody line taking on the angular lines of Brecker's sax. The musicians fly on this track. 'Amelia' is sung solo, to an amplified guitar, and is sadder, more meditative than the original. Metheny joins in towards the end, complementing rather than taking over. The music then segues into 'Pat's Solo', a free-form improvisation on the song, reminiscent, of all things, of late sixties Fleetwood Mac, Peter Green and Danny Kirwan drifting out into the cosmos together. The band go straight into 'Hejira', with pattering congas, and Joni singing as if out of a dream. She sings of "strains of Michael Brecker coming through the trees," and he plays saxophone on cue. Music that drifts in the breeze. 'Dreamland' is an early attempt at World music, with its chorus of percussion and vocals, no instruments.

Joni introduces the band, then follows up with a ghostly rendition of 'Furry Sings the Blues', slipping twice into Furry's toothless rant. "We'd like to rock 'n' roll you now" – dirty sax, a torrent of harmonies, and Joni revisits her wild youth with a cover of 'Why Do Fools Fall in Love'. We're back with Frankie Lymon, and Joni does a convincing, hard-voiced impression of a fifties kid. In contrast, the full version of 'Shadows and Light' comes on like a Buddhist chant, with synthesiser backing and rich, gospel vocals from the Persuasions. Only the applause at the end reminds you that such a fabulous musical concoction was actually recorded live. No studio enhancement here.

'God Must Be A Boogie Man' is taken straight from the PA mix, and is wonderfully rough, less careful than the studio original, so better. 'Woodstock' completes proceedings – the CD omits three tracks, no great loss – and puts a jazzy inflection both in her voice and her amplified rhythm guitar. A wistful rendition, with hope at the end. Joni's voice floats on "golden," and she ends the song willing us to get back "to some semblance of a garden," which draws huge applause. Just like when Dylan sung the line "even the President of the United States sometimes must stand naked," just after Watergate.

Joni's next two press sightings witness her public acceptance by two, entirely different, types of elder statesman. In 1980, she jammed with blues maestro Albert King at the Bread and Roses Festival at Berkeley, California. In February 1981, she went back home to Canada to be inducted by prime minister Pierre Trudeau into the Juno Hall of Fame. The new decade was not to be kind to her, however, and it began with an omen. As Joni told Phil Sutcliffe, "I started the 1980s by going to a party with the theme 'be nice to the eighties and they will be nice to you.' Everyone realised at the brink of it that it was going to be a hideous era. I had this car, my beloved '69 Bluebird, and I was driving past Tower Records on Sunset, it was that royal blue time of night, just before it goes black. I stopped and ran into the store because I just had to listen to a Jimmy Cliff record. When I came out, there was an empty slot where my car had been. Never saw it again."

It is both ironic and prophetic that this car left the production lines in 1969, when Joni was the coming thing. The same year as Woodstock.

"It was all downhill from there. It's like the anti-Christ is running things in this era."

Well, Johnny Rotten did say....

It was 1982, Joni was approaching the dread age of forty, and Ronald Reagan was firmly ensconced in the White House. Greed and snobbery were back in fashion. The 'we're all in this together' feel of the sixties had yielded to the 'look at me', self-centred seventies, and now it was the 'F-you' eighties. From *Woodstock* to *Wall Street*. Joni too was going through some big changes. The affair with Don Alias was over, as was her love affair with jazz. Her new record, *Wild Things Run Fast*, was mainstream rock 'n' roll, and on bass was her new husband, Larry Klein, some thirteen years her junior. Joni had signed with David Geffen's new, heavily corporate label – modestly named after himself. She was shortly to break with long-time manager Elliot Roberts, who had nurse-maided her career from early Greenwich Village days. Joni tried, once again, to handle her own business affairs, but after a few weeks appointed Peter Asher as her personal manager.

Asher, brother to actress and cake-baker Jane, had been half of a particularly wimpy sixties duo, Peter and Gordon, and had discovered James Taylor while briefly head of A&R at Apple. Having your sister go out with Paul McCartney was a smart career move. Asher recognised Taylor's potential early, and followed him back to LA, where he became an extremely successful promoter of the whole Laurel Canyon music scene.

Joni married Larry on November 21st in Malibu, just as her new album was released in Britain. It was a moderate success, reaching Number Twenty-Five in the US album charts, and Thirty-Two in Britain. In December, '(You're so Square) Baby I Don't Care', originally sung by Elvis in his 1957 film *Jailhouse Rock*, was released as a single, and made the American Top Fifty. Just. Joni celebrated her new domestic harmony by setting off to play the world's major rock arenas. It was to be her last major tour. For the rest of the decade, Mitchell was to slip in and out of the shadows of public notice, running her career on two-star petrol, slowly getting angry.

The cover of *Wild Things Run Fast* seems to presage this retreat. On the back cover, Joni has kicked off her high heels, as if set on staying in. The CD re-release has wiped away the series of song titles and the Geffen logo previously inscribed on the wall behind, which is vaguely unsettling. Joni's shoes have a poignant, Van Gogh-like feel to them. The high life, discarded. On the front cover, Joni poses in what looks distressingly like a shell suit, watching TV in a drab, barely decorated room. The TV shows wild, white horses, plunging through the surf: Joni's own expression is resigned, pensive, the corners of her mouth slightly turned down. On the inside cover, she cradles Larry Klein – looking dark and saturnine with his droopy moustache, an Oliver Reed smugness to his (literally) devilish good looks. Across the lyric sheet, two horses nuzzle each other in much the same way, though all three paintings have the same vaguely washed out and sickly feel as the music contained within. The most intricately painted is a fourth sketch, of watercolour paints, and a book lying open with a reproduction of Matisse's dancers in a ring, propped up on a chair, ready to be copied. Joni's second career, on which she was now to concentrate.

Don Alias is nowhere to be found on *Wild Things Run Fast*, though he has left his mark on the rhythm arrangement for 'Be Cool'. Bizarrely enough, another old flame – John Guerin – reappears on drums, from which Alias supplanted him on the previous tour. Larry Carlton and Wayne Shorter are back, and new faces include Steve Lukather on hi-tech electric guitar, and two synthesiser players, Russell Ferrante and Larry Williams. Next step, Thomas Dolby. The much-maligned (in song) James Taylor helps out on backing vocals, as does Lionel Richie. Another schlock-master, Kenny Rankin, helps provide a "whisper chorus." Joni thanks Elliot Roberts for personal direction – not for much longer, mate – and Larry Klein for "caring about and fussing over this record along with me." Yuk. The results caused critical distress.

Richard Cook, in *NME*, was unmoved. He felt "that she's slumming in the cheapest throes of dime-novel romance," and thought it ludicrous that such facile music should come from somebody capable of so much more – *Hejira*, for example. *Sounds* is slightly less inhibited: "A truly menopausal record. Like a faded old tart, Joni Mitchell uses the cheap cosmetics of brass and hunky guitar to give her sagging musical figures a much needed lift – and the result is cheap trash." But apart from that... Carol Clerk, in *Melody Maker* did attempt grudging praise. Mitchell was making music with the "realistic and graceful perception" of somebody realising that "this is 1982" – i.e. that things had moved on. As 1982 was close to being a musical graveyard, this is not exactly comforting. *Wild Things Run Fast* is a record of looking back, both for Joni and for Clerk. "I listen to Joni Mitchell's voice these days with a fleeting pang of nostalgia. Flitting from one plaintive note to another, fluttering up and down the scales like a moth on a tour of a chandelier, it brings back echoes of a distant time, when our only responsibilities were to ride on buses all round town with a copy of *Blue* beneath our arms."

Wild Things Run Fast mines similar areas of nostalgia and regret, though emotionally it seems oddly muffled. It sounds great, with a superb rock band, and Larry Klein leading from the bottom. His bass playing isn't as slithery as Jaco Pastorius: it's more architectural, like Jack Bruce, or Free's hugely underrated Andy Fraser. Written to a childhood friend, 'Chinese Cafe' starts matter of fact, and cuts deep. A song of middle age. Joni makes a public confession about the child she gave away for adoption: "I bore her but I could not raise her." There is also a new sense of political anger. In 'Big Yellow Taxi' they put up a parking lot: here the whole of her childhood is going under concrete. The song hankers for lost innocence, and recreates it in the poignancy of 'Unchained Melody', broadcast as if from the cafe jukebox. Here is the theme of the album – "I need your love." The rest of *Wild Things Run Fast* expands this theme, considering exactly what goes on between a man and a woman. The final track puts this in its full religious context, courtesy of St Paul, a definition of love which is beyond sex or conquest, and ever giving. The whole album has the cinematic quality for which Joni has long been seeking, "a modern form comparable to a symphony or sonata."

'Wild Things Run Fast' opens like heavy rock, with hints of Mick Ronson's flash guitar on Rolling Thunder, then Joni's exuberant vocal, thundering through the speakers as if she is in the room. Woman, not man, is the hunter, the male of the species her tender prey. At the end, Joni briefly imitates Reg Presley of the Troggs, singing 'Wild Thing'. In 'Ladies Man', her high harmonies sound like Jimmy Somerville, though the song title is hardly appropriate. Joni's rival here is not another woman, but a drug: cocaine, though not as lazily hymned by JJ Cale. Closer to Bowie's *Station to Station*: disorientated, distant, dulled.

'Moon at the Window' begins with the aftermath of a robbery, ironic for one raised on it. This is the jazziest track, with Wayne Shorter blowing flurries of notes, and Joni's lazy voicings like Sade. The first use of the word "faucet" in rock since Joni's early song 'Marcie', with covert references to cocaine use again in the middle eight, and the same kind of exhausted sophistication. It is love that has been stolen here: never can the word "cheerful" have been sung with such misery. 'Solid Love' is prophetic about Joni's own life, replacing "fly-by-night romance" with a serious attempt at a long-term relationship, which was to last. The love which breaks here is "unbelievable," a miracle. The rhythm is almost reggae, and Joni sings with her most tender, open voice, just about held under control.

'Be Cool' sounds vacuous at first hearing. Then you notice how Shorter's soprano sax sounds like the late lamented Chris Wood, of Traffic – that same haunted, lonesome tone. Joni's lyrics are about disguising pain by freezing emotion. Cool is halfway between fire and ice, Dante's twin tortures in *The Divine Comedy*. This is not so fanciful a conceit, when a 'whisper chorus' seems to echo Joni from the underworld. The final chord is reminiscent of the end of Fairport's monumental *Sailor's Life*, a harbour found after emotional storms. That song's surface is fifties pop, and the real thing follows, a cover version of fellow rock craftspersons Leiber and Stoller's '(You're So Square) Baby I Don't Care'. The song is not accidentally placed. "Square" is the antithesis of "cool", and the "toot" the lover here rejects is cocaine. Joni's vocal is nicely ironic, yet affectionate, with a fine doo-wop chorus, of herself, and Larry Klein going berserk on bass at the end. Maestro time.

'You Dream Flat Tires' also starts with virtuoso bass, and is just plain weird. An exuberant musical conversation with schlock-master Lionel Richie, it plumbs depths of punning known only to Elvis Costello at his very, very worst. "Coming in on a rim and a prayer," no less. The basic scenario examines a man having cold feet about a relationship. Joni takes the anti-feminist line that men suffer more than women at the end of an affair – all too true in my own experience, and something to do with the survival of the species. 'Man to Man' deals with the singer's own promiscuity. Under the sweet surface, a deeply pensive song, Joni looking herself full in the face. Perhaps as a forfeit, she employs James

Taylor – one of her most prominent former lovers – in the chorus line, just as Carly Simon did with Mick Jagger in 'You're So Vain', which might just be about him. This song, though, accuses only herself, and the way Joni's voice almost fails on "I hope can care" is heartbreaking when the listener has realised what is going on.

On a cursory listen, 'Underneath the Street Light' could be anybody singing. It contains Mitchell's worst line – "gayboys with their pants so tight" – and the best that can be said is that it only lasts two minutes and fourteen seconds. As ever, love is a form of dancing, but it is the sheer ferocity of her declaration here that startles. It's a song totally lacking in ambiguity (or poetry, or a tune, for that matter) but in context, an outpouring of total, unalloyed joy. 'Love' reveals everything, slightly recasting the language of the King James Bible. Paul's letter to the Corinthians is a little too dense for a pop song, and the musicians drift in the wind. It's better than Siouxsie Sue's deconstruction of the Lord's Prayer, which saw the emergence of Sid Vicious, but you can't really hum it, and it would have been far more effective sung acappella. This remnant of Joni's short-lived conversion to Christianity is an oddly unsettling note on which to end so sure-footed and melodic a record.

In 'Chinese Cafe' and all that follows, Joni is asking the same question as her old friend Neil Young in 'Rust Never Sleeps'. Is it better to burn out or to fade away? The answer given here is to make a full-tilt assault on love, to hold on to somebody, cherish them, and hope for the best. At least try to ride those wild horses on the cover, even if you drown in the process.

There have been a few, wan attempts to rescue this album from oblivion. Debbie Pead, in *Record Collector*, sees it as Joni's recovery from a writer's block, and also as a return to "the safety of rock." On a generally optimistic LP, 'Chinese Cafe' stands out, "moving and haunting; it is a nostalgic look-back from graceful middle age."

As Joni was to say, "I was singing love songs when the fashion was for cynicism." Years later, talking to David Wild, Joni found that the album marked some kind of watershed. "The critics have gotten into the scheme of reducing *Wild Things Run Fast* to 'I Love Larry' songs. You know, this flippant, stupid way that they have of tearing things down. That song, 'Love', does not deserve to be reduced that way. U2

228

flipped when they heard that. Among the musicians it is comprehended occasionally. But the business is kind of painful, it has disintegrated into a bunch of crap. And what made America great was ingenuity, new ideas. But it kills; it now eats its young alive – and its old, its middle-aged. It eats the good ideas alive. It's like America is Las Vegas now."

Perhaps this is a bit on the excessive side. Even if the album did usher in the dark ages of the American soul, it also heralded a long period of emotional stability, and chronicles Joni's flickering need for some kind of religious faith. "I was kind of lonely at the time. And I actually prayed. I don't pray that often. I said 'Look, God. I know I don't write. I don't call. I don't need that much. All I need is a real good kisser who likes to play pinball.' So two days later, Klein says to me 'How would you like to go to the Santa Monica pier and play video games?' And I looked up at the sky and I said 'Close enough.' And he said 'I beg your pardon?' And we never looked back. So I look at it as divine intervention."

In December 1982, *NME* printed a long interview with Joni, conducted by Kristine McKenna. It is headed with a colour photo by Norman Seeff, in which Joni wears male attire, a check shirt and tie (at half mast), no makeup, and tousled blonde hair. She looks like a female Richard Branson, without the beard! Joni is sitting in an office on Sunset Boulevard, but this is no faded prima donna, living on past memories. She answers questions honestly, and with great humour. What are her latest themes? "Well, there's ecology, although I did throw cigarette butts out the window the other day so I have no right to talk. Of course, the anatomy of the love crime is my favourite subject. The big hurt and the big pay-off seem to be the most popular form of love."

Joni continues to explore her own inner landscape, whereas many of her generation have become "numbed out adrenalin addicts." She admits to being an "overly-sensitive person. I have a kind of loud antenna and sometimes I pick up too much, to the point that it becomes chaotic. My wonder is still intact, and I laugh a lot." She finds it difficult to work up any enthusiasm for the "more public" aspects of her chosen career, touring and giving interviews. The worst aspect, though, is an unwanted celebrity.

"Fame does cause you to get very unnatural responses from people. Somebody will call you an asshole in a public place, then someone tells that person who you are and they light up like a Christmas tree. I receive an inordinate amount of affection, which is a lovely thing, but sometimes, depending on your own undulating patterns of self-esteem, it can be terrifying. It's like someone you feel nothing for telling you they love you. It has taken me ten years to learn to deal with it: when people looked at me I wanted to shrivel up. But I insist on my right to move about the world and I go to a lot of places by myself – as a writer, you have to. My relationships really depend on how comfortable the other person is with my career. If they're too impressed by me what usually happens is the first time I show any signs of being human they're disappointed, and they attack (laughter)."

Musically, the most important thing is to keep things fresh – just like a love affair, in fact. "I like to hear every musician play with a ripe, blooming personality rather than lock them into a military drill." If only we all had bosses like Joni! As to her own singing, she is acutely sensitive to "false sexuality or false emotion." Most of what she now hears reminds her of the musical nadir a decade earlier, between Elvis and the Beatles. She and Dylan had done their best in "growing up the American pop song, but I don't find much deep thought in the music on the radio right now." The current album is "the first of five I'll do for Geffen – and there are days when I regret making that commitment. David's pretty good with me, though. We're friends – we lived together for a few years. I don't think he'll pressure me. But when I make a commitment I pressure myself. I haven't made an album too many people could relate to for a long time."

Joni began her world tour – the last she would undertake – in February 1983 with concerts in Japan. She went on to play in New Zealand, Australia and Europe, concluding back in the States five months later. The tour included two highly-praised nights in Wembley in April. The bootleg *Dreams are Shivering Down My Spine*, taped in Verona, is an interesting mix of old and new, six songs from *Wild Things Run Fast*, shuffled in with old favourites like 'Both Sides Now', 'Woodstock' and 'Big Yellow Taxi'. There's even a cover version of 'I Heard It Through the Grapevine', a Tamla Motown hit for Marvin Gaye. An portentous choice: Gaye died the following year, slaughtered by his own father.

230

Earlier, Joni had told McKenna that she was dreading going back on the road. It was a young woman's game. "Elliot Roberts gave me a pep talk the other day. Run Joan! Swim Joan! He says that when you're pushing forty you have to run back and forth like Mick Jagger. I told him to just push me out in a wheel chair, and I'd do the whole set sitting down." She was starting to feel like an antique. "There seem to be large numbers of kids turning out right now to see the old guard perform before they croak. Maybe I'll just go out there and throw paint at a canvas and hum."

Which is exactly what she did. In November 1985, *NME* writer Alan Jackson attended 'Joni Mitchell, New Paintings New Songs: an evening benefit for the Museum of Contemporary Art' at the James Corcoran gallery, Santa Monica Boulevard, Los Angeles. The event was held in a low building nestling among liquor stores and restaurants. A small crowd outside watched limousines disgorge celebrities. "Inside, faces are watching faces. Larry Klein, handsome eyes shining, is talking with Pat Metheny. Shelley Duvall is looking earnestly at a work called *The Marriage of Church and State*, which features a soiled crucifix hammered onto an American Flag. Within the Stars and Stripes there stands a small army of toy-shop tin generals, tacked on by hand." Joni herself arrives, in trademark black beret, waves of people radiating around her wherever she moves. "Life's been pretty good to you?" a dark-haired girl is asking Jack Nicholson, as he lounges in a doorway. "Yeah," replies Jack, giving that slow, wicked smile and tilting his shades forward a little. "Life's been fucking great..."

Joni's new album, *Dog Eat Dog* plays continuously. Introduced to Sheena Easton – the subject of Prince's semi-obscene 'Sugar Walls' – she cranes forward in rapt conversation: "You're from a small town too, aren't you..." A knot of people pauses on the sidewalk outside, still discussing the paintings they have just seen – "I expected them to be more figurative somehow, like her record covers" says one man. Mitchell herself will later say of them, her tongue heavily in her cheek, that "you could think of them as party decorations for the release of the new album. At their most trivial, they are at least that good."

BBC2 sent Richard Skinner to interview Joni in her studio. Answering his obvious bemusement, she described the show as "largely satirical." She performs an action painting for the camera, flicking paint at the canvas with her brush, then using a bottle to create swirls as it rolls across. Ironically, this pastiche was the one the gallery experts most immediately responded to.

The resulting TV show provides a different kind of gallery, with live clips from various times in her career. In 1970, a fresh-faced Joni, with every blonde hair scraped into place and wearing a long pink dress, sings solo to a worshipful, seated audience. The intensity of 'My Old Man' is almost painful, her eyes screwed tightly shut. Four years later, her hair is permed, and she's wearing another floor-length dress, this time embroidered with flowers. She has loosened up both visually and musically as she stands – backed by the LA Express – swaying in time to the music. A 1980 concert video intercuts 'Coyote' with footage of that beast chasing a tiny mouse, but failing to catch it. Joni is in high heels and a blue trouser suit, fronting a wild band which includes Don Alias toiling on congas, and Jaco Pastorius, all white bellbottoms and long hair tied in a head band, swaying to the rhythm. On 'The Dry Cleaner from Des Moines', Alias is behind a drum kit, and the band take off like a jazz-rock supergroup, as Joni dances on the open air stage.

Cut to 1983. Mitchell, all bare arms and styled hair, wears a man's pinstriped clothes, and plays solo electric guitar. On 'A Case of You' she sits strumming a dulcimer across her knees, like a washboard. The following year, she's in a black dress at her piano; the tension and love between her and Larry Klein – weaving bass lines – can almost be touched. She faces the camera straight, and gazes at her audience direct and imploring, an icon of sexuality and soft hair, breathing out the words. The show ends with the extraordinary video for 'Good Friends', in which she eats, smokes, drives a car, and dances with Klein. The images are straight out of surrealism – disembodied male and female hands, a burning wedding ring, day blinking into night: a black and white photo of Joni on the wall suddenly blinks. The effect is hi-tech but distant. That fragile, giggly young girl from 1970 is now shrouded in dark glasses, and somehow part of the furniture. Such, perhaps, is progress.

The next day, Jackson took tea with Joni at the offices of Peter Asher Management, in North Doheny Drive. Sitting behind a large glass desk in a small side office, Joni looks tired but alert. "You know, I'm just one of those Spock babies. We do everything a little late. It took a long time for me to remarry, to find the stability of a partner again. So with that taken care of, you begin to look around you." She laughs as she talks, an odd mixture of schoolgirl and philosopher. "The Western world has all the symptoms of downfall if you compare it with all the other civilisations that have gone under. There are the youth cult obsessions, a greater openness regarding homosexuality, the decadent theatre. Look at German theatre before Hitler. It's very similar to MTV with all its black studs. Dominantly savage." As to her own strange musical journey, "I felt I should write in my own blood. The closer it was to my direct experience, the less it was going to be hearsay, the more poignancy it should have. I am a witness to my times. The world had become so mysterious from the vantage point of the seventies. The disillusionment, the killing of the president, the stain of the Vietnamese war. It was a natural thing for people to look into themselves."

She remains happy to act as a representative of the 1960s, an era now derided. "We really broke from our elders. There was a clear cut. A line was drawn. This generation kind of resembles my parents' generation, like a throwback, which often happens. Their aim is to get a job and hold it. We came up in the greatest pocket of affluence, post-Second World War. The country was rich, the economy was in good shape, and we were raised on certain philosophies. Like, spare the rod. Yes, do spoil the child. So we never really reached adulthood in a certain way. We were a kind of freaky generation, very self-centred as a rule, in a good way and a bad way."

As Joni talks, one thinks inevitably of the end of *Easy Ride*: "We blew it." It is as if that kind of freewheeling lifestyle, paid for by drugs, has finally to face its own contradictions. The random violence at the end of the movie is a metaphor for what any such attempt at freedom will eventually run into – envy, and the urge to destroy. Such reactionary forces are now firmly in control. "So now it starts to get really scary," she says, leaning forward and jabbing the air with her cigarette. "We're only a hairline and a few laws from incredible

233

censorship." Unless people start speaking out, the freedom of expression that so many fought for, some even died for, might be closed off forever. Suddenly her mood lightens, as she remembers an article she read recently about a new right-wing women's group.

"It was Christian women linked to getting the devil's language out of rock 'n' roll. They like being housewives. They're anti-feminist. And they were in training to go out and visit the media, because some of them had appeared on television and had felt awkward. The training programme consisted of a woman standing up and saying" – here her voice adopts a prissy, Miss Manners tone – "'Now remember girls, on TV your knees are your best friends. Keep them together... Take out your pocket mirrors, girls. I want you to notice that if, when you're speaking, you raise your eyebrows up and down, your voice takes on a more melodious quality.' The women prayed, they sang songs, and then they looked at an aborted foetus, and I thought, God, this is a new movement? It's just as sick and limited as the old one." Such concerns were bang at the centre of her new album, *Dog Eat Dog*.

1985's *Dog Eat Dog* was co-produced by English synthesiser ace Thomas Dolby, who also supplies keyboards: the sound is metallic, heavily modern, driven. The LP peaked at Number Fifty-Seven in the UK album charts, and Sixty-Three in the States. The cover art is also a drastic departure, seething with violence. In an amalgam of photography and paint, Joni throws her arms up in a mixture of despair and triumph, while wild dogs – in whom the wolf seems resurgent – bare their teeth, and prowl around a wrecked car. Those on the back cover are flecked with blood, presumably emanating from the unfortunate driver. On the inside of the LP, Joni smiles down on two slavering hounds, which grin back, while another dog smokes a cigar, suggesting that these canines are humans in disguise. The CD booklet features photographs instead, two of them unretouched originals from the front cover.

One thinks immediately of wolves howling on the *Mingus* album, and of the final lines from 'Jericho', "the wild and gentle dogs/kennelled in me." We're back in the mean streets from the back cover of Joni's first album, but there is no escape now in peacocks or magic ships. The distance between the high and pure vocals of that recording and the feral growl she adopts for most *Dog Eat Dog* can be measured in more than years. The production – almost by committee, with Dolby, Joni, Larry Klein and Mike Shipley contributing, but no sign of Henry Lewy – and the use of Galaxy studios rather than A&M in Hollywood, gives a high-tech sheen to the sound. As a result, this album sounds more dated now than her earlier work, and the warmth and clarity of *Wild Things Run Fast* has evaporated. So, too, have many of her pool of musicians, with only Wayne Shorter and Larry Klein retained. Vinnie Colaiuta appears on drums – Don Alias and John Guerin now discarded – while drum samples, Fairlight, and synthesiser predominate.

Reviewers were highly impressed by what they saw as a return to form. In *Melody Maker*, Helen Fitzgerald even told purists not to worry, "she hasn't gone electrobop," the synths merely adding precision and background to her narratives. The LP presents a "disenchanted vision of the eighties by a saddened sixties idealist." Similarly, *Beat* magazine wondered "what holds her fast to the principles most of her generation abandoned." Tony Mitchell was surprised that Thomas Dolby's efforts had proved controversial, as "he seems to have only the most gentle and, dare I say it, positive influence on the resulting sounds, restrained electronic percussion, the odd wistful Fairlight flute or keyboard line, and other bits of background and sampling. But this, and the presence of (shock, horror) chunky guitar distortion on a couple of tracks, will be enough to convince more deaf ears that Joni's got metal. Whereas, what Joni's actually got is angry." Mitchell continues to offer "much-needed relief from major chords and minor talents."

Dog Eat Dog begins with a song about friendship, and ends with one about love. Between them is a sequence of waking nightmares. The album sounds harsh and metallic, electronic drums like a migraine, much like Martin Hannett's ground-breaking production for Joy Division's *Unknown Pleasures*. It shares much of that band's sense of alienation in the middle of a loveless and threatening world. Urban and nervous breakdown. On the other hand, it pulls off the Human League trick, by making its human elements all the more melodic and affecting for being set against a techno backing. Joni has rediscovered her gift for melody, even if it takes a few plays for the songs to enter the bloodstream.

'Good Friends' opens with solo voice – treated, so that it could be genderless – and echoed chorus, before opening up into a driving electronic beat. Former Doobie Brother Michael McDonald brings his own whiff of AOR to the exercise, but the song's swagger yields to the understanding that this friendship is over, and that the chorus of "good friends you and me" is already ironic. 'Fiction' takes its main riff from Grieg's music for the ballet *Peer Gynt*, about a man ruined by self-delusion. Joni's voice is siren-like in its blandishments from the world of TV adverts and unreal images – she used to be a New York salesgirl, and it shows. The 'song as list' idea was taken to its illogical conclusion on Roy Harper's 'The Lord's Prayer', where it became a litany. Here it is more of an amphetamine rush, half-lost in echo, along with distorted electric guitar and anonymous male voices. 'The Three Great Stimulants' opens with the rhythm of a heartbeat, and Joni singing one of her most gorgeous melodies, with deeply unpalatable words. She has never sounded so uninvolved. The lyrics are almost stream of consciousness, a cry of pain. The basic rhythm is like a steam engine, chugging along through the song, like the train she used to wave at during her childhood. The sharp, self-doubting tone which enters her voice towards the end of the song is a dead ringer for Tracy Chapman, or the Michelle Shocked of songs like 'Anchorage'.

'Tax Free' is another song which rambles into shape. It has some of the inner fire of *Infidels*, an album which looks increasingly to be Bob Dylan's artistic swansong, a long, slow scream against the dying of hope. Here, hellfire preachers (much like Dylan himself on 'Slow Train Coming', ironically) are the source of conflict. Rod Steiger is off the waterfront and into the pulpit, willing on his congregation to nuke Cuba. The song begins like a drone, in slow motion, then Joni's voice soars, like a balloon set free. The irony of her own tax hike, and the fact that such religious charlatans and bigots pay no tax on their takings fuels the anger here. Of course, many of these Reaganite preachers – "church and state hold hands" – were later brought to court for sexual and financial chicanery. Pink Floyd once announced their intention to compose a rock symphony from found sounds, the like of the cigarette machine which provides the percussion on this track. They abandoned the attempt, as Joni should have – for though this aggravating minute or so does capture the dull ache of addiction, it merely comes over as pretentious and empty. *Dog Eat Dog* returns to Joni as prophet railing in the wilderness, and to the "snakebite evangelists" of 'Tax Free'. All set to a tune which Madonna would kill for, with a catchy chorus. One can picture long-term Joni Mitchell fans deserting in droves, and in disbelief, and failing to notice her new-found intensity, and continued tunefulness. If the message herein also seemed a little hysterical back in 1985, the last ten years have brought her warnings home to a workforce prone to 'downsizing', watching the rich tower like pharaohs, and the poor all around them. The line about all that is genuine being "scorned and conned and cast away" is extremely true to my own experience of the last decade.

There's a disco beat to 'Shiny Toys', and an annoying perkiness to the music which is matched by a scatter-gun protest element to the lyrics. The production makes her voice shrill, a difficult achievement that must have taken many hours and thousands of dollars. 'Ethiopia' is at the other end of the scale, deeply felt and touchingly sung, though the lyrics lack bite or definition, only hitting the spot when they come back home – "every Sunday on TV." The tune is circular, like a tape loop. An interesting aural soundscape, and one ahead of its time, with its sampling of native voices and sounds. 'Impossible Dreamer' opens with churchy keyboards, and Joni's deep growls at their most sensual. It's an abstract take on the previous song, more mysterious and far more affecting because rooted in another person. Wayne Shorter's sax weaves through the song like a silver fish in a dark pool. The song could well be about John Lennon – "give peace a chance" (sung almost subliminally) – rubbed out in New York at the start of the decade, an omen if ever there was one.

'Lucky Girl' sounds almost like Kylie Minogue, backed by a large and super-cool jazz ensemble, as Joni's voice answers itself, and the whole thing sashays like the best of *Wild Things Run Fast*. Larry Klein's bass proudly stalks the song, in which, single-handed, he becomes an antidote to wise guys and woman beaters everywhere. Lucky man. In this song – for all the horror outside, perhaps because of it – Don Juan's restless daughter has finally learnt to stay happily at home.

In hindsight, *Dog Eat Dog* proved prophetic. Indeed even the title was endlessly recycled, most recently as a crime novel by a star of the cult movie *Reservoir Dogs* – a double irony – and as the name of a rock band who combine rap vocals and hardcore guitar. For Timothy White, Mitchell was a Joan of Arc figure, assailing the "smarmy triumvirate of TV evangelists, advertising executives, and junk bond salesmen busy brokering America's moral fibre." Joni herself, talking to David Wild, realised that "probably the album that will date the most, ultimately, is *Dog Eat Dog*. That was me looking out at what was going on in the world because nobody else was."

All of the records Joni made with the Geffen label had cost a lot to make. None had yet recouped their outlay, "which is dangerous, because you're maintaining the integrity of your product, but you're becoming indebted to the company store. And just before Christmas (1990) the worst happened; the accountant deemed that two of my albums hadn't sold, and they dropped them."

The albums in question were *Wild Things Run Fast* and *Dog Eat Dog*, ironically the two best that she had recorded for the label. With the help of Geffen President Eddie Rosenblatt, they were reinstated onto catalogue, despite the "horrendous press" which they had received at the time. "There are people who are afraid to stick their necks out and like something without being told it's hip. And that's gotten increasingly worse over the last two generations. There has been a general decline of independent thinking and integrity." As in all media, artists were increasingly divided between a few famous and super-rich household names, and the rest, including Joni.

Talking to Bill Flanagan, Sting – who abandoned the white reggae of the Police to go full tilt into jazz stylings – was notably ungrateful for her undoubted influence on his work. The Queen of Pain had yielded to the King, and he was out for murder. "Joni Mitchell I'm not so sure about. I think she's a bit lost. I haven't heard her new album but I've read the lyrics. I think she's kind of lost her centre. But then again I'm not sure what I'm going to write about next. I'm not sure what there is to write about." Joni got her own back later: Sting "is like James Taylor's and my baby."

Years later, talking to Barney Hoskyns, Joni told a story at Sting's expense, which blows him out of the water, frankly. "I go to see Sting because my beloved Vinnie Colaiuta is drumming with him, but poor Vinnie's all alone up there. It put me in a kind of bad mood, this show. I kept going out and smoking in the wings. Afterwards there was a party, and I was the first to get there. I see Don Henley sitting by himself in a long, long, long booth. So I walk over as if to sit down with him and he does this thing where he looks left and right, with a very worried look on his face. And I know exactly what that means, that he's saving the place for Sting. So I say something casual and go sit at another table with Vinnie and Bruce Springsteen and his wife." The mention, as if in passing, of Springsteen is masterful. Sting arrives, and Henley eventually sends over an emissary to tell Joni that she can come and sit with him. "So I launch myself into the air, and I yell 'Never.' The idea of that kind of political lamination gags me with a spoon. It's so tragically hip, and I think it's the enemy of art. I'm not impressed by stars, you know. I'm impressed by heart and fun." As to the album, she told a Japanese interviewer that "America is a land of ostriches and somebody's got to be Paul Revere." *Time* called it an adolescent work, yet it contained two of their subsequent cover stories.

As the media circus fed increasingly on itself – dog eat dog, indeed – its demands became pre-eminent. Joni flew over to England just before Christmas, not to play any concerts, but to conduct some press interviews. Mick Brown found "the wheaten hair and cornflower-blue eyes, the air of winsome candour" all intact. Joni now dresses designer expensive, though, and other things have changed. Two years ago, she received a tax demand that effectively put an end to her residual faith in government. "It was like finding out that daddy goes to hookers." While admitting that there was little sympathy for rich rock 'n' roll singers – "we're the devil now" – and that it had not seriously affected her wealth, the unfairness of all this awoke her to the crookedness of government, and a power struggle, to the death. "This country is going very conservative, very right-wing, and a lot of the progress made in the sixties through liberal law-making is being undone. I think there is a sense of powerlessness developing among people. A lot of people I talk to say they feel angry. I do myself." Even in rock music, there had been a clamping down: the business had become a business: "I've learned that the record business is very simple. If a corporation can make a profit on what you do, they'll leave you alone. If this does well, I can afford to do it again next year. If it doesn't, it will be back to Joni and her guitar..."

B ack to Alan Jackson, interviewing Joni on home turf. How had times changed? "There'll never be another Woodstock. Every time there's been one of those large gatherings of people, they've been entirely different. Collectively, each of those crowds had its own personality. Live Aid was much more commercialised. They were flashing up the band's latest album after every song. I don't think people were weeping in the wings. I don't think there was the same poignancy surrounding the event." Having taken part in the Canadian 'Band Aid', she felt uncomfortable about the way the songs written specially for the event "were more about us, the performers and the contributors of money, than they were about the people of Africa themselves," or the underlying dangers, which are worldwide in their possible impact. "Terrible things are being done in the name of commerce. The rainforests are coming down around the globe. We're going to have deserts springing up all over the place. It's not just going to be in Ethiopia."

Here speaks a child of the Canadian wheat belt. Jackson pursues her views on another contentious issue, that of feminism. "I've had a good relationship with my father. I enjoy men's company and I grew up enjoying it. My best friendships, generally speaking, were with men. I'm driven, as women go, so I relate more to driven men. Feminism was too divisive, but it did something to open things up. I like the idea that a man and a woman can sit and for a moment all of these sexual considerations are bypassed, and you have an open dialogue. I have basically tried to live my life in that way." Outside, Larry Klein lounges in a chair, chatting with office staff. He smiles to see her. The world might be rotting at its core, but her personal happiness remains undogged.

B ack to *Dog Eat Dog*. Joni told Adam Sweeting it was a very domestic album: "Mainly it was written married, settled down, staying home a lot, watching a lotta television. You are a recipient of communications that are going out that a lot of people are picking up." One of these was a need for religious assurance of some kind. "I guess people, finding that there was an emptiness in their lives and a lack of community, turned to the churches. They turned to this idea of the paternal figure at the head of the family." The perfect father was Ronald Reagan, of course. "Neil Young thinks he's a nice guy. He's an actor, y'know." She rocks back in her seat, laughing.

Mitchell was particularly concerned with the "toxic crap" now flooding the earth. It was difficult trying to articulate such views through pop music, rather than literature. Indeed, she was trying to write short stories, and immersing herself in the work of Raymond Carver and John Cheever. "My work is a combination of fiction, autobiography, a lot of the names are the actual names of friends and acquaintances, some are fictionalised and some aren't." Similarly, painting was becoming an increasingly important part of her life. It was like crop rotation, and if the rock star part of her existence came to an end, so be it.

In January 1986, 'Good Friends' – the most obvious, radio-friendly single from the album – stalled at number 83 in the US Hot 100. Two months later, she announced that "under the terms of my record contract I have three more albums to do, then I'll retire altogether and concentrate on painting. It's gotten too complicated for me. It's time to grow old gracefully. I don't want to be part of a neurotic pop youth culture any more."

Little was heard publicly from Joni until April 1988, when her new album, *Chalk Mark in a Rain Storm*, was released. It reached Number Forty-Five in the US album charts, and twenty-six in the UK. Produced by her and Larry Klein, the LP was a return to a more timeless sound, the only hi-tech element being drum programming by Mitchell, and guitar programming by Klein. Recording had spanned the Atlantic, taking place – courtesy of Peter Gabriel – at Ashcombe House, Bath, and the Wool Hall, Beckington, and in seven studios in LA and Santa Monica. These included a return booking at the trusty old A&M studios, Hollywood. Manu Katche played percussion and African talking drum, Steven Lindsey organ, and Larry Klein bass and keyboards. Michael Landau provided guitar, and Wayne Shorter saxophone. On vocals were an extraordinary line-up including Peter Gabriel, 'Iron Eyes' Cody, the Eagles' Don Henley, Tom Petty, former

Car Benjamin Orr, original punk Billy Idol, and the king of 'outlaw country', Willie Nelson, who appeared on the 1930s song 'Cool Water'. All other songs were by Joni, apart from 'Corrina, Corrina', here rearranged as 'A Bird That Whistles'. The young Dylan had recorded a yearning version of this traditional song on *Freewheelin'*.

Chalk Mark in a Rain Storm is about looking back, coming to terms with one's past. Peter Kane, in *Sounds*, found the album returning to simpler, more accessible music, though his review has a sting in its tail: "Her obsessions these days are the easy ones of saying 'no' to war and the modern ethic of 'you are what you earn', while the melodies rarely take root. But something approaching normal service has been resumed. Is anybody still listening?" The album is packaged mysteriously. On the front cover, Joni poses, Nico-like, in a man's broad-brimmed hat, with full lips and shielded eyes. Her shoulders are shrouded in an Indian blanket, and behind her stretches a dark forest. The sun is either just rising or setting behind the hills. Inside the LP gatefold (and on the back cover of the CD), Joni sleeps out under the night sky. Bottom right, a snake much like that on *The Hissing of Summer Lawns* slithers in her direction. Only the song lyrics stand between the two striped, coiled figures, oddly alike. The album's production has the technical sheen of Peter Gabriel's own work, while sharing the Genesis refugee's interest in third-world rhythms. Gabriel is largely responsible for the WOMAD festivals, having bailed them out with his own money on more than one occasion.

Caravan's first album opens with 'A Place of My Own', about somewhere to crash after taking LSD. The opening song in *Chalk Mark*, 'My Secret Place', is also about finding refuge, in a far less innocent world. A duet with Gabriel, it seems to be a dialogue between a young girl and a New York-born thug, hiding out. The sound is creamy, and richly layered, like a cake. Joni told Timothy White that the song was about the magic of young love: "You're on the same wavelength. That's the time where you're liable to say the same thing at the same time, and giggle a lot about it. It's a psychic period of bonding."

'Number One' is 'Dog Eat Dog' revisited, with sampled (and tricksy) African rhythms. Mitchell's massed voices combine to exhilarating effect, taking one's mind off the banality of the words they sing.

'Lakota' performs the same trick with native American source material, to wit, the vocals of 'Iron Eyes' Cody. The sound prefigures the recent *Sacred Spirit* CD: both combine Indian chants with gleaming technology. 'Coyote' calls again, but this time it is the real animal, its very existence endangered by strip mining. The song itself is 'Big Yellow Taxi' inflated to a global context, with a new backbeat.

'The Tea Leaf Prophecy' mines Joni's own past, taking her conception right back to basics, her parents' first meeting. The trouble is that the story reads better than it sings, missing out the gypsy's further prediction that Joni's mother will suffer an agonising death. The song also presents her mum as a prototype Joni, with her own "urge for going," except that she never actually gets to leave. There is something dirge-like about this track. 'Dancin' Clown' is an amazing contrast, all electric bounce, like Abba. Billy Idol provides a mean punk shout. The lyrics are silly enough to make Olivia Newton-John's songs in *Grease* seem profound. Compared with the bite and drive and musical brilliance of Zappa's 'Dancin' Fool', this song doesn't even reach the dancefloor.

There must be some reason for an update of 'Cool Water', but I can't think of one myself. It's wonderful to hear Willie Nelson's vocals, though – the voice of a man who's been to hell and back and learnt dignity somewhere along the way. That, and memories of Elvis, make Joni's singing a particular delight, even if the keyboard riff does start to grate well before the song takes its leave. 'The Beat of Black Wings' is also based on one of Joni's long-told stories, and again loses in the musical telling. Her vocals are surprisingly perky for such a dark song: the sense of futility in the final verse strikes deep, and entrances the listener, as does Joni's precise voicing of the 'F' word.

'Snakes and Ladders' moves along at a fair lick, vocally helped on its way by Don Henley, but this re-run of 'Harry's House' – even the snake is present – lacks any of the delicacy that first brought Joni to fame, as does 'The Reoccurring Dream'. A 'collage' of voices, it brings a jazz tinge to its exposure of the false world of advertising, hardly a novel theme. 'A Bird That Whistles' is a rewriting of the traditional song 'Corrina, Corrina'. Wayne Shorter's duelling saxophones sound a bit like the break in 'Penny Lane', while the words relate to Joni's seaside home, but are as shockingly vacuous as the performance. This is the kind of music that could only be made by somebody who has completely lost touch with her natural audience. All those studios, and all that technology leave the listener with a pleasant set of noises, well sung and played, but Joni's artistic nadir, at least until her next album.

For Timothy White, though, the album was lucid and sublimely sung, a powerful statement "pretty to the ear but upsetting in its content." It certainly makes great background music. He talked with its creator over chicken salad sandwiches one March evening in 1988, in a dimly-lit studio in North Hollywood. Joni was "jumpy", due to an attack of hypoglycaemia, but relaxed once she had digested her food, and grew touchingly sentimental. The album's title was an "image of impermanence. A young soldier delivers it, and he's drunk in a tavern somewhere, talking to anyone who'll listen." She met the real thing in Fort Bragg, Carolina. At a time when most of her friends were peaceniks, she was playing for gung-ho boys coming from and to Vietnam. "He was like a Tennessee Williams character, very young and short. I walked into the room and he was red in the face, livid, his fists clenched, and he said to me in a drawl, 'You've got a lotta nerve sister, standing up there talking about love, because there ain't no love. Not where I come from. Love is gone, love is dead, and I'm gonna tell you where love went.'"

Kyle was mentioned in her song 'Cactus Tree' as a man who "sends her medals/he is bleeding from the war." He came back into Joni's mind as she was recording the album, at Peter Gabriel's home studio near Bath. "On the other side of the valley from the studio is an army base, from which US planes attacked Libya. So it crossed my mind that, if there was any retaliation, we might very well be the target. Also, the radiation from the Chernobyl accident was drifting toward us. It was a very pensive time for Yanks in England, and gave everyone an awareness that this planet is a tiny place indeed. Accidents from one country and wars in another now affect us all."

Little more was heard from Joni for another year. On June 1st, 1989, the single 'Spirit of the Forest' was released by Virgin, to focus attention on the plight of the Amazonian rain forests, as some of the songs on *Chalk Mark in a Rain Storm* had (however incompletely carried through). All proceeds went to the Earth Love fund. Musicians joining Joni on the record included Kate Bush, the Ramones, XTC,

Brian Wilson, and Bonnie Raitt. Her efforts on behalf of charity were not all so successful.

In 1986, she had appeared at Meadowlands in New Jersey, in aid of Amnesty International. Placed between U2 and the Police – that Sting again – she concentrated on new songs, and drew a hail of missiles for her pains. Talking to David Wild, the bruises were still there, inside. "I went on as a pitch hitter. That crowd was throwing stuff all day. It just happened that by the time I got out there, they'd had a lot of practice. Their aim was getting better. I picked the perfect material – 'The Three Great Stimulants', which addressed the cause. Well, nobody's there for the cause. That's heartbreaking. And in the back room, the managers are squabbling over position. They're kicking U2 out of their rightful spot to put the Police on top with their reunion, and it's ugly. And I did a song called 'Number One'. And in the middle of it – if you see the videotape – my face kind of lights up. I'm thinking, Holy shit, if they stone me now it will be so fitting. But those big charity shows always end up being competitive situations, and me, I'd rather compete against myself. I'd rather play pinball."

In July 1990, Joni took part in Roger Waters' extraordinary recreation – under Berlin's open skies – of Pink Floyd's *The Wall*. She had barely performed in public since the Amnesty concert. Waters' gloomy masterpiece had taken on fresh significance with the demolition (literally) of the Berlin Wall, and (symbolically) of the Iron Curtain. The performance – including her version of 'Goodbye Blue Sky' – was broadcast live around the world, and later released as a double LP. It was a day of bizarre ironies. Jack Barron's eyewitness report for *NME* was titled 'Wall of Confusion'. The full impact only sank in "when the last styrofoam brick in the 600-foot long, 100-foot high wall, on the biggest stage ever erected – on the former no-man's land between West and East Berlin – had been loosed from its mooring, when the final firework had burned out above the heads of the 200,000 or so people gathered in Potsdamerplatz."

For some, Waters that night represented all that his rock opera tried to reject, "the ultimate example of corporate rock as artistic fascism." A small remaining section of the Berlin Wall was newly put to use as a barrier, dividing fans from 'celebrities'. "Backstage in the VIP area, Jerry

Hall drifts by. Mel Smith puffs on a cigar. Derek Nimmo scowls at me. Across the way stands the marquee of the Hard Rock Cafe, whose organisers have got all today's main performers to sign a tablecloth." It had taken a large team of soldiers and former border guards to clear the site of land-mines and grenades. Armed security guards roamed the site, confiscating cameras.

Onstage was a motley collection of rock eccentrics, drawn together by a shared sense of taking part in something larger than themselves, just like Live Aid, The Last Waltz, Woodstock even. Besides Joni, here were Paddy Maloney of the Chieftains, three founding members of the Band, Cyndi Lauper, Thomas Dolby on an elasticated rope, Sinead O'Connor, Van Morrison, Marianne Faithfull, and Bryan Adams. Here, too, were Waters himself – dressed as a tinpot South American dictator – the flautist James Galway, Group Captain Leonard Cheshire VC, actors Albert Finney and Tim Curry, the East Berlin Radio Choir, and the Military Orchestra of the Soviet Army. Quite apart from the distended cartoons and costumes, designed by Gerald Scarfe, one image in particular haunted Barron: "Hundreds of people in wheelchairs in front of the grandstand light sparklers and spliffs. Things like this melt cynicism and transform this night from a mega-bucks farce into the biggest musical fantasy ever." At the end of the show, 2600 styrofoam bricks lay discarded on the ground, constituents of a fake Wall, demolished by German bulldozers.

Strangely, it was Terry Hughes of *Hello* magazine – a dentist's waiting room read, with its snout deep in the trough of the very kind of cheap fame which she had always run a mile from – who got closest to Joni and her feelings. "The coming down of the wall here in Berlin is such a momentous event. The main concern in a single person is 'where is my love?' If you're lucky enough to find a stable relationship, you have all this energy going free for family and larger concerns. Your energy's not being used up out combing the bars looking for romance!"

Another focus for this new energy was Joni's re-involvement with art. In September of the same year, her work formed a major component of 'Canada in the City', an exhibition at the Rotunda gallery in London's Broadgate centre, EC2. She showed 20 or so canvases, painted that summer when she had taken Larry Klein on a sentimental journey to the Canadian outback. As she told David Sinclair, "I photographed the lakes of my childhood: the farm machinery, the grain elevators, which we call prairie skyscrapers – tall wooden structures, painted bright greens and oranges and burgundies, with yellow roofs." These images were then sandwiched with a series of self-portraits. "You get a bluff of trees in the eyes and it looks like heavy eye makeup, or a road going up my nose, and there's a field of wheat with my husband standing where my nose is, and my eye becomes a moon. Oh, there's some really profound stuff." See *Night Ride Home* for examples.

Joni filled in more details for Terry Hughes: "I started studying painting at the age of nine. At the beginning of the decade, when Larry and I got together, my painting was mainly figurative. In a lot of the early work, Larry is the subject matter." As the decade wore on, she moved more towards abstract expressionism, though never without a figurative element. We hardly need Joni to tell us this, as her own LP sleeves trace a similar process. What is less well known is how successful these 'diaries of a day' were becoming in the art market: a recent show in Japan had pushed up the average price of each canvas to around £35,000. Joni came over to London to launch the show, and talked to Robert Sandall of the *Sunday Times*. Was she now principally a painter or musician?

"I'm not anything. I'm a mutt," she explains, then cackles, slapping her blue jeans. "The spirit of eclecticism in my music runs through everything I do. I went to art school in Calgary and I always thought I'd be a painter. Back then folk music was easy. Pick up a guitar and six months later you were on stage and getting invited to lots of parties. But I had no career in mind. It was unheard of. So when I have writer's block now, it doesn't bother me at all. I just paint." What bothers her more is the low level of her competitors, as rock stars who paint. Ron Wood, Bob Dylan, and a leading disco queen all also sell pictures. "Donna Summer's painting badly works against my credibility. If you have a famous signature, the art world hates you, but you're guaranteed to draw a crowd. I drew more people at the Corcoran than any of the big boys, like Jasper Johns. But that's OK, because in the past, it's always been difficult for women painters."

A considerable understatement: Germaine Greer wrote

magnificently in *The Obstacle Race* about the constraints on female artists of the past. Conversely, many of the most interesting young painters (and musicians, for that matter) are women. Joni was herself an important role model, "busy being free." Whereas it was once merely amusing that, say, Tommy Steele was a (fine) sculptor, rather like watching a dog dance on its hind legs, there is now a far greater interplay between rock music and fine art. Like Joni, Don Van Vliet (aka Captain Beefheart) showed early talent as an artist, but jumped tracks into the world of rock, led into bad ways by Frank Zappa. With his self-imposed retirement from rock music, Van Vliet once again became a full-time artist, and is now taken extremely seriously. He commands high prices, the sign of success in any art form. He is one among many – manic John Cleese lookalike Humphrey Oceans, one of the foremost portraitists of his generation, once played bass with Kilburn and the High Roads (where he was replaced by a dwarf). In just the same way, Nick Cave or Richard Hell require no special pleadings as professional novelists, and Patti Smith and Lou Reed were both published poets long before they were rock stars.

For all this, the life of any female artist – in whatever form – requires particular sacrifices, and Joni reveals exactly what she has had to abandon along the way. She talks openly for the first time about Kelly, the daughter she gave up for adoption. "Anyone could have raised that child better than me in those first years. I would have had to give up my life. I would have been a waitress. It would have been one cranky woman bringing up another cranky woman. I celebrate her birthday – it's near St Valentine's Day. And reach out to her once in a while in my songs, to soften the blow." Whether for her or Kelly is not made clear. It is a cruel world in which to grow up. "The world's a mess. Not to be anxious in these times is not to be alive. In the eighties, the heart went out of life." The nineties are a reaction against all this, as is her forthcoming LP, *Night Ride Home*. "I played the album at the restaurant where I eat every day and it was really well received by the kids there," she reveals proudly, happy that her music is reaching a young audience who tell her that her songs make them want to open bottles of champagne and light candles. "It's got tunes – it's not just sentimental," she hastens to point out.

Her ability to switch art forms is mutually nourishing. "I apply a lot of painting theory to music." After the sonic clutter of *Chalk Mark*, she now opts for clarity of line. "It's just a lot sparser than the last one, me and a guitar mainly." It is doubtful if she will go back on the road, though: "Touring's a young person's business. I had polio in my back when I was nine, and I've never been supposed to lift anything that weighs over five pounds. If I can get my back strong enough to hold a guitar for two hours, I'll do it. But I won't be leaping around like old tricky Mick, that's for sure."

In March 1991, *Night Ride Home* – produced, again, by Joni and her husband – debuted in the UK album charts at Number Twenty-Five, and began its slow rise into the US Top Fifty. The musical mix was much as before, with Larry Klein, Michael Landau, and Wayne Shorter all present and correct, and Vinnie Colaiuta back on drums. New faces included Alex Acuna on percussion, and pedal steel guitarist Bill Dillon. Joni herself had added oboe, billatron and omnichord to her musical palate. She also wrote all the songs, apart from the music to 'Nothing can be Done' – by Larry Klein – and WB Yeats's poem 'The Second Coming', which she renamed 'Slouching towards Bethlehem', and supplied a tune for.

The critical reception was welcoming, this time around. *NME* noticed "a return to her roots, via hard-edged acoustic strums and soft vocals meant for clubs where the only competitive noises stem from stirred coffee cups. Joni's just a folkie again, albeit a more sophisticated one." *Rolling Stone* thought that any modern folkie owed an enormous spiritual debt to Joni Mitchell. "Mitchell may have been an incurable romantic obsessed with charting the erratic graph of love life, but she was nobody's wimp." Tom Sinclair found the album contained some of Mitchell's prettiest melodies in years, even if its innate tastefulness was sometimes close to New Age music at its most cloying. "A few rough edges would have been nice."

The album presents itself with restraint and mystery. On the front cover, Joni's face is superimposed on a spectral photograph of a lakeside scene – much like *Clouds* – with a male face, presumably Larry Klein's, in silhouette, chewing a match, more menacing than supportive. There is an ominous quality to Joni's grey-blue eyes, and to the inner cover, where lyrics are printed white on black. Joni's face looms above them, cut off just below the eyes, larger than life, pale as death. On the inner bag of the LP – an artefact that still refuses to die, despite the best attempts of those who control market forces – Joni's face is integrated with a rotting barn and a car's wing mirror, like the more outlandish conjunctions of JG Ballard's mutant science fiction.

Crickets chirp, guitars strum, Larry Klein's bass plunges earthwards, and Joni puts on her best nursery tale, hypnotic voice. The title song of *Night Ride Home* – the album's 'mission statement', in contemporary slang – is a song of contentment. It is Independence Day, and Joni sets off for the open road, but alone no longer. 'Passion Play' is a low-key replay of the themes of *Dog Eat Dog*, but Joni sounds half asleep. The real subject here is muffled, perhaps that of Joni being sued by her housekeeper, in which case the song is about the ingratitude of the modern servant class. Very Woodstock.

'Cherokee Louise' is told by a young girl about her missing friend, victim of a sexually abusive father, who has literally gone to ground. Wayne Shorter's sax takes us back to earlier glories, but the near total lack of a tune and leaden pace proves a major stumbling block. Joni by numbers. One reviewer thought that 'The Windfall (Everything for Nothing)' was sung from the viewpoint of a woman divorcing a gold digger. Close, but no cigar. It is actually a direct attack on her ex-housekeeper, and as such is really a private narrative. Talking to Phil Sutcliffe, Joni explained the story behind the song. "Then my housekeeper decided to sue me for $5 million. She was ripping me off. She was a Guatemalan and I'd paid for her to go home twice. The second time, she didn't even go, she went to Europe, so she'd been lying. Finally, I kicked her in the shins. But I can't do that as a public person. She went to the criminal court and they threw it out because it's just so laughable. But she's still after me, though she's on her fifth lawyer." The song lacks the healing spite of, say, Dylan's 'Positively 4th Street', or the universal quality of that weird sixties film *The Servant*. After all, the theme of master and servant reversing roles is as old as literature itself, dating back at least to the drama of ancient Greece.

Some of our greatest poets were revolutionaries. John Milton was close to being executed as a regicide, while WB Yeats was closely involved in Ireland's war of independence, and sat as a senator in the Irish Free State. Had things gone differently, he would undoubtedly have been shot by the British. His poem 'The Second Coming' is a terrifying polemic about coming anarchy, and a metaphor for fascism (for which he had some sympathy). One can imagine it being howled out by Nick Cave, say, or slurred aggressively by Shane MacGowan. Joni retitles it, as 'Slouching Towards Bethlehem', gives it a vapid tune, provides a counter-melody like Joan Baez in sexual congress, and wimps out. Even the drums sound limp. Cilla Black or the New Seekers could improve on this. A career lowlight.

'Come In From The Cold' is far more sinister, based on the firmer ground of Joni's childhood. It's a triumph of multi-tracked, choral singing, and the kind of middle-aged love song which dignifies the album, the linked theme of Side Two of the vinyl release. There are still "bonfires in my spine." A shame, then, that the music too has a middle-aged plod to it. 'Nothing Can Be Done' continues to hit that same vein. It has the benefit of a passage from the Desiderata, a series of truisms which has never recovered from Viv Stanshall's exact parody of it as 'Deterioata'. Joni sounds here as if she is singing to and for herself, having forgotten her audience. Sleepy-time music.

'The Only Joy in Town' is set in Rome. Musically, the experience has kick-started Joni, and she sounds at least half-awake here. In the mildly interesting lyrics, she has found herself a real toy boy, albeit one painted by Botticelli many centuries before. 'Ray's Dad's Cadillac' takes us back again to her childhood. Elsewhere she damned Bruce Springsteen with faint praise as a folk carpenter, "a very nice craftsperson," but this is very much in his territory, though without the charged power of even his most cliched material. The song quotes rock 'n' roll, but doesn't evoke it. One thinks enviously of how, in his horrid way, the late Frank Zappa would have used the same title to conjure up a far more specific memory of adolescence, probably involving snot or some similar body secretion. Joni's attempt sounds airbrushed.

The album drips to an end with 'Two Grey Rooms'. It opens with sad, David Accles-like piano, and shares some of that near-forgotten genius's ability to evoke melancholy and loss. The love object here could possible be a phantom – he fades so fast – but then so could the singer, relocated to a cheap apartment. Joni's cello-like voice meshes well with the string arrangement – as, in a radically different context, does Elvis Costello's – and the song satisfyingly undercuts the

251

optimism of the title track. The weekend and public holiday there looked forward to are now the subject of dread. In fact, as an album, *Night Ride Home* would make a good single, with those two tracks alone. Before and after. Along with *Chalk Mark in a Rain Storm*, this is the only Joni Mitchell record I would not immediately replace after a robbery. I admit to writing her off artistically at this point.

Some critics were farther-sighted, seeing glimmerings here of Joni's renaissance. For David Sinclair, there is a chirpy quality to songs like 'The Only Joy in Town' which recalls the lightness of touch she had brought to 'Big Yellow Taxi'. Talking to David Wild, Joni described her new concern as writing "middle-aged love songs. Like Desiderata says, surrender gracefully the things of youth. But it's easy for him to say. He was a monk, you know. He wasn't in show business. If I must desperately protect my youth in order to have credibility, then I have no dignity and the whole thing is stupid, and I may as well quit. On the other hand, perhaps I can write material that's suitable for this period of my life. Sinatra has had a long run. It remains to be seen who among my generation will be allowed that. It's hard, because a lot of the young listeners can't seem to make up their minds, and the direction they're getting is so bad, so shallow."

Talking to Mick Brown, Mitchell launches into a detailed account of the book of Revelations, and its relevance to the Gulf War as the final judgement of God (a trifle premature, in retrospect). "I don't want to be Doomsday Joan or anything, but all the images hook up. I've been struggling to warn everybody my whole career, and now it's here. My songs are just full of ecological catastrophe and romantic collapse." As an owner of four expensive homes – in New York, British Columbia, Beverly Hills, and a beach house at Malibu – Joni has found a way to retain her spirituality while still having a "nice living room." Or four, for that matter. The royalties for her songs 'Lakota' and 'Ethiopia' are paid into a charitable fund. Even the cigarettes that Joni chain smokes are called 'American Spirit', come in a sky-blue pack, and are environmentally friendly.

Such was the increasing sophistication of cross-marketing that the *Night Ride Home* album had its own visual companion in the *Come In From The Cold* video. Eight current songs, from her latest two albums, were mixed together with film footage, Joni's spoken introductions between the songs, and still photographs. When Matt Johnson of The The did the same with his *Infected* album – the most savage, sexual and humorous dissection of eighties tawdriness in any art form – he created a masterpiece. The leading video directors he employed found perfect visual correlations to the songs, and locations which ranged the world. Joni was more self-reliant, less innovative. As Max Bell wrote, "the voice and the cheekbones are intact and the songs are airily beautiful, but the cinematography is banal, much of it looking like high grade commercials. The paean to the Indians and their buffalo gods in 'Lakota', brought to life with evocative Hopper-esque landscapes, does at least add a sense of purpose to the heart wrenching. Trouble is, when video usurps all imagination, it becomes just another marketing ploy. Stick to the album."

The albums remain in print, the video does not, Phil Sutcliffe re-emphasises why: marking out of ten, he awards a lucky three. "The video features eight spine-tingling songs, but also reveals her as a novice tentatively exploring the promo form. There's a lot of monochrome, arty chiaroscuro and not much happening." One plus is her boogie round the kitchen, and a definite minus is her continued propensity to dress up in black face, as here in 'The Beat of Black Wings'. Her performance as a Vietnam vet "detracts absurdly from the song's wounded beauty."

The unkindest cut of all comes from Lucy O'Brien, who skewers the cultural product thus: "Joni hangs out with her hippy friends and says, 'Gee Chuck let's not do the normal pop video thing, let's get an intellectual perspective.' This means Mitchell's face is superimposed on her own fine art photography, tasteful muted brown, soft focus log fires and shimmering water. She wears designer black, pearl earrings and introduces each song facing the camera." Every picture might tell a story, but the limpid direction here barely helps convey any excitement or energy. It is not until the end of the video that Mitchell recovers any of her innate authority, with 'Lakota', "a song that roots out her squaw ancestry. It's only this sparky, less restrained footage that marks her out from her MTV peers."

Spectacularly unfair, when Joni chose U2's favourite photographer, Anton Corbijn, to interpret 'My Secret Place' because of a shared love of the Russian director Tarkovsky. "It's hard on the tailbone, but it

253

lingers in your mind." Unlike Dylan or Neil Young, Mitchell's wish to direct her own movie remains as yet unfulfilled.

An interesting point. It was for MTV that the videos on *Come In From the Cold* had been first intended, and Joni was very much of an age now to be an elder of her tribe, the Woodstock-era rock singer. Perhaps the greatest test of any creative artist is what kind and number of imitators they leave behind them, that being the sincerest form of flattery. This confers immortality, so that Woody Guthrie can live on in the voice of Bob Dylan, or Robert Johnson in the blues of Eric Clapton. Having been herself first seen as little more than an amalgam of Joan Baez and Judy Collins, Joni fought hard to establish her own identity. Her influence, both directly in terms of music, and indirectly through her very stance as a woman of self-reliance and tough grace, has indeed proved enduring (and endearing) in a whole new generation of female singer-songwriters.

This was already becoming obvious by the turn of the decade, when Robert Sandall asked her what she thought of "the new Joni Mitchells?", almost as if the current model was now out of production. "Joni Mitchell grins, sucks appreciably on another cigarette and thinks hard, as she often does, before speaking. "Well, Dylan spawned his imitators right at the outset. I guess it's just taken 20 years for mine to come along. Remember that there weren't that many women in the business when I started out. There was maybe Laura Nyro and myself. There were plenty of women. But there weren't any women writers. Sure, they came up with a coupla songs now and then, but you couldn't really call Joan Baez or Judy Collins a writer." Unfortunately for them, the same precise discrimination, turned on contemporary musicians, is just as cutting. Joni, now aged forty-six, may still exemplify the "dreamy, genial air" of an old hippie, but she is not laid back at all when the names of those she is alleged to have influenced are listed: Suzanne Vega, Tracy Chapman, Tanita Tikaram, Michelle Shocked. The lady herself isn't having any of it.

"My music is nothing *like* any of these girls," she almost snorts. "They don't have my chordal sense. Most of them don't have any idea of architecture in their chordal movement. Tracy Chapman wrote a coupla good songs, but generally speaking, she's not that musically gifted. And Suzanne Vega, well... " Sandall is sparing about what exactly these dots replace. It appears that Joni has attempted what she herself calls "a good adjudication" on the evidently thorny subject of Vega (whose own popularity far outweighed Joni's at that precise point in time, though not now). Neurotic, chilly, heartless, overly influenced by Leonard Cohen while lacking his black humour; these are merely some of the charges laid against the pretender to Mitchell's crown. And she is merely the leader of the pack. As Joni said elsewhere, "they're gonna run every girl with a guitar past me at one point or another." She concludes firmly, "and now there are dozens of them. But I don't hear much there, frankly. When it comes to knowing where to put the chords, how to tell a story and how to build a chorus, none of them can touch me."

Talking with David Sinclair, Joni adds further details about her own musical abilities, quite rightly, but without any overdue sense of modesty. It was her explorations integrating jazz, folk and rock which, she now believes, lost her a large chunk of her audience. This is an allegation she had herself hotly denied to journalists at the time, and it is difficult to warm to her sense of injustice here, however well founded. "I've pretty much been stricken from the history of rock 'n' roll in America," she says ruefully. "However, I am being written up in some classical music textbooks. They include me along with Stevie Wonder, Duke Ellington and others, as twentieth-century composers. I am one of the pioneers of music with a broader harmonic sense than rock 'n' roll, but I don't fit into any of the handy pigeonholes. That's why it's taken twenty years for me to spawn imitators, and even they have a hard time getting started, the poor dears."

In conversation with Bill Flanagan, she sounds less uncharitable, more sympathetic to those coming up – like her – the hard way. Flanagan first contends that while fifteen years before it was acceptable "for a man to sing about the whole range of his emotions," that is no longer true. A strange contention, when one thinks of, say, Elvis Costello, continuing to further extend and deepen both his musical horizons, and his responses to an increasingly complex world. Figures as diverse as Jackie Leven, Lyle Lovett, Jarvis Cocker, Julian Cope, even Oasis, are exploring in different ways what it means to be a man in a woman's world. Imperial warlords who have lost their empire.

That said, it is true that one feels – in all art forms – that male responses to the world are becoming, in general, tired and repetitious. Flanagan instances Aimee Mann – how ironic a name! – as perhaps the most interesting new voice to emerge recently. Joni replies. "Yeah exactly! Because nobody for a long time has really dared to put back the anxiety." Flanagan points out how most male artists measure themselves against Bruce Springsteen, while missing the essence of his work. 'Born in the USA' was a song that he delivered with irony and pain, but most imitators merely see a macho pose and bombast, and reproduce it. No one can come out from nowhere now, and 'expose himself' in the way that James Taylor once did. (If, of course, they literally exposed themselves, in the way that Jim Morrison or Iggy Pop once did, they would be immediately arrested!) Yet, he alleges, people accept it from a woman.

Joni demurs: "I don't know. The feedback that I get in my personal life is almost like 'You wanted it, libertine!' I feel like I'm in the same bind. That's not going to stop me, I'm still going to do it but I don't feel I have the luxury because of my gender to do this. It's just as hard." She feels that what most appeals to her as a writer is just this kind of detail, things that "would make a novel or screenplay good and have some depth as opposed to just being a caricature. I sacrifice myself to them. I'd never really say that was easy. I just don't know any other way to be. If I could think of a way to change and get consistently strong so that I could sing about strong things. It's a delicate thing. I wouldn't go putting it into a gender bag at all."

Her peers agree. Linda Rondstadt saw Joni as the first woman to match any man on his own terms, whether as "songwriter, guitar player, or as an incredibly magnetic human being." Tom Rush thought that any human being, of whatever gender, could relate to her, and "if a man hasn't gone through it, maybe he knows somebody who has." Though, as Stephen Stills once said, Joni "reaches down and grabs the essence of something very private and personal to women." As she grows older, she most resembles her friend, the great woman painter Georgia O'Keefe, who lives alone in the desert, producing huge canvases of flowers and skulls.

Joni is coming out fighting, and this newly positive, aggressive persona – who has learnt, in turn, from some of the new female voices coming through – is given full rein on her forthcoming album *Turbulent Indigo*.

S peaking of aggressive personas, Barney Hoskyns asked if Joni had ever worked with Prince, a noted Mitchell fan. "No. He sent me a song once called 'You are My Emotional Pump, You Make My Body Jump'. I called him up and said 'I can't sing this.' He's a strange little duck, but I like him." Nevertheless, Joni did record "a load of unreleased stuff" under Prince's direction with Wendy and Lisa, doyens of psychedelic soul. One of the reasons for fewer guest stars appearing on *Night Ride Home* and the new album was that both records were, literally, home grown. She had built a home studio – the Kiva – in her Bel Air house, which made the whole process cosier, but less open to chance. Billy Idol, for example, had been recording in an adjacent studio during the making of *Chalk Mark in a Rain Storm*, and she dragged him in as the bully in 'Dancin' Clown'. People in England saw this as opportunistic on Joni's part – "because he was big at the time and my stock was down" though it had been just one of those things that kind of happens. Prince phoned her, to ask who the guy "whooping and hollering" was. He could, of course, have read the sleeve credits. When she told him, his reply was "Oh, that's a good idea."

Another good idea was that of leaving Geffen records, and moving back to Reprise after a gap of 23 years. "I had the choice to give this record to Geffen and call it my swansong, to head up into the Canadian backbush and get on with my painting. But because Geffen hadn't done too much with me in the time I was with them – I was just kind of hired and forgotten, on a lot of levels. And Mo Ostin at Warners was very enthusiastic about having me back." Not surprising, as he had helped discover her in in the first place. Joni felt a special buzz about *Turbulent Indigo*, even before its release. "See, in my entire career, there hasn't been a lot of excitement about my albums coming out. There is excitement about this one, for some reason. People are ready to listen, they're more ready to take something a little more to heart and to mind than they have in the past. And unlike some of my peers, I haven't hit a writers' block; when I hit a block I just paint, which is an old crop-rotation trick. So since I haven't lost my voice, and since I'm over the middle-age hump and at peace with becoming an elder... although, of course, I did ask myself whether a woman of my age could continue in this youth-orientated genre. It's such a shallow and fickle business."

The LA riots had helped inspire the new record, as had another major source of disruption in her life. Joni had just separated from Larry Klein, her husband of twelve years standing. "Klein and I spent twelve years together. We were good friends in the beginning, then we were lovers, then we were husband and wife. I love Klein; there's a mutual affection there and I can't imagine what would destroy it." Those not immune to Californian psycho-babble should skip the next paragraph, though there is genuine pain underlying her answer. "My main criterion is: am I good for this man? If at a certain point I feel I'm causing him more problems than growth, then if he doesn't have the sense to get out I have to kick him out! The 'Mr Mitchell' thing, of course, is prevalent. I was in New Orleans one night and we were partying and this Greek guy came up and asked me to dance. And he said to me 'In Greece they say Joni Mitchell she doesn't need a man.' I said 'Oh, is that right? All of Greece says this?'"

Joni had started in the music business ultra-feminine, but the need for her to handle many tough situations herself had made her a kind of hybrid, "both male and female to myself." A public image. "So it takes a specific kind of man who wants a strong and independent woman. Klein did, but at the same time there were things about living with 'Joni Mitchell' – not with me – that pinched on his life in a certain way that made me think he needed a break. Our separation, I think, was wholesome – painful and occasionally a little mean, but never nasty or ugly. There was a certain amount of normal separation perversity – he'd spent a third of his life with me, after all, and I'd spent a quarter of mine with him – but for the most part it was a wonderful growth experience for both of us. Klein would say the friction created a pearl." As he has never granted an interview, this must remain guesswork.

chapter 6:

Mood Indigo

Turbulent Indigo was issued in late 1994. The title could not have been more apt: Joni and Larry Klein had separated on the day before sessions for the album were due to begin. This made recording particularly difficult, as it took place at the marital home (as was). One can only imagine the domestic difficulties that ensued, like a situation comedy played for real. No wonder that, on the front cover of the CD, Joni has painted her self-portrait in the style of Van Gogh, wounded but determined.

Joni conceived *Turbulent Indigo* as a leavetaking, a grace note to her career. As already noted, the record appeared on Reprise, the label to which she had been first signed way back in 1967: not so much a different time as a different planet. In fact, it sold well, and re-established Joni as a major artist, at the forefront of contemporary issues. Joni appears on keyboards and 'high strung guitar', which might or might not also be a pun on her notorious temperament. Larry Klein might have just quit her life, but he co-produces the album with her, and appears on bass, organ, and percussion. Both the sound and guest list are sparser than on recent records, due largely to the recording venue. Friends only. Michael Landau reappears, joined by Stuart Smith on 'orchestral electric guitar' and Greg Leisz on pedal steel. Bill Dillon plays something called guitorgan, and Wayne Shorter plays sax. Drum duties are shared between the legendary Jim Keltner and Carlos Vega (presumably no relation to Suzanne, whose work Joni had skewered in recent interviews). Backing vocalists included Seal, who had made his reputation in electro dance. The circle goes round and round, and who should reappear as a co-writer of one song but

Dave Crosby, producer of Joni's first LP.

Rod Campbell recognised that the album focused largely on women's issues. The lyrics of 'The Magdalene Laundries' deal with the incarceration of Irish women by the Catholic Church. As she told Campbell, the song had caused great consternation to the Chieftains when she appeared with them (and briefly with Dylan) that same year in Osaka at the Great Music Experience. "It was a difficult decision for them to decide whether they would play with me. It caused a little bit of controversy in Ireland, I guess. It's a touchy subject." Other songs deal with racism, family violence, rape, injustice. "My songs have always been relationship-orientated between a man and a woman, not women's issues. It just turns out that there was a lot more battering and decapitating, *bobbiting*. Children packing guns, it was very strange times."

The album had been very carefully produced, for long-term impact. "There's a minimal amount of layering on this album and it's designed to take a lot of listening. It's not designed to impart everything at first hearing. It's very sparse. All of the verses are just voices and guitar. It only thicks and thins along the way to give it more symphonic dynamics. I usually write music first and set the lyrics to it; it's harder that way but more interesting. That way you know by the score, so to speak, the complex emotion of every chord and the release of it. Because that's what they are: emotions releasing into other emotions. I tuned the guitar to the sounds of the British Columbia coastline – to the birds, to the tonality of the day."

Strangely enough, the least enthusiastic review came from a woman, Charlotte Greig, writing for *Mojo*. The album was "overwrought and ambiguous." Songs "meander along like a drunk zig-zagging home, throwing punches and hazy philosophical cliches at the air." What Greig most disliked was the major change in Joni's stance, her new role as a "doom-laden seer." Well, compared to Matt Johnson or Mark E Smith, she's still a happy bunny. Certainly, the political commitment which has always been part of the rich weave of her work is here foregrounded, although *Dog Eat Dog* was, if anything, more savage. There is a sadness and weariness here – shared by contemporaries like Dylan, Neil Young and Leonard Cohen – which is new. Such a world view might not be shared by Greig, but it responds to my own feelings, and those of many old friends I talk to. Joni has once again touched the pulse of a generation.

'Sunny Sunday' starts just like Fairport's version of 'I Don't Know Where I Stand', then a minor chord, and Wayne Shorter's mournful sax bring us back to the nineties, and this cold, cold song. Joni's vocals catch the boredom and desperation of the subject here, literally shooting out the lights. A vision of endless hell – and tomorrow will be exactly the same – oddly reminiscent of a notorious Tony Hancock 'half hour', when a Sunday afternoon in East Cheam drips into eternity. In 'Sex Kills', this preference for darkness over light becomes endemic, in a world as far removed from the rich simplicities of *Ladies of the Canyon* as night from day. The song takes off on an ominous lope, a Meters'-like strut, with Joni sounding oddly exhilarated, and Michael Landau's cityscape guitar underlying everything. If sex, or at least free and equal love, was seen to be the answer in the sixties, now it is merely another lottery ticket for death. A protest song without a solution, other than its own exuberance.

'How Do You Stop', written by Dan Hartman and Charlie Midnight, asks much the same question. Joni's vocal alternates between swoon and flutter, deep and masculine as compared to Seal's high male falsetto. The title track ties in with the album cover, Joni *sans* right ear, grim faced and heavily framed, a painting she proudly displays inside, all sandals and grin. In the song, we're back in the world of 'Sunny Sunday', except that here the gun has been turned on oneself, in suicide. It's a conventional song about the privations and hardships of genius, given life by the details – pissing on bourgeois fireplaces – and Wayne Shorter's sax flourishes, which paint pictures all of their own. Joni's vocal is oddly intimate, as if whispered.

'Last Chance Lost' is particularly odd, a musical duet between Mitchell and Klein, on a song about the death of their marriage, as if Lady Di had put her feelings about Charles to music, and broadcast it on *Panorama*. Even here, violence is (literally) in the air, as the couple bicker on a "rifle range." Even more personal is 'The Magdalene Laundries', which mythologises Joni's time as an unmarried mother. An extraordinary song, which few of her contemporaries would have the sense of historical resonance to think of, let alone write, let alone perform with such charged emotion.

Larry Klein's bass booms like a funeral bell, and keyboards circle like a prayer, as Joni brings to light a scandal of the Irish church, where young girls come pregnant – some by their own fathers, or the parish priest – to a prison-cum-sweatshop. There is a horrid contrast between the girls' fecundity, which brought them here in the first place, and the aridity of their warder nuns, wilting the very grass they walk on. Joni brings the horror home by singing in the first person, and her voice resonates dull routine, undercut by the secret delight with which she brands herself as "Jezebel" and "temptress." Her wordless vocals at the end are full of sexual abandon.

'Not to Blame' was described by Charlotte Greig as "a dull anti-rape number," which leaves this mere male speechless. Written about OJ Simpson, or somebody very like him, it is in fact about male violence to women, and the way it is excused. The rubber gloves here are not only literal. Joni's sudden pretence to be a three-year old child is horrifying – the way she sings "daddy" could be tacky and is in fact deeply disturbed, like Tony Perkins at the end of *Psycho*. As in the previous song, we end up looking over a "lonely little grave." The song has the same finger-pointing insistence as early Dylan exercises like 'Who Killed Davey Moore' or 'The Lonesome Death of Hattie Carroll', but – like the latter – also shares a genuine emotion, welling up from somewhere deep inside the singer, and reflected in voice rather than words. One wonders from the barely controlled anger here – the way she half chokes on "despise" – whether Joni actually knew the people concerned.

For Arlo Guthrie, the borderline is something to cross with illegal drugs. For Bruce Springsteen, the border between California and Mexico has proved increasingly a key motif, between poverty and riches. For Richard and Linda Thompson it was a metaphor for death. Mitchell's 'Borderline' is the dividing line between what is and is not acceptable, and which the unnamed assailant of the song has breached. Here words are like bullets – "you snipe so steady" – to continue the album's theme. 'Borderline' was described by Greig as "trite state-of-the-planet moans," which means that she might have heard the song, but she certainly hasn't felt it. The very way in which keyboards and pedal steel weave a lament behind Joni's edge of the grave vocals means that the song would lose little if it was sung in

Swahili. Indeed, it has the same charged feeling as some of the more emotive outpourings of Salif Keita, and other singers of an emergent Africa.

'Yvette in English' has the same toytown atmosphere as Kevin Ayers' first LP, sharing the same love for all things French, and the theme and air of intense happiness, as his song 'May I'. It's a return to the city of 'Free Man in Paris', where anything is possible, even "a little bit of instant bliss," though the song is oddly unresolved, which is its point. The girl is nervy, insecure, but the battle here has turned into the old one of love, not a bullet (real or metaphorical) in sight. The guitorgan sounds increasingly like an accordion, and Joni like a crooner found in some smoky Left Bank haunt, dreaming awake.

'The Sire of Sorrow (Job's Sad Song)' is subject to a final attack by Greig, that Mitchell "uses global concerns to mask her own disappointments. She refuses to let the undercurrents of her own fear of ageing and death get through and give the song some emotional honesty." In which case, neither did Shakespeare use the figure of King Lear to bear some of his own terror and guilt. Not the simplest or most hummable of songs, this is in fact a huge cry of hope, both in the lyrics – Job after all patiently endured all that his God inflicted, and never lost belief – and in Joni's vocals, answering a doubting chorus of herself. She might be confronted by "everything I fear and everything I dread," but the grain of her delivery is joyous survival. Driven by Klein's bass and Joni's bass drum, we are back in the musical landscape of *The Hissing of Summer Lawns*, full of dissonant melody.

Much the same atmosphere lurks in the landscape paintings for which the CD booklet forms a kind of private view. Apart from one, reproduced in miniature and in black and white, of Larry nuzzling a cat where his moustache usually is, and one of a picnic table laid for two (with Van Gogh's chair drawn up, ready), these are mood indigo landscapes, of sea, sky and land, brooding, touched by divinity, endless and vast, hugely empty. Not a single human being disturbs a vision of earth either before or after its colonisation by man.

The world depicted on *Turbulent Indigo* has its own logic too. As in the Eagles' earlier masterpiece of decadent arousal, 'Hotel California', Los Angeles serves as a metaphor for decline and fall. In tone, the closest parallel is Lou Reed's *New York* – the soundscape of a city in free fall – or Leonard Cohen's *The Future*, which does not see one. Mitchell's own health problems – to which the last song must surely allude – chime in with what she observes outside herself, a world ripe for riot and bloodshed, full of division and borders, both between the races and between individual human beings.

As with the Eagles, this feeling is offset by a weird enjoyment of the spectacle, taking pleasure – or 'jouissance' as French literary critics would have it – in the very fact of creation and performance. Joni has not sounded this animated and committed since, well, *Hejira*. After a run of half-achieved studio outings, this is the real thing. The end of the long love affair with Larry Klein – so movingly begun in the songs on *Wild Things Run Fast* – seems to have led her again to put her full essence into her work, giving full commitment to the anonymous listener.

Folk Roots noted the odd fact that since 1982 Joni had released one album every three years, the same gestation period as an elephant! She had just played the Edmonton Folk Festival in Canada, only her second gig of the year following her performance with the Chieftains in Osaka. Indeed, she had only played a handful of concerts since 1982. The audience's response had been warm and heartfelt. "I really loved the audience. There was so much comment right after the new songs. I was very pleased. The new songs should communicate. I don't want to become a living jukebox where people are coming to relive their childhood. I intend to be a vital artist until I lose it."

Backstage at Edmonton, a week before the 25th anniversary of Woodstock, she updated Rod Campbell on the last decade. "I had poor health for most of the eighties. Every decade I have a few rounds with death, you know. There's a thing called post-polio syndrome. Your physiology is affected, and I've an allergy to air conditioning. So flying, which heavy touring requires, had to be held to a minimum. But I'm putting my toe in the water again." For all that, she chain-smokes filter-tipped Players, to ward off evil spirits, she claims. "If you knew the history of my smoking cures – every time I quit I break a leg. It just seems I'd be healthier to keep smoking."

Her laughter is warm and disarming, while there is a sparkle in her eyes, like sapphires. Mitchell is on top of her career again, with a hot new album in *Turbulent Indigo*, and looking forward with hope into the future. One surprising claim is that she sold more records than Elvis Presley. "Not after his death, but when I was the queen of rock 'n' roll. I sold more than he did when he was the king."

Follow that!

One of the most positive responses to the album came from Barney Hoskyns, also in *Mojo*. This was the seventeenth recorded episode in a career as "distinguished and diverse" – why does Joni always inspire alliteration? – as any in the rock canon. Here are songs full of "beguiling beauty and trenchant indignation." The best of them "rank with the most compelling and compassionate musical statements ever made about the things human beings do to themselves and to each other." The final track, based on the Old Testament, literally raised the hairs on the back of his neck when he first heard it.

Hoskyns interviewed Joni in LA. She bounded into the room like a spring colt, having just posed for a photo on the streets of West Hollywood, just outside Peter Asher's palatial offices. Hoskyns had heard "whisperings" that she was seriously ill with lung cancer – aren't people nice! – but her exuberance and prodigious intake of cigarettes knocked that out of court. Like the late Frank Zappa, she obviously regards nicotine as a health food. Joni sat down at an oak table, and the verbal tennis match began.

"In a lifetime, I think everyone sinks to the pits. If you've been to the bottom, you have an opportunity to be a more compassionate person. I have had a difficult life – no more difficult than anyone's else's but peculiarly difficult all the same. A life of very good luck and very bad luck, with a lot of health problems and therefore a lot of contact with medical carelessness. But I don't think I've ever become faithless, though I can't say what orthodoxy I belong to." She had been thinking about many themes and images for a long time, but was only now ready – or cheerful – enough to tackle subjects like the Book of Job, as she does in the concluding track of the album.

Had this priestess of the love generation yet purged the hatred she once admitted she held in her heart? "You've got to cleanse yourself.

Krishnamurti said an interesting thing, that the man who hates his boss hates his wife, and I think that's true. If you're holding dark feelings about anyone, they carry over into your relationship; you burden them with your bitterness. The eighties were very difficult for me, physically and emotionally." Problems included poor health – she had been "butchered" by a dentist – and financial betrayal. All in all, she had felt like a prisoner of war, "what with the physical and mental pain and general climate of mistrust." She had first articulated these concerns in *Dog Eat Dog*, though few had noticed. "No-one was ready for that at the time. They were all into ra-ra-Ronnie Reagan. Maybe the greed of that decade was supposed to descend on me more heavily, or more irrationally, than on other people. But I did feel like Alice with the Red Queen. I felt I was in a world where irrational law was coming at me from all directions."

The nineties had seen this malaise spread. Even the yuppies had at last noticed that material goods could only bring happiness up to a point. And as to love: "All human relationships are so malformed at this point, especially heterosexual relationships. You have to wonder why it is that men are so frustrated that they're beating on women and feel they have the licence to do so. Contemporary music is full of woman-hatred. Rap grew out of the pimp tradition, 'My bitch is badder than yours.'"

'Tomboy' Joni had never embraced feminism – though one could argue that she enacted it as well as anyone – but now found that "things between men and women have gotten so out of line in America. We don't know if OJ Simpson killed his wife, but we do know that he battered her frequently and was kind of smug about it, like he was above the law. So the precariousness of my gender at this particular time was something that was hard for me to sidestep; precariousness in the office, in the streets, even in public swimming pools." It is as if the hissing beneath summer lawns has become a full fledged roar. One thinks of Joni floating alone and safe in her own pool on the inner sleeve of that album.

Perhaps reflecting this kind of "precariousness", Hoskyns noticed a new vulnerability and huskiness to her vocals on the new album. "I'm finally developing enough character in my voice, I think, to play the roles I wrote for myself – even 'Both Sides Now', which I wrote when I was twenty-one and is better sung by a person in their fifties or sixties reflecting back on their life." Now that Joni is herself approaching that age, she too is looking back. She can see a musical development running through it, like a river. Born in the 'swing' era, "when I got my legs back after I had polio, I rock 'n' roll danced my way through my teens. My music was always very rhythmic, it just had no drums. But my first songs went back to my first roots, which were classical. My friends who only knew me as a party doll thought 'What is this, and where is it coming from?' My music started off as folk music, then it got more Celtic, and even like German lieder when I added the piano. Only then did it really begin to swing. Sometimes it takes a long time for your influences to show up."

After the ludicrous exercise of Woodstock Two – like a Hollywood sequel, totally missing the point of the original – she was clear about not wanting to be some kind of nostalgia trip. "I understand how people's memories – particularly of their youth and their best years – are wrapped up with the music they listened to then. They also tend to listen to music less and less as they get older. But I like to keep moving forward. I don't want to become a 'duty player', as Miles Davis would have said." Besides, who could provide corporate sponsorship, besides tobacco companies! She laughed raucously. She also admitted to having become, at one point, contemptuous of her audience, the one unforgivable sin in any art form.

"At the time of *For the Roses*, I was really mad at show business. I realise now that I'd entered into show business with a bad idea of what it was all about. I liked small clubs. I am a ham and an enjoyer. But on the big stage you get sonic distortion and my open tunings are a pain in the butt, so it's not very enjoyable." Appearing at the Edmonton Folk Festival had rekindled her appetite. "Songs like 'Circle Game' and 'Big Yellow Taxi' have almost become nursery rhymes. I didn't write 'Circle Game' as a children's song, but I'm very pleased to see it go into the culture in that way."

Joni herself was very much a part of contemporary culture. People on the street would feel able to communicate direct, without any sense of her being a 'star', and thus set apart. "In New York, strangers used to holler at me like someone in your class at school: 'Hey Joni, when you gonna do a concert?!' They didn't suck in their breath when they saw me. In the folk clubs, you could finish a set and go down and have a drink with people, and maybe even listen to music at their houses. That's the kind of ordinary I'm talking about. You haven't lost your access to life. Once you're trapped in your hotel room, it's all over." That said, her public image remains ambiguous, the chronicler of 'Woodstock nation' but also something of an outsider, looking in.

"I was the queen of the hippies, but in a way I wasn't really a hippy at all. I was always looking at it for its upsides and downsides, balancing it and thinking, here's the beauty of it, and here's the exploitive quality of it, and here's the silliness of it. I could never buy into it totally as an orthodoxy. If you go from the hippy thing to more of a Gatsby community, so what? Life is short and you have an opportunity to explore as much of it as time and fortune allow. I feel I belong to everything and nothing, so how could you define my environment?" Barney Hoskyns ties this kind of restlessness into her attitude to relationships. He instances the song 'Man to Man', which features not only her husband (then!) but two former lovers, James Taylor and John Guerin.

She ruefully agrees. "Oh, I always do that, I'm terrible at that! And they're all looking at me like 'You asshole', because the boyfriend and I wrote the song, and the old boyfriend who introduced me to Klein is on the drums. I don't know, artists are a strange lot."

In December 1994, Joni made a rare flight over the Atlantic to appear on BBC2's Late Show. Between solo versions of 'Sunny Sunday' and 'Love Kills', she talked with Tracey McLeod. Producer Mark Cooper remembers that Joni seemed to respond particularly well towards men, was charming, professional throughout, and without any apparent ego. Dressed richly, with a beret hiding her greying hair, and with perfect skin (cue Lloyd Cole), her voice is a bewitching blend of California cool and precise Canadian vowels. She speaks quickly, as if intensely nervous.

"It's not me that has gotten pessimistic, it's the times that have got more difficult, I'm just a witness. Los Angeles is at the centre of change. Right now it's a dangerous city to live in. The climate when I wrote my early work in California was so very different, people were courteous drivers, we didn't lock our doors at night. If you signalled to turn left, people said 'oh please, be my guest.' Now it's a very mean driving town. If you signal, people feel that you're trying to get ahead of them, and nobody is going to get ahead of anyone in LA. The song 'Sex Kills' deals with it. You can feel in urban traffic that everyone hates everyone. It wasn't this way in the sixties. People's nervous systems are shot, we're overpopulated. You can't remove yourself, it's totally random. I've had follow-homes, things like that, it's everywhere."

As if taken aback by the vehemence of all this, McLeod switches the ground to a discussion of technique. How do Joni's music and her paintings interrelate? "Joni's weird chords are aubergine, chartreuse, puce, whatever this colour is (points to her dress). They're muted colours, just opposed against each other, but moving by, so my colour sense musically and my colour sense as a painter tends towards the smokey – there's a continuity there – but generally I don't tend to paint the same things that I write about, because the poetry is deeper and darker. I'd rather not do that in the painting, I keep the themes generally more portraits of friends, landscapes that I like."

So how about the title of her new album, *Turbulent Indigo*? Cobalt, rather than indigo, was the shade of blue Van Gogh used so much, for the boiling skies he painted. "In a way, that's where the term comes from. Also it's psychology. To be a great artist, you have to be able to tap into emotional disturbances, channel them, you have to lassoo the hurricane." McLeod again changes the subject, and throws in a curve ball. Is she still careful to avoid the role as a spokesperson for women? There is a mild hint of reproof here, McLeod toeing the feminist line, which Mitchell abhors.

Joni smiles sweetly, and comes out all guns blazing. "No, I don't think I ever was careful about it, I just don't think I wrote for women. I wrote for relationships, I wrote to both men and women, in terms of their relationship. I was never a feminist, because it was too apartheid. Any feminists that I ever met were man-haters, they saw it in terms of them and us, where I was constantly in the company of men, usually large entourages of men, and ninety-nine per cent of the time I preferred their company to women, because I was more used to it. From being in men's company so much I was no longer a normal woman. Women seemed kind of foreign to me, up until recently actually."

McLeod (herself the antithesis of dourness) asks, "at the risk of sounding like a dour feminist," whether Joni would have had an easier life if she had been a man. Her reply, once again, drifts into unexpected areas. "Yes, absolutely. A gypsy, a Sikh, came up to me in a booth in New York one day and insisted on telling me about my past lives, he said they were sticking out all over me, and I said I didn't want to know. 'Are you going to tell me I'm Cleopatra or something?' 'No,' he said, 'it is is your first incarnation as a woman.' In my last life I was a bird, in the life before that I was an English gent, of all things, and in the life before that – he said this with considerable distaste – I was an Arab rug merchant. And that's the one I thought, 'that's true,' because I have this affinity for textiles. I could sit all day with a samovar of coffee, wheeling and dealing and feeling fabric."

Joni acknowledges that, with a thirty-year career already behind her, she is entering uncharted waters. She doesn't herself have many role models. "Lena Horne. There's a few women, you know, jazz singers mostly. We will see if the pop, quote unquote, world will allow me to survive." It is not a challenge that greatly excites, or worries her. "There is a prejudice against middle-aged women. Also, for the last fifteen or twenty years, depending on what country you're talking about, I've been out of favour, which is just typical of pop. No matter what I do, no matter how good my work is, it's not good enough, so there's a possibility that I will not sell enough records to have a contract. In which case I'll paint. I've always wandered out of this business."

Even if Joni wanted to quit the rock business, it refused to quit her. In December 1995, Natalie Merchant performed a "seriously strained" version of her song 'River'. The Indigo Girls were playing the same song in concert – two Jonis for the price of one – and a spirited version is captured on their recent live CD. It was as if this song of escape struck a chord in the late nineties, as something devoutly to be wished for.

For those who had lost contact with her music, *Turbulent Indigo* was almost like a return from the dead. If so, it is a rebirth that continues. In a major interview for *Billboard*, Timothy White captured a Joni Mitchell full of hope and plans. They held a series of meetings, stretching over six months, sitting in her hacienda-like Bel Air home, which serves now both as studio and art gallery. One thinks of the dying Frank Zappa, sorting through vaults of tapes to re-order his own musical heritage, though Mitchell is in some ways only just starting. Her walls are hung with images of the Canadian wilderness, painted during winter retreats at the lakeside home she still owns in British Columbia. "The luminous canvases are steeped in auburn and alabaster sunbeams that intensify as they rebound between water, frosty glaze and sky." They seem to reflect the inner turmoil of her recent battle with her own body, and what doctors have identified as post-polio syndrome.

"My compensation with yoga and other methods was good for about forty years, but now the wiring in my central nervous system is overtaxed and when I don't conserve my energy, the disease manifests itself in loss of animation. Last year I was experiencing a lot of muscle aches, joint aches, and extreme sensitivity to temperature changes. When I fly, I have to layer up and peel off assorted clothes as the plane is going up and down, because my body doesn't regulate its own temperature like a normal person's." A regime of holistic treatment has seen her resume a life she could enjoy, rather than endure.

"I've had Chinese acupuncturists and a Hawaiian kahuna working on me, and I'm doing kombucha mushroom treatments, so I've eliminated a lot of the pain I was experiencing. I feel good right now." Mitchell is now divorced from Larry Klein, though they remain good friends, as couples who split up often do, when there are no children involved. Her sociability remains intact. As White interviews her, friends – mainly young actors and musicians – begin arriving for a potlatch dinner, bearing dishes of pasta, fried chicken, vegetable salad, and bottles of red wine. Visibly cheered up, Joni begins to dance the Lindy Hop to an old Tamla Motown song on the radio, taking each guest by the hand. She then launches into a new song of her own, 'Happiness is the Best Facelift'. Pausing in mid-verse, she explains that it's about a "Romeo and Juliet situation," a love story set against parental disapproval.

It seems also to deal with Joni's own blossoming relationship, with Donald Freed, a 45-year old singer-songwriter and librarian from

271

Prince Albert, Saskatchewan. Hardly Romeo and Juliet, more Darby and Joan, especially as Joni's mother actually introduced them. The words play back the theme of 'Both Sides Now', viewed from experience.

> *Oh the cold winds blew*
> *At our room with a view*
> *All helpful and hopeful and candle light*
> *We kissed the angels*
> *And the moon eclipsed*
> *You know happiness is the best facelift.*

If nothing else, Joni has learnt to know love by now, when it happens. Her poignant rendition stills the small crowd, freezing them with its emotion, until Joni herself breaks the spell with laughter. Her hands flutter as she shoos her guests out onto the patio, where a fire is already blazing out against the dying of the day.

Like a naughty pair of schoolchildren, Joni and White go off to her studio, at the rear of the house. She unveils her new pride and joy, a specially modified, bright green Fender Stratocaster. "This instrument is going to be my saviour." The guitar has been built by Fred Walecki at Westwood Music, and hooks up with the "computerised brain" of a digital Roland VG8 unit. Joni controls this technical marvel with foot pedals. She will now be able to control at the flick of a switch the myriad special tunings which her songs demand on stage. She had previously decided to quit live performances, for good. She certainly looks fit as she bops back onto the open patio, and sits by the fireglow, "her high, unlined cheekbones starkly silhouetted against the flames."

Her career, so long on hold, seems about to enter its second flight. She is already planning surprise gigs – to road-test new songs – and negotiating with Reprise for the release of a box set. If this were to be along the lines of Crosby, Stills & Nash's magnificent four-CD retrospective (essential even for people like me, who have no huge affection for their music), packed with rare tracks, carefully annotated and comprehensive, it would be a peach indeed. From what is already known to exist in the vaults – early live concerts, out-takes and demos

– a skilled compiler could do for Mitchell what similar exercises also did for the Byrds, Dylan, and Jefferson Airplane. A box set is the cardboard equivalent to entry into the rock 'n' roll hall of fame. It redefines an artist's whole career and cultural significance. For someone who has never even issued a 'Best of' – except briefly in New Zealand – it would fill a particular and much-needed gap.

A quick glance at the Joni Mitchell sites on the Internet reveals over 2000 entries, ranging from set lists of her rare concert appearances, to personal testimonies to her music, to lyric sheets and dialogues about what her songs actually mean. It is ironic that someone who came up on the coffee-house circuit should now be lauded at Internet cafes, attracting the same kind of intense scrutiny and intimacy, in so radically different a context. From the basements of Yorktown and Greenwich Village to the phone lines of the world.

It is strange, when tribute albums to a single artists are so prevalent, that one has never been devoted to Mitchell herself, among the most influential songwriters of her age. Neil Young has inspired at least one, Leonard Cohen at least two, and Dylan a couple of dozen. Unlike those three friends and rivals, she does not even inspire a fanzine as yet, though I hope that the publication of this very book will remedy that, by playing its own small part in redirecting attention back to this wonderful artist.

In New York on 6th November, 1995, Joni Mitchell gave an unexpected live concert. She performed at the Fez, deep in the heart of Greenwich Village. It was a kind of homecoming, and the Internet buzzed for months afterwards with reviews of, and reactions to, the evening. A select audience of 200, including old friends like Eric Andersen and Carly Simon, and new fans like Natalie Merchant and Chrissie Hynde, were lucky enough to have procured tickets. Accompanied only by her own magic Stratocaster and jazz drummer Brian Blade, Joni offered a "bravura" selection of songs old and new.

It was her own version of MTV's *Unplugged*, jolting her career onto another set of tracks. Through *Unplugged*, Dylan was reborn as a sharply-dressed, focused prophet of doom, and Neil Young took time out after a feedback-drenched *Crazy Horse* tour to play the simple country boy, pumping out 'Hurricane' on a wheezy harmonium. Such exposure – and the inevitable follow-up soundtrack album – is exactly what Mitchell now needs. Perhaps it is about to happen. On the phone to Timothy White the following afternoon, Joni told him that she had just collaborated with Don Freed on a new song called 'Love Cries', the refrain declaring "When that train comes rumbling by, no one can hear love's cries." A song based on her childhood memory of waving at the train as it passed by each day, off to unknown territories and empires, in whose wake Joni had since followed, exploring the world. A gleeful Mitchell giggled down the phone line, and asserted that everything was still to play for in her life and career. "The impossible is now possible."

Joni continues to inspire those on the cutting edge of rock music. In January 1996, Seal named her in the Guardian as his favourite musician. "She might be talking about something completely unrelated to anything in your experience, but then there'll be a line that will be worth waiting the whole song for. She has an amazing ability to record parts of her life in a way that people will understand. She can write about anything. We're friends now and she's everything you'd imagine her to be from her songs."

Such emotional honesty has also infected a whole generation of women singers. Both Annie Lennox and Madonna have testified to her influence, though Joni has remained characteristically sharp-eyed, especially about the latter. Talking to David Wild, she admits. "Well, she's a great 'star.' She's got that whore-Madonna thing built in (laughs). She's like a living Barbie doll but a little on the blue side. There's always been that type of female. There's always been a market for it, but the danger is that she thinks she's a role model. And it's a *terrible* role model. It's death to all things real." Joni prefers Sinead O'Connor, bane to most of Joni's generation after her attempt to disrupt that holy of holies Bob Dylan's fiftieth birthday concert. Joni likes, and empathises with, her spikiness. "She's a passionate little singer. And I understand her saying 'I hate this job.' People don't realize how horrible it is. Making music is great. The exploitation of it is horrible. And I think you've got to be as hard as nails. Maybe that's where Madonna has the edge on us. I think it's degrading, humiliating – so does Sinead. Whereas Madonna's above being degraded or humiliated. She *flirts* with it... but at what cost to her soul, is my question."

Joni's real heirs are female revolutionaries like the Slits – their very name an affront – Liz Phair, who reinterpreted male dinosaurs the Stones' 'Exile on Main Street' for women, and Chrissie Hynde, who shredded a male lover in 'Private Life'. Mitchell has become the spiritual godmother to a new generation of confrontational women singer-songwriters: PJ Harvey, Courtney Love of Hole, Tori Amos even. Ironically, it was Joni's non-confrontational image at the time – as compared to Janis Joplin, say – which enabled her to get away with the soul-baring of albums like *Blue*. Under its surface sweetness, that album declared that women could be as free, as self-determining, as musically independent and as sexually choosy and demanding as any man. Yoko Ono, oddly enough, was saying much the same, but in albums recorded on her husband's record label, and barely listened to at the time (or now, come to think of it). Joni's particular gift was to put all this to a good tune.

She also reflects a particularly Canadian perspective, a more literate culture (dare one say it) than the USA, less media obsessed – though Joni once admitted that her favourite TV show was *Looney Tunes*! On this cultural cusp between the rest of North America and Europe, there is a kind of sadness which seeps from the northern sky into the work of Leonard Cohen, Neil Young, Robbie Robertson, visiting draft dodger Jesse Winchester, and the folk sisters Kate and Anna McGarrigle. There is a sparking generation of new Canadian singer-songwriters just now breaking through, who range from Ron Sexsmith – his lazy vocals sound like a retread of Phil Ochs, of all people – to Sarah McLachlan. *Fumbling Towards Ecstasy* draws on trance dance, and there is a male svengali in the wings, but McLachlan's vocals are astonishingly intimate, a waterfall of naked emotion. The UK issue of the CD adds a final track, no less than a cover version of 'Blue', even more haunted than the original.

A less acknowledged influence is on kd lang, though her song 'Save Me' has been described as Patsy Cline meeting Joni Mitchell. lang has done for country what Joni did for jazz, by bringing it into conjunction with rock, and has faced the same charges of an icy non-involvement with her material. Both share a largely female audience, and although lang has always worn her alternative sexuality on her sleeve, both are in their different ways lesbian icons. Particularly ironic in Joni's case, since her involvement with men is, to put it mildly, firmly on the record.

Alanis Morissette is also a fellow Canadian. Like Joni, she too underwent a drastic image change, destroying her public's perception of her as a template of bright-eyed innocence with just one album. The multi-million selling CD *Jagged Little Pill* – which won four Grammys, including that of album of the year – a saga of oral sex, twisted love, and bitter vengeance. A soundtrack for the millennium. In the uncredited and unaccompanied song which concludes the CD, she visits her ex-boyfriend's house while he is out. Like a female stalker, she strips off, puts on his bathrobe and cologne, and goes through his CDs. What does she play, to remind her of their lost love? His Joni Mitchell records, naturally...

Joni Mitchell has survived all that life has thrown at her: unimaginable riches and emotional agony, mass adulation followed by apparent public indifference. Those who have talked to her recently report a confident, friendly and determined person. She has recently parted with manager Peter Asher, and is infused with the desire to resuscitate her career. Along the way to her current lonely eminence, she has lost as much as she has gained. In Spring 1996, she revealed on Canadian TV that she was searching for Kelly, the daughter she gave away for adoption when she was nineteen, and who would now be in her early thirties. In a desperate bid to locate her via the media, a tearful Joni declared "I just want to tell her I didn't give her up for lack of love."

Of her old friends, James Taylor has indeed seen his hairline recede. David Crosby endured a self-induced crucifixion on crack cocaine and firearms charges, spending time in prison, and came back a sadder and thinner man to join Stills and Nash in a CSN now grey and nostalgic, with all the flash of youth long gone. Neil Young has continued to perform the unexpected, becoming a kind of grandfather of grunge. Dylan continues to stumble from one live performance to the next, though with a renewed sense of purpose. David Geffen is one of the richest men in the world, and is setting up a new record label with Stephen Spielberg.

The LA riots and Reaganite economics have turned uptown

California into an armed camp, with little time for community or love, except behind locked doors. The days of free festivals are well and truly over: rock music is now a corporate business, costed to the last dollar. The coffee houses are long gone as folk venues; indeed, the only venue now to offer that kind of nurturing is a web of arts-centres and small concert halls, themselves under financial constraint, and an unspoken Government imperative not to encourage the outspoken or voices of protest. Music is now a leisure choice, not a tool for change. As Joni predicted, people are increasingly nervous about speaking their minds in a world increasingly managed and conformist.

Even the BBC is succumbing to the voodoo of managerialism, with tightly defined 'core audiences', and woe betide anyone over 25 who dares listen to Radio One. Joni would now be slotted onto Radio Two, as middle-aged nostalgia. The kind of knowledgable DJ who would naturally have played her new work – like Johnny Walker – has been expunged, or relegated to a night-time slot.

Her appeal continues to be reflected in magazines like *Q* and *Mojo* – and indeed *Rolling Stone* – whose journalists and readers have grown up with rock music, and she would find a ready spot on TV shows like *Later* which smash gleefully through false musical boundaries. Hopefully, initiatives like this book will help to persuade her to re-enter the arena, however fierce the media lions waiting to bare their jaws at this proponent of long-derided follies like peace, and love, and friendship, and the vagaries of the human heart. Her determined retreat from the music scene has created a vacuum that no-one else has ever been able quite to fill.

Part of Joni's 1994 solo concert from Toronto recently surfaced on the *Just Ice* bootleg CD. Between songs Joni jokingly refers to her propensity to write sad material, just to cheer herself up! Particularly refreshing are two new songs: 'Love Cries' is a collaboration with Donald Freed and looks back to her childhood; 'Happiness is the best Facelift' is magnificent and heart rending all at once. Painfully based on an updating of the generation gap, the song describes the middle-aged Joni coming back to Saskatoon with Donald Freed in unwedded bliss only to meet her mother's continuing disapproval over the "moral issue" of their living together. Set on Christmas Day the song updates her earlier *The River*. There it was a means of escape, here water unites the two lovers as a harmonic.

In August 1996, *Acoustic Guitar* magazine carried an interview with Joni by Jeffrey Pepper Rodgers, which brought out her secret history as a guitar maestro. In her hands it becomes an orchestra, "the treble strings become a cool jazz horn section; the bass snaps out syncopations like a snare drum; the notes ring out in clusters that simply don't come out of a normal six string". Her new Roland guitar has infused her new songs. What emerged from this state of the art computer wizardry were memories. "Swinging brass, pulled through Miles Davis and different harmonic stuff that I absorbed in the 50s."

The first song to emerge was 'Harlem in Havana', "about two little girls in my hometown getting into this black revue which was an Afro-Cuban burlesque kind of show that you weren't supposed to stand in front of, let alone go in." Joni also reveals that she is working on a CD anthology of the best of her past work and a complete songbook. Her renaissance as an artist continues and is starting to be noticed by the wider world. Joni won two Grammy awards in 1996, one for Best Pop Album for *Turbulent Indigo*.

Even Joni's personal life seems to be echoing earlier achievements. According to extraordinary press statements circulating in late 1996, Joni Mitchell, at the age of fifty-two, has given birth to a daughter, more than thirty years after the arrival of Kelly. The 'circle game' indeed.

We will leave the last word to Joni herself, coming as close to a career definition as she has ever done. Bill Flanagan relates a scene from the film *After Hours*, directed by Martin Scorsese (responsible also for *The Last Waltz*, in which a whole era draws to a sad close). The hero has suffered just about everything a man could. A woman invites him back to her home, which he finds to be festooned with peace symbols on every wall, a throwback to the sixties. She even puts a Monkees album on the hi-fi. "He's sitting there depressed, and she goes. 'Oh you're crying!' He says 'Yes, I've been through a tough experience.' She goes 'Don't worry' and runs over, takes off the Monkees, and puts on 'Chelsea Morning'."

Joni's response is immediate, and full of quiet wit. "It's a pill. Like a Kleenex. I remember Paul McCartney said he didn't mind being an aspirin for a generation at all." And neither does she.

Discography

As Joni told Timothy White: "I have nothing to do with the choosing of tracks for singles. Generally speaking, I don't agree with the selections and there are tracks that never get played on the radio that I regret won't get the exposure. 'Car on a Hill' was one I thought would have been a good single; I wish that I was circulating in the goldie oldies department because it has a vitality today, it would work, 'Trouble Child' too and 'Just Like This Train', which I'd rather hear on the radio than 'Raised on Robbery'.

"My record company always had the tendency to take my fastest songs on albums for singles, thinking they'd stand out. Meanwhile I'd think that the radio is crying out for one of my ballads!"

UK 7-INCH SINGLES

REPRISE

RS 20694 Night in the City/I Had a King	July 1968
RS 23402 Chelsea Morning/Both Sides Now	August 1969
RS 20906 Big Yellow Taxi/Woodstock	June 1970
K 14099 Carey/My Old Man	August 1971
K 14130 California/A Case of You	April 1972

ASYLUM

AYM 511 You Turn Me On (I'm a Radio)/Urge for Going	November 1972
AYM 515 Cold Blue Steel and Sweet Fire/Blonde in the Bleachers	March 1973
AYM 524 Raised on Robbery/Court and Spark	January 1974
AYM 525 Help Me/Just Like This Train	March 1974
AYM 533 Free Man in Paris/Car on a Hill	October 1974
AYM 5337Big Yellow Taxi(Live)/Rainy Night House (Live)	January 1975

K 13035	In France They Kiss on Main Street/Boho Dance	March 1976
K 13048	You Turn Me On (I'm a Radio)/Free Man in Paris	July 1976
K 13072	Coyote/Blue Motel Room	February 1977
K 13110	Off Night Backstreet/Jericho	February 1978
K 13154	The Dry Cleaner from Des Moines/God Must be a Boogie Man	June 1979
K 12478	Why Do Fools Fall in Love (Live)/Black Crow (Live)	October 1980

GEFFEN

GEF A2950	(You're So Square) Baby I Don't Care/Love	November 1982
GEF A3122	Chinese Cafe/Unchained Melody, Ladies Man	February 1983
GEF A3122	Chinese Cafe/Ladies Man	February 1983
GEF A6740	Good Friends/Smokin' (Empty, Try Another)	November 1985
GEF A7124	Shiny Toys/Three Great Stimulants	April 1986
GEF 37	My Secret Place (Edit)/Number One	May 1988
GEF 4	Come in from the Cold (edit)/Ray's Dad's Cadillac	July 1991

UK EPs
REPRISE

| K 14345 | Carey/Both Sides Now/Big Yellow Taxi/Woodstock | May 1974 |

UK 12-INCHES
GEFFEN

| TA7124 | Shiny Toys/Three Great Stimulants | April 1986 |
| GEF 37T | My Secret Place/Chinese Cafe/Unchained Melody/Good Friends | May 1988 |

UK CD SINGLES

GEF 35CD My Secret Place/Chinese Cafe/Unchained Melody/Good Friends

	May 1988
CD GFSTD Come in from the Cold/Ray's Dad's Cadillac	July 1991
CD GFSXD ditto, in special flip pack, with four prints	

PROMOS: US SINGLES

Reprise PRO 333 Clouds – radio edit	1968
Reprise PRO 337 Chelsea Morning – promo	1968
Asylum E452447 Carey/Jericho – promo	1975

PROMOS: US 12-INCHES

| GEF PROA 1081 Wild Things Run Fast – sampler | 1982 |

GEF PROA 2386	Good Friends – promo (with Michael McDonald)	1983
GEF PROA	Shiny Toys –promo	1985
GEF PROA 3018	Snakes and Ladders –promo	1988
GEF PROA 3116	My Secret Place –promo	1988

PROMOS: US CD SINGLES

GEF PROCD	Cool Water – radio edit	1988
GEF PROCD 4213	Come in from the Cold – promo	1991
GEF PROCD 4291	Nothing Can Be Done – promo	1991
GEF PROCD 7220	How Do You Stop – promo	1994

PROMOS: UK SINGLES

Geffen Promo	Chinese Cafe/Ladies Man/An Interview (double single)	1983
Geffen Promo	My Secret Place – radio edit	1988
Geffen Promo	Come in from the Cold/Ray's Dad's Cadillac – promo box with CD	
and Video		1991

UK ALBUMS (Release dates given on British CD reissues refer instead to US issues).
JONI MITCHELL (SONG TO A SEAGULL)
Side One: I Came To The City:
I Had a King, Michael from Mountains, Night in the City, Marcie, Nathan La Franeer.
Side Two: Out of the City and Down to the Seaside:
Sisotowbell Lane, The Dawntreader, The Pirate of Penance, Song to a Seagull, Cactus Tree.

LP: Reprise RSPL 6293	June 1968
Reprise K 44051	July 1973
CD: Reprise K 244051	January 1988

CLOUDS
Side One: Tin Angel, Chelsea Morning, I Don't Know Where I Stand, That Song About the Midway, Roses Blue.
Side Two: The Gallery, I Think I Understand, Songs to Ageing Children Come, The Fiddle and the Drum, Both Sides Now.

LP: Reprise RSPL 6341	October 1969
Reprise K 44070	July 1973
CD: Reprise K244070	January 1988

LADIES OF THE CANYON

Side One: Morning Morgantown, For Free, Conversation, Ladies of the Canyon, Willy, The Arrangement.

Side Two: Rainy Night House, The Priest, Blue Boy, Big Yellow Taxi, Woodstock, The Circle Game.

LP: Reprise RSPL 6376	May 1970
Reprise K 44085	July 1973
CD: Reprise K 244085	March 1988

BLUE

Side One: All I Want, My Old Man, Little Green, Carey, Blue.

Side Two: California, This Flight Tonight, River, A Case of You, The Last Time I Saw Richard.

LP: Reprise K 44128	July 1971
CD: Reprise K244128	January 1987
Reprise CD Box set/book, ltd to 2500 copies	1988

FOR THE ROSES

Side One: Banquet, Cold Blue Steel and Sweet Fire, Barangrill, Lesson in Survival, Let the Wind Carry Me, For the Roses.

Side Two: See You Sometime, Electricity, You Turn Me On (I'm a Radio), Blonde in the Bleachers, Woman of Heart and Mind, Judgement of the Moon and Stars (Ludwig's tune).

LP: Asylum SYLA 8753	December 1972
Asylum K 53007	June 1976
CD: Asylum K253007	August 1984

COURT AND SPARK

Side One: Court and Spark, Help Me, Free Man in Paris, People's Parties, The Same Situation.

Side Two: Car on a Hill, Down to You, Just Like This Train, Raised on Robbery, Trouble Child, Twisted.

LP: Asylum SYLA 8756	March 1974
Asylum K 53002	June 1976

CD: Asylum 253002   August 1984

Special Pressings:
Asylum EQ 1001: US Quad Mix
Nautilus Audiophile NR 11   1982

MILES OF AISLES

Side One: You Turn Me On (I'm a Radio), Big Yellow Taxi, Rainy Night House, Woodstock.

Side Two: Cactus Tree, Cold Blue Steel and Sweet Fire, A Case of You, Blue.

Side Three: Circle Game, Peoples' Parties, All I Want, Real Good for Free, Both Sides Now.

Side Four: Carey, The Last Time I Saw Richard, Jericho, Love Or Money.

LP: Asylum SYSP 902	January 1975
Asylum K 63011	June 1976
CD	US issue only

THE HISSING OF SUMMER LAWNS

Side One: In France They Kiss on Main Street, The Jungle Line, Edith and the Kingpin, Don't Interrupt the Sorrow, Shades of Scarlett Conquering.

Side Two: The Hissing of Summer Lawns, The Boho Dance, Harry's House/Centerpiece, Sweet Bird, Shadows and Light.

LP: Asylum SYLA 876	November 1975
Asylum K 53018	June 1976
CD: Asylum K253018	October 1987

Special Pressings:
Asylum EQ 1031 US Quad mix
Asylum/Nimbus Audiophile Pressing 1984 – sold through Practical Hi-Fi mag

HEJIRA

Side One: Coyote, Amelia, Furry Sings the Blues, A Strange Boy, Hejira.

Side Two: Hejira, Song for Sharon, Black Crow, Blue Motel Room, Refuge of the Roads.

LP: Asylum K 53053	November 1976

CD: Asylum 253053   October 1987

DON JUAN'S RECKLESS DAUGHTER
Side One: Overture – Cotton Avenue, Talk to Me, Jericho.
Side Two: Paprika Plains.
Side Three: Otis and Marlena, The Tenth World, Dreamland.
Side Four: Don Juan's Reckless Daughter, Off Night Backstreet, The Silky Veils of Ardor.

LP: Asylum K 63006   January 1978
CD: Asylum 263006   August 1987

MINGUS
Side One: Happy Birthday 1975 (Rap), God Must be a Boogie Man, Funeral (Rap), A Chair in the Sky, The Wolf That Lives in Lindsey.
Side Two: It's A Muggin' (Rap), Sweet Sucker Dance, Coin in the Pocket (Rap), The Dry Cleaner from Des Moines, Lucky (Rap), Goodbye Pork Pie Hat.

LP: Asylum K 53091   July 1979
CD: Asylum K253091   October 1987

SHADOWS AND LIGHT
Side One: Introduction, In France They Kiss on Main Street, Edith and the Kingpin, Coyote, Goodbye Pork Pie Hat.
Side Two: The Dry Cleaner from Des Moines, Amelia, Pat's Solo (Pat Metheny), Hejira.
Side Three: Black Crow, Don's Solo (Don Alias), Dreamland, Free Man in Paris, Band Introduction, Furry Sings the Blues.
Side Four: Why Do Fools Fall in Love, Shadows and Light, God Must be a Boogie Man, Woodstock.

LP: Asylum K 62030   September 1980
CD: US issue only (Asylum 704-2). US CD issue omits Black Crow, Don's Solo, Free Man in Paris.

WILD THINGS RUN FAST
Side One: Chinese Cafe, Unchained Melody, Wild Things Run Fast, Ladies' Man, Moon at the Window, Solid Love.

Side Two: Be Cool, (You're So Square) Baby I Don't Care, You Dream Flat Tires, Man to Man, Underneath the Streetlight, Love.

LP: Geffen GEF 25102	November 1982
Geffen 9020191	September 1986
Geffen GEF 02019	January 1991
CD: Geffen 902 0192	July 1988
Geffen CD GEFD 02019	January 1991

Special Pressings:
Geffen GUS 2019 Pure Vinyl pressing

DOG EAT DOG
Side One: Good Friends, Fiction, The Three Great Stimulants, Tax Free, Smoking (Empty, Try Another).
Side Two: Dog Eat Dog, Shiny Toys, Ethiopia, Impossible Dreamer, Lucky Girl.

LP: Geffen GEF 26455	November 1985
Geffen GEF K9240741	October 1987
CD: Geffen CD 9240742	May 1986
Geffen CD GFLD	March 1993

Special Pressings:
Interview album, Geffen promo LP — 1985

CHALK MARK IN A RAINSTORM
Side One: My Secret Place, Number One, Lakota, The Tea Leaf Prophecy (Lay Down Your Arms), Dancin' Clown.
Side Two: Cool Water, The Beat of Black Wings, Snakes and Ladders, The Reoccuring Dream, A Bird That Whistles.

LP: Geffen WX 141	March 1988
CD: Geffen CD K9241722	March 1988
Geffen CD GEFD 24172	January 1991

Special Pressings:
Inside Information: Geffen promo box set for Chalk Mark – package includes CD, cassette, photos and biography.

A Conversation with Joni Mitchell – Geffen promo CD   1988

NIGHT RIDE HOME
Side One: Night Ride Home, Passion Play (When All the Slaves are Free), Cherokee Louise, The Windfall (Everything for Nothing).
Side Two: Come in from the Cold, Nothing can be Done, The Only Joy in Town, Ray's Dad's Cadillac, Two Grey Rooms.

LP: Geffen 24302   March 1991
CD: Geffen GEFD 24302   March 1991

TURBULENT INDIGO
Sunny Sunday, Sex Kills, How Do You Stop, Turbulent Indigo, Last Chance Lost, The Magdalene Laundries, Not to Blame, Borderline, Yvette in English, The Sire of Sorrow (Job's Sad Song).

CD: Reprise 9362-457862   October 1994

RADIO CONCERTS
JONI MITCHELL/JAMES TAYLOR: POP SPECTACULAR
BBC Transcription Services   1970
JONI MITCHELL/JAMES TAYLOR: WESTWOOD ONE POP CONCERT 88-25 13.6.88

COMPILATIONS

THE WORLD OF JONI MITCHELL
NZ Reprise 5-5260 (New Zealand issue only. The only compilation of her work yet to be released, anywhere!)

Also appears on:
THE BAND: THE LAST WALTZ: Triple LP
WB K66076   April 1978
CD reissue K266076   March 1988
Includes Coyote with conga by Dr John. She also sings background vocal on Neil Young's Helpless.

ROGER WATERS: THE WALL: LIVE IN BERLIN
Mercury LP 846-611-1   August 1990

Mercury CD 846611-2
She performs one song, Goodbye Blue Sky (Waters).

FRIENDS
Reprise CD 9362-460082   September 1995
Joni performs Big Yellow Taxi (Traffic Jam Mix).

MESSAGE TO LOVE: THE ISLE OF WIGHT FESTIVAL 1970: Double CD set
EFD CD 327   December 1995
She performs Big Yellow Taxi and Woodstock.

UK VIDEOS
COME IN FROM THE COLD:
Castle   1991
A collection of promo videos, now deleted.

MESSAGE TO LOVE: THE ISLE OF WIGHT FESTIVAL 1970
VIDEO PNV 1005   October 1995

UK RADIO SESSIONS:
Top Gear, BBC Radio One, 29th September 1969, with John Cameron, piano; Harold
McNair, saxophone; Tony Carr, drums; Danny Thompson, bass.
Chelsea Morning, Gallery, Night in the City, Cactus Tree.

UK RADIO CONCERTS
BBC Radio One: London, 29 October, 1970, with James Taylor.
BBC Radio One: In Concert 1972, James Taylor second guitar.

SELECTED UK TV APPEARANCES
BBC2 In Concert: 1970, solo.
BBC2 In Concert: 19th November, 1974, with Tom Scott and the LA Express.
BBC2 Old Grey Whistle Test Special: 1985. Richard Skinner interview, film of Joni
painting in her studio, and clips from the two BBC TV concerts, a 1980 open-air festival
with Jaco Pastorius, three songs from a 1983 solo concert, a live-in-the-studio version of
Chinese Cafe with Larry Klein from 1984, and the Good Friends video.
BBC2 The Late Show: 12th December, 1994. Tracy McLeod interview and solo
versions of Sunny Sunday, Sex Kills.

BOOTLEGS

The whole question of bootlegs – as compared to pirate copies – is a legal and moral minefield. Official CDs like Dylan's Basement Tapes and the Beatles Anthology series would probably not exist without feeding an appetite whetted by bootleg tapes. Some official releases, like the Who's Live at Leeds are even packaged with bootleg-like roughness. Misattributions of songs are often comic: bootlegs range from complete rip-offs to the productions of devoted fans, with annotations that would put a college professor to shame.

I am not aware of any studio out-takes in circulation. The records listed below are all taken either from radio broadcasts or live performances. The records listed below are of USA origin, apart from the CD, made somewhere in the EEC.

BOOTLEG LPs

THE POSALL AND THE MOSALM: WMMR Interviews 1966, March 1967, October 1967, Second Fret 17 March 1967, 12th October 1967, all mono, coloured vinyl.

Side One: Circle Games, Old Paintings – Interview, London Bridge, Joni's Coke Commercial, Eastern Rain, Just Like Me, The Bagel Game, The Posall and the Mosalm.

Side Two: Brandy Eyes, Drummer Man, Winter Lady, Mr Blue, Urge for Going, Approximately Sugar Mountain – Interviews.

The most intriguing of all her bootlegs, with lots of unrecorded songs, and an early version of 'Urge for Going'. Is The Bagel Game a mishearing of The Circle Game, or something else entirely? I'd love to hear this record, for research purposes only, of course....

WINTERLADY (FLAT)

Canada 1967, mono.

Side One: The Circle Game, London Bridge, John's Coke Commercial, Eastern Rain, Just Like Me.

Side Two: Brandy Eyes, Drummer Man, Winter Lady, Mr Blue, Urge for Going, Sugar Mountain.

FOR FREE (Midnite Records)/Lennie and Dom Songs (TAKRL)

NET TV Broadcast, LA 1969, mono

Side One: Chelsea Morning, Cactus Tree, Night in the City, Marcie, Nathan La Franeer, Rainy Night House, Blue Boy.

Side Two: For Free, Get Together, The Fiddle and Drum, I Think I Understand, Both Sides Now.

Lennie and Dom Songs reverses the two sides.

IN PERFECT HARMONY (Escargot Records)/TAKES TWO TO TANGO (SE)
BBC broadcast, misattributed to the Royal Albert Hall. With James Taylor.
Side One: Steam Roller, The Gallery, Rainy Day Man, Night Owl, The Priest, Carey, Carolina on my Mind.
Side Two: California, For Free, Circle Games.

A mysterious release, which I cannot comment on, having never heard or seen it. Presumably the Albert Hall is a misnomer for the Royal Festival Hall, but this is a different selection of tracks to the CD release For Free. If the song titles are correct, tracks one, three, four and seven on side one are James Taylor songs.

LIGHTS OUT IN GEORGIA (Trade Mark of Quality)
No details of date or venue available.
Side One: Lights out in Georgia, Gift of the Magi, I Can't Go Back There Anymore, Morning Morgantown, Ballerina Ballerina
Side Two: Seagulls, Both Sides Now, Plays Real Good for Free, And So Once Again.

A complete mystery, combining songs which predate the first LP with For Free, written much later. The last song is obviously The Fiddle and the Drum and track three side one is I Had a King.

BY HER OWN DEVICES (TAKRL)
BBC Radio One: In Concert 1972, James Taylor second guitar
Side One: This Flight Tonight, Electricity, Big Yellow Taxi, See You Sometime, That Song about the Midway, Gallery.
Side Two: The Priest, California, Carey, You Turn Me On (I'm a Radio), For the Roses.
The first two songs on side two feature Taylor.

SPRING SONGS (Berkeley Records)
Duke University, Durham, North Carolina February 1974, mono
Side One: You Turn Me On (I'm a Radio), Free Man in Paris, Same Situation
Side Two: Just Like This Train, Rainy Night Man, Woodstock
Side Three: Big Yellow Taxi, Peoples' Parties, All I Want
Side Four: A Case of You, For the Roses, Cold Blue Steel and Sweet Fire

CALIFORNIA (L-100)

Greek Theatre, Hollywood 16th September 1979: mono, 250 copies only

Side One: In France They Kiss on Main Street, Coyote, Free Man in Paris, Goodbye Pork Pie Hat.

Side Two: Dry Cleaner from Des Moines, Furry Sings the Blues, God Must be a Boogie Man, Raised on Robbery, Why Do Fools Fall In Love.

From the same tour captured on the official release Shadows and Light, a double LP with nine extra tracks on the original vinyl outing (and an Introduction), recorded at Santa Barbara County Bowl in the same month.

DREAMS ARE SHIVERING DOWN MY SPINE (Neon)

Verona, Italy 7th May 1983

Side One: Cotton Avenue, You Turn Me On(I'm a Radio), You Dream Flat Tires, Songs for Sharon, Big Yellow Taxi

Side Two: God Must Be a Boogie Man, Amelia, Wild Things Run Fast.

Side Three: Raised on Robbery, Refuge of the Road, (You're so Square) Baby I Don't Care, Solid Love, Love.

Side Four: Chinese Cafe, Unchained Melody, Both Sides Now, I Heard It Through the Grapevine, Woodstock.

BOOTLEG CDs

FOR FREE (Sacem, 1991)

BBC Radio One: London 29 October 1970, with James Taylor.

That Song about the Midway, Gallery, Rainy Day Man (wrong title, wrongly credited to Taylor), The River, My Old Man, The Priest, Carey, A Case of You, California, For Free, Circle Games (mis-credited to Taylor).

LP SESSIONS

A selection of LPs by other artists on which Joni Mitchell is featured, either as singer, musician, cover artist, or even dedicatee.

Eric Andersen: Blue River, 1973: vocals

Be True to You, 1975: vocals

The first of this pair is a wonderfully miserable record, and Joni wails in the background where appropriate. Andersen is an old friend from the Canadian folk scene.

Joan Baez: Gracias A La Vida, 1974: vocals
Diamonds and Rust, 1975: vocals
Early influence and long-time rival. The hatchet is buried here.

David Blue: Com'n Back for More, 1975: vocals
A fellow folkie whose first LP is an unconscious parody of Highway 61, with one difference: where Dylan takes vocals where they never before went, Blue simply can't sing. Where Dylan brings to rock lyrics his deep knowledge of folk, blues and the poetry of TS Eliot, Rimbaud and the Surrealists, Blue simply strings odd words together. He got better, and appears – shortly before his death, playing a pinball machine – in Dylan's movie Renaldo and Clara.

Jackson Browne: For Everyman, 1973: piano
Joni's protegee from the 1972 tour. He performed a similar role to the Eagles as she did to CSNY, as songwriter and inspiration.

Dave Crosby If Only I Could Remember My Name: unspecified
A typhoon of sound, with all the great West Coast musicians jamming like crazy.

Crosby and Nash: Graham Nash David Crosby, 1972
Dedicated to Miss Mitchell from two former boyfriends.

Crosby, Stills and Nash: Replayer: cover painting

Paul Horn Visions, 1974: vocals, keyboards

LA Express Shadow Play, 1976: vocals
Repaying the compliment to her backing group.

Graham Nash Wild Tales, 1973: vocals, back cover painting

Seemon & Marijke Son of America, 1971: vocals
A weird record by two remnants from The Fool who helped design the Beatles Apple store, before it was all given away. Ultimate hippies.

James Taylor Mud Slide Slim and the Blue Horizon, 1971: vocals
Taylor repays the compliment by playing on Blue, whose title song is about him.

291

Jimmie Webb Letters, 1972: vocals
Lands End, 1974: vocals
Webb is an MOR supremo, turned singer-songwriter.

SONGS ABOUT JONI MITCHELL ON OTHER ALBUMS

Crosby, Stills and Nash 'Lady of the Island' (Nash); 'Genevieve' (Crosby) 3rd verse
Crosby Stills and Nash (1969)

Crosby, Stills, Nash and Young 'Our House' (Nash)
Deja Vu (1970)

Graham Nash 'Simple Man' (Nash)
Songs for Beginners (1971)

Neil Young 'Sweet Joni' (unreleased)
'Stupid Girl' (Young)
Zuma (1975)

COVER VERSIONS OF JONI MITCHELL SONGS
These are wildly varying, from 'easy' listening to full-tilt rock 'n' roll. I have listed some of the high and low lights: Clouds and Both Sides Now are, of course, the same song.

Ronnie Aldrich:	Both Sides Now
Big Country:	Big Yellow Taxi
Max Bygraves:	Both Sides Now
Glen Campbell:	Both Sides Now
Clannad:	Both Sides Now
Judy Collins:	Michael from Mountains, Both Sides Now
Christine Collister:	Shades of Scarlett Conquering
Bing Crosby:	Both Sides Now
Dave Crosby:	Yvette in English
Crosby & Nash	Urge for Going
CSN&Y:	Woodstock
Neil Diamond:	Both Sides Now
Bob Dylan:	Big Yellow Taxi
Fairport Convention:	I Don't Know Where I Stand, Chelsea Morning, Night in

the City, Marcie, Eastern Rain

BB Gabor:	Big Yellow Taxi (Canadian new wave)
Go Betweens:	Clouds
Benny Goodman:	Both Sides Now
Davey Graham:	Both Sides Now
Amy Grant:	Big Yellow Taxi (1995 surprise hit single)
George Hamilton IV:	Urge for Going, Both Sides Now
Noel Harrison:	Nathan La Franeer
Ian and Sylvia:	The Circle Game
Indigo Girls:	River (Live version)
Low Noise:	Jungle Line, features Thomas Dolby
Mantovani:	Both Sides Now
Matthews Southern Comfort:	Woodstock
Barry McGuire:	Clouds
Sarah McLachlan:	Blue
Nazareth:	This Flight Tonight
Willie Nelson:	Both Sides Now
Mary O'Hara:	Both Sides Now
Minnie Ripperton	Woman of Heart and Mind
Tom Rush:	Tin Angel, Urge for Going, The Circle Game
Frank Sinatra:	Both Sides Now
Sir Douglas Quartet:	Big Yellow Taxi
David Snell:	Both Sides Now set for the harp
Dave Stewart & Barbara Gaskin:	Amelia
Barbra Streisand:	I Don't Know Where I Stand
June Tabor:	Fiddle and the Drum
Kiri Te Kanawa:	Both Sides Now
Alan Tew Orchestra:	Woodstock
Dave Van Ronk:	Clouds
Andy Williams:	Both Sides Now
Paul Young:	Both Sides Now

Bibliography

Where items have been published in Great Britain, I have given details of that, even if a US issue predates it.

ALLEN, MIKE 'The Boho Dance', LIQUORICE 7, 1976.

ANON 'New Pop Albums – Clouds', MELODY MAKER, 27 September 1969.

'She is destined to paint with words', MUSIC NOW, 29 August 1970, Warner Reprise supplement.

'The Complete Folk Singer', DISC 8, August 1970.

ATLAS, JACOBA 'First Lady of the Canyon', MELODY MAKER, 26 April 1975.

BARRON, JACK 'Wall of Confusion', NME, 4 August 1990.

BARRY, R 'Joni's Code of Life', MELODY MAKER, 31 July 1971.

BOUCHER, CAROLINE 'Joni: My Personal Life is a Shambles', DISC, 10 January 1970.

BRADSHAW, STEVE Cafe Life: Bohemian Life from Swift to Bob Dylan, Weidenfeld 1978. ('Neon, Jukes, Heavenly Blue', pp 180-90.)

BROWN, MICK 'The Flowering of Joni Mitchell', TELEGRAPH MAGAZINE, 23 February 1991.

BURT, ROB & NORTH, PATSY (eds), West Coast Story, Hamlyn 1977, pp 63-67.

CAMPBELL, ROD 'Mitchell In', FOLK ROOTS 137, February 1995.

CHARONE, BARBARA 'By the Time We Got Through Neasden', SOUNDS, 21 September 1974.

CLAIRE, VIVIAN Judy Collins, NY Flash Books, 1977

CLARKE, STEVE 'The Importance of Being Joni', NME, 2 February 1974.

'Our Lady of the Silences' NME, 27 April 1974.

'Both Sides of Joni', Turning On: Rock in the Sixties, Orbis, 1985. (pp 143-5.)

CLERK, CAROL 'Wild Things Run Fast', MELODY MAKER, 27 November 1982.

RAY COLEMAN 'Joni Mitchell', EVENING STANDARD, 22 August, 1970; Festival Funbook p 19.

COOK, RICHARD 'Songs for Ageing Children', NME, 27 November 1982.

COON, CAROLINE 'New Singles', MELODY MAKER, 24 April 1976.

CRESCENTI, PETER 'Who's Frail and Blonde and Rocks like a Bitch', SOUNDS, 20 March 1976.

CROSBY, DAVID Long Time Gone: The Autobiography, Doubleday 1986.

CROUSE, TIMOTHY 'Blue', ROLLING STONE, 5 August 1971. Reprinted in Rolling Stone Record Review Volume II, 1974, NY, Pocket Books.

CROWE, CAMERON 'The Interview: Joni Mitchell', ROLLING STONE, 1979, reprinted in Ben Fong-Torres' The Rolling Stone Interviews, St Martins Press, NY 1981 pp 376-91.

DALLAS, KARL 'Joni, the Seagull from Saskatoon', MELODY MAKER, 28 September 1968.

DENESLOW, ROBIN When The Music's Over, Faber, 1989, p 263.

DEVOSS, DAVID 'Rock's Woman of the Heart and Mind', TIME.

de WHALLEY, CHAS 'She's an Artist, She Don't Look Back', NME, 29 November 1975.

ECHOLS, ALICE '30 Years with a Portable Lover', LA WEEKLY, 25 November-1 December 1994.

EINARSON, JOHN Neil Young: The Canadian Years, Omnibus 1993.

ESCOTT, COLIN Good Rockin' Tonight: Sun Records and the Birth Of Rock 'n' Roll, Virgin, 1992, p 106.

FITZGERALD, HELEN 'Dog Eat Dog', MELODY MAKER, 23 November 1985.

FLANAGAN, BILL Written In My Soul, Chicago 1986, pp 267-284.

FLEISCHER, LEONORE Joni Mitchell – Her Lives, Her Loves, Her Music, Flash Books, 1976. ISBN 0 8256 3907 7, pbk 79pp.

The above book is a superficial biography which concentrates on the influences of the various men in Joni Mitchell's life. Her songs are dealt with in passing, as are her albums up to 1975, and there are some unusual photographs. It is the sole biography and major source of information on a major artist, but unfortunately it fails to give the space, time and sensitivity required to do justice to the subject.

FONG-TORRES, BEN 'The Interview – David Crosby', ROLLING STONE, 23 July 1970.

GAAR, GILLIAN She's A Rebel: The History Of Women In Rock & Roll, Blandford Press, 1993.

GAMBACCINI, PAUL Masters Of Rock, Omnibus 1982.

GASKELL, JOHN 'Mingus Minus', CAMBRIDGE EVENING NEWS, 15 August 1979.

GILBERT, JEREMY 'A Triumph for Joni', MELODY MAKER, 24 January 1970.

'Joni Still Feels the Pull of the Country', MELODY MAKER, 10 January 1970.

GILL, JOHN 'Shadows and Light', SOUNDS, 11 October 1980.

GOLDSTEIN, DAN 'Big Yellow Taxi', Unplugged, Castle, 1996, p 30-34.

GREIG, CHARLOTTE 'The Charismatic Siren Gives Way to the Doom-laden Seer',

MOJO, November 1994.

HEYHOE, MALCOM 'The Perpetual Marriage of Granite and Rainbow', LIQUORICE 8, 1976/77.

HIGGINS, MJ 'Mail Bag', MELODY MAKER, 24 June 1972.

HINTON, BRIAN 'Message to Love', Castle, 1995, pp 138-9.

HOLDEN, STEPHEN 'A Summer Garden of Verses', ROLLING STONE, 28 February 1974.

HOPKINS, JERRY Festival, Collier Books, NY 1970.

HOSKYNS, BARNEY Across the Great Divide: The Band and America, Viking 1993.

'Our Lady of Sorrows', MOJO, December 1994.

100 GREAT VOICES (Mojo Music Guide 2, no 62).

Waiting for the Sun: The Story of the Los Angeles Music Scene, Viking 1996, especially chapter 6, 'Ladies and Gentlemen of the Canyon'.

HOT WACKS BOOK XI, Babylon Books, 1986, pp 185-6.

HUGHES, TERRY 'Canada in the City: Joni's Painting', HELLO, date unknown.

HUMPHRIES, PATRICK 'Still Dark in the Tunnel', MELODY MAKER, 27 September 1980.

JACKSON, ALAN 'Portrait of the Artist', NME, 30 November 1985.

JAMES, VIOLA 'Joni's Miles of Aisles Breathes Life into her Legend', CIRCUS, date unknown.

JEWEL, DEREK 'Joni's Masterwork', SUNDAY TIMES, 5 February 1978, reprinted in The Popular Voice, Deutsch 1980, p 214.

KENT, NICK 'Wembley Report', NME, 21 September 1974.

'Dunno. Ask Joni Mitchell', NME, 11 January 1975.

The Dark Stuff, Penguin 1994, p 313.

KING, V, PLUMBLEY, M, TURNER, P 'Isle of Wight Rock: A Music Anthology', IOW Rock Archives 1995, p 92.

KUBERKIK, HARVEY 'Band's Last Stand', MELODY MAKER, 11 December 1976.

LAING, DAVE 'Troubadours and Stars', in The Electric Muse: The Story of Folk into Rock, Methuen 1975, pp 69-71.

LAKE, STEVE 'Return of the Woodstock Spirit', MELODY MAKER, 20 April 1974 interview with Graham Nash.

LEBLANC, LARRY 'Joni Takes A Break', ROLLING STONE, 4 March 1971.

LEWIS, ALUN 'How True Is Blue', MELODY MAKER, 13 May 1971.

LITTLE, HILARY & RUMSEY, GINA 'Women and Pop: A Series of Lost Encounters' in Zoot Suits and Second-hand Dresses, ed Angela McRobbie, Macmillan 1989.

LOGAN, NICK 'Joni is Supreme', NME, 28 November 1970.

LOTT, TIM 'The Top of the Iceberg', SOUNDS, 27 November 1976.

MCDOUGALL, ALAN 'Beautiful, Sensitive Joni', NME, 21 March 1970.

MACKIE, ROB 'From Folk Waif to Rock & Roll Lady', SOUNDS, 27 April 1974.

'Joni's Prize Blooms', SOUNDS, 4 May 1974.

MACKINNON, ANGUS 'Joni: It's a Labyrinthine Affair', STREET LIFE, 27 December 1976.

'Joni's Vision of Mingus; Lost in the Haze', NME, 23 June 1979.

MANN, IAN 'Joni', ZIGZAG 15, September 1969.

MASLIN, JANET 'Joni Mitchell's Reckless and Shapeless Daughter', ROLLING STONE, 9 March 1978.

'Singers/Songwriters', in The Rolling Stone Illustrated History of Rock & Roll, ed J Miller, Picador 1981, pp 340-1.

MILWARD, JOHN 'Joni Mitchell' in Rolling Stone Record Guide, ed Dave Marsh, Virgin 1980, p 251.

MINGUS, CHARLES Beneath The Underdog, Knopf 1971. His autobiography.

MITCHELL, JONI Joni Mitchell Complete I. Music and lyrics to Joni Mitchell, Clouds, Ladies of the Canyon.

Joni Mitchell Complete II. Music and lyrics to Blue, For the Roses, Court and Spark. Anthology, Warner Brothers, 31 songs.

MITCHELL, TONY 'Joni's Enigmatic Innervisions' SOUNDS, 24 December 1977.

MURRAY, CHARLES SHAAR 'Gentle Joni Does It Again', NME, 16th December 1972.

O'BRIEN, LUCY She-Bop, Penguin 1995.

O'HAGAN, SEAN 'Idol Talk', NME, 4 June 1988.

PEAD, DEBBIE 'Joni Mitchell', RECORD COLLECTOR 62, October 1984.

PEEL, JOHN 'Joni – A Leader Once Again', SOUNDS, 22 December 1973.

PENMAN, IAN 'Switch to Mitchell – and Make it Live', NME, 27 September 1980.

PHILLIPS, SANKY & WILSON, DAVE 'Talking with Joni Mitchell', ZIGZAG 69, February 1977.

PULIN, CHUCK 'Joni Mitchell', SOUNDS, 23 February 1974.

REYNOLDS, SIMON & PRESS, JOY The Sex Revolts: Gender, Rebellion and Rock'n'roll, Serpents Tail 1995.

RICHMOND, DICK 'The Lawn Ranger Rides Again', SOUNDS, 31 January 1976.

ROBERTSON, SANDY 'Scared to Dance', SOUNDS, 30 June 1979.

ROCKWELL, JOHN All American Music: Composition in the Late Twentieth Century, Kahn and Averill 1985, p 240.

RODGERS, JEFFREY My Secret Place: The Guitar Odyssey of Joni Mitchell

ROGAN, JOHNNY Neil Young: The Definitive Story, Proteus 1982.

ROSEN, STEVE 'Joni in Person', SOUNDS, 9 December 1972.

SANDALL, ROBERT 'Still the Leading Lady of the Folk Canon', SUNDAY TIMES, 9

September 1990.

SARLIN, BOB Turn it Up (I Can't Hear the Words), NY 1973. British edition, Coronet books 1975, pp 105-115.

SEAL 'Essentials', GUARDIAN, 5 January 1995.

SHELTON, ROBERT No Direction Home: The Life and Music of Bob Dylan NY, Beech Tree Books 1986. Rolling Thunder Revue.

SHEPARD, SAM Rolling Thunder Logbook, Penguin 1978, p 82.

SHEVEY, SANDRA Ladies Of Pop-Rock, NY Scholastic Bk Services 1972.

SIEGEL, JULES 'Midnight in Babylon', ROLLING STONE, 18 February 1971.

SINCLAIR, DAVID Rock on CD: The Essential Guide, Kyole Cathie 1992, pp 217-221.

SMITH, JOE Off the Record: An Oral History of Popular Music, Sidgwick and Jackson 1989, pp 305-7.

SPITZ, BOB Dylan: A Biography, NY, McGraw Hill 1989, pp 495-6.

STAMBLER, IRWIN Encyclopedia of Pop, Rock and Soul, St James Press 1974, pp 352, 353.

STEPHENS, MG 'Natural History', ROLLING STONE 30 April 1970, poem.

STOKES, GEOFFREY 'The Sixties', Rock of Ages: The Rolling Stone History of Rock and Roll, Penguin 1987, pp 453-5.

SUTCLIFFE, PHIL 'The Q Interview: Don Juan's Reckless Daughter', Q, 20 May 1988.

SWARTLEY, ARIEL 'Mitchell: The Siren and the Symbolist', ROLLING STONE, 10 February 1977.

SWEETING, ADAM 'Dog Day Afternoon', MELODY MAKER, 4 January 1986.

TAYLOR, GRAHAM 'Of Robbers and Angels', LET IT ROCK, 25 January 1975.

TAYLOR, PAUL Popular Music Since 1955: A Critical Guide to the Literature, Mansell 1985, p 326.

TOBLER, JOHN 'Clouds', 100 Great Albums of the Sixties, Little Brown 1994. p 92.

TRAUM, HAPPY Interview, ROLLING STONE, 17 May 1969, insert pp 8-9.

VALENTINE, PENNY 'Joni overcomes disaster threat' , SOUNDS, 13 May 1972.

'Joni Mitchell', SOUNDS, 3 June 1972.

'The Lady who Walks on Eggs', SOUNDS, 10 June 1972.

'Joni: Roses and Kisses, SOUNDS, 17 February 1973.

VASSAL, JACQUES Electric Children: Roots and Branches of Modern Folkrock, NY 1976, pp 215-9.

WALKER, BILL 'Contemporary Songwriters: Joni Mitchell', SOUNDS, 9 January 1971.

'Beautifully Blue', SOUNDS, 3 July 1971.

WATTS, MICHAEL 'Glimpses of Joni', MELODY MAKER, 19 September 1970.

'Priestess Joni', MELODY MAKER, 13 May 1972.

'Court and Spark', MELODY MAKER, 26 January 1974.

'The Divine Miss M', MELODY MAKER, 27 April 1974.

'A Bigger Splash', MELODY MAKER, 29 November 1975.

'Joni: Summer Lawns, Grey Gardens', MELODY MAKER, 27 November 1976.

'A Fallible Magician', MELODY MAKER, 24 December 1977.

'Joni... er... um', MELODY MAKER, 16 June 1979.

WELCH, CHRIS 'New Pop Singles', MELODY MAKER, 25 November 1972.

WERBEN, STUART 'The Interview – James Taylor & Carly Simon', ROLLING STONE, 4 January 1973.

WHITE, TIMOTHY Rock Lives: Profiles and Interviews, NY 1990. British edition, Omnibus books 1991, pp 328-339.

'A Portrait of an Artist', BILLBOARD, 9 December 1995.

WIGGINS, NEVILLE 'Blue' in The Perfect Collection, ed T Hibbert, Proteus 1982, p 150.

WILD, DAVID 'A Conversation with Joni Mitchell', ROLLING STONE, 30 May 1991.

WILLIAMS, RICHARD 'Sense and Sensuality', MELODY MAKER, 9 December 1972.

'Mingus Dies', MELODY MAKER, 13 January 1979.

WILSON, DAVE Interview, BROADSIDE, 1968.

YORKE, RICHIE Axes, Chops & Hot Licks: The Canadian Music Scene, Edmonton, Hurtig 1971, pp 121-5.

Index